Algebra I
Course Workbook

2021-22 Edition

Donny Brusca

www.CourseWorkBooks.com

Algebra I
Course Workbook

2021-22 Edition

Donny Brusca

ISBN 979-8-71161-796-9

www.CourseWorkBooks.com

Table of Contents

Introduction

ABOUT THE AUTHOR

Donny Brusca founded CourseWorkBooks in 2010.

He has retired from teaching and school administration after about 30 years of employment, mostly on the high school and college levels. He has a B.S. in mathematics and M.A. in computer and information science from Brooklyn College (CUNY) and a post-graduate P.D. in educational administration and supervision from St. John's University.

His college-level instructional experiences include Brooklyn College, Pace University, and Touro College Graduate School of Technology. His high school teaching experiences include public, charter, Catholic, and Jewish schools.

His administrative experiences include serving as the Student Data Systems Manager at a charter management organization and high school and as the Academic Dean and Mathematics Chairperson at a Manhattan business college. For several years, he was responsible for student scheduling in a high school of about 1000 students.

He has taught courses in basic mathematics, logic, algebra, geometry, probability, discrete structures, computer programming, web design, data structures, switching theory, computer architecture, and application software. He has taught all three Regents level mathematics courses and AP Computer Science A and AP Computer Science Principles.

He owned and operated a successful part-time disc jockey business (Sound Sensation), performing personally at nearly 1000 weddings and private events over a 12 year span.

He has managed and coached high school baseball teams, after playing for over 40 years in organized baseball and softball leagues. He currently works part time as a baseball umpire.

He lives in Staten Island, NY, with his wife, Camille, and their cats.

ABOUT THIS BOOK

The topics in this book are aligned to the national Common Core high school curriculum (C.C.S.S.). The book is intended for use in any state, but it is specifically arranged to correspond to the scope and sequence of topics established by New York State for the successful completion of a course leading to the state Regents examination.

Every topic section begins with an explanation of the Key Terms and Concepts. I have intentionally limited the content here to the most essential ideas. The notes should supplement a fuller presentation of the concepts by the teacher through a more developmental approach.

Calculator Tips explain how to use the graphing calculator to solve problems or check solutions. Keystrokes include button names in rectangles, STO▸, alternate button features in brackets, [SIN⁻¹], and on-screen text in larger rectangles, NUM . Directions for selecting on-screen text (arrow keys and ENTER) are usually omitted. Screenshots from a TI-84 Plus CE are shown by default, but differences from the TI-83 or other TI-84 models are noted.

Topic sections include one or more Model Problems, each with a solution and an explanation of steps needed to solve the problem. Steps lettered (A), (B), etc., in the explanations refer to the corresponding lettered steps shown in the solutions. General wording is used in the explanations so that students may apply the steps directly to new but similar problems. However, for clarity, the text often refers to the specific model problem by using *[italicized text in brackets]*. To make the most sense of this writing style, insert the words "in this case" before reading any *[italicized text in brackets]*.

After the Model Problem are a number of Practice Problems in boxed work spaces. These numbered problems are generally arranged in order of increasing level of difficulty.

A supplemental text, Algebra I Regents Questions, containing all Common Core exam questions related to each chapter of this book, is available at CourseWorkBooks.com. Both books are available in digital format as eWorkBooks, allowing students to not only read the books online, but also write directly onto the pages and save their work as PNG files.

Answer Keys are also available at CourseWorkBooks.com.

My goal is to have an error-free book and answer key and I am willing to offer a monetary reward to the first person who contacts me about any error in mathematical content. Simply email me at donny@courseworkbooks.com and be as specific as possible about the error. Corrections are posted under "Errata" at CourseWorkBooks.com.

NEXT GENERATION LEARNING STANDARDS

Several years ago, the New York State Education Department (NYSED) proposed changes to the state mathematics learning standards, which they called **Next Generation**. Despite the name change, there was no major overhaul -- most of the Common Core based standards from 2011 remain intact or were only slightly modified. The introduction of the updated standards has been delayed multiple times, most recently due to the virus pandemic. Here is the most recent timeline for implementation:

Timetable for Next Generation Regents Exam Administration in New York State

Regents Exam	First Administration of Exam Aligned to Next Generation Standards	Last Administration of Exam Aligned to 2011 Standards
Algebra I	June, 2023	June, 2024
Geometry	June, 2024	June, 2025
Algebra II	June, 2025	June, 2026

The following topics will be **added to** the Algebra I curriculum when the Next Generation standards are implemented. They are marked by a [NG] in the section titles.
- Operations with Radicals [NG] (Section 6.2)
- Rationalizing Denominators [NG] (Section 6.3)

These topics will be moved from the Algebra II curriculum.

The following topics will be **eliminated from** the Algebra I curriculum when the Next Generation standards are implemented. They are marked by a [CC] in the section titles.
- Compound Inequalities [CC] (Section 1.4)
- Residuals [CC] (Section 8.7)
- Recursively Defined Sequences [CC] (Section 12.3)
- Factor a Trinomial by Grouping [CC] (Section 13.4)
- Solve Quadratics with $a \neq 1$ [CC] (Section 14.7)
- Vertex Form with $a \neq 1$ [CC] (Section 15.6)
- Cube Root Functions [CC] (Section 17.3)

All but the first two topics above will be moved to the Algebra II curriculum.

The following expectations will also modified when the new standards are implemented:
- Sequences will be written in subscript notation only, *not* function notation.
- Completing the square will be limited to cases where b is even, to avoid fractions.
- Students will not be expected to factor by grouping.
- Horizontal stretches of function graphs, $f(kx)$, will be eliminated.

Chapter 1.   Equations and Inequalities

1.1   Properties of Real Numbers

KEY TERMS AND CONCEPTS

Identities: The word "identity" comes from the Latin *idem*, meaning the same.

The **additive identity** is zero, because when you add 0 to a value, the value remains the same.

The **multiplicative identity** is one, because when you multiply a value by 1, the value remains the same.

$$a + 0 = a \qquad\qquad a \times 1 = a$$

Inverses: When an operation is performed between a value and its inverse, the result is the identity for that operation.

So, the **additive inverse** of a number is its opposite, since adding a number and its opposite results in zero, the identity for addition: $a + (-a) = 0$

The **multiplicative inverse** of a number is its reciprocal, since multiplying a number and its reciprocal results in one, the identity for multiplication: $a \times \frac{1}{a} = 1$

Examples: The additive inverse of 2 is -2, and the multiplicative inverse of 2 is $\frac{1}{2}$.

The **Commutative Property** states that for an operation, the order of the operands doesn't matter. Addition and multiplication are commutative; subtraction and division are not. In other words, for addition, $a + b = b + a$, and for multiplication, $ab = ba$.

The **Associative Property** states that when performing the same operation on three operands, the order in which we perform the operations (grouping by parentheses) doesn't matter. Addition and multiplication are associative; subtraction and division are not. In other words, for addition, $a + (b + c) = (a + b) + c$, and for multiplication, $a(bc) = (ab)c$.

The **Distributive Property** states that when a value is multiplied by a sum, we get the same result if we were to multiply the value by each addend separately and then add the products. In other words, $x(a + b) = xa + xb$.

The **Reflexive Property of Equality** states that a value is equal to itself. That is, for all real values of a, $a = a$.

The **Symmetric Property of Equality** states that if we switch the two sides of an equation, the equation remains true. That is, if $a = b$, then $b = a$.

Note that if we switch the two sides of an *inequality*, we must also *reverse* the inequality symbol in order for it to remain true. This is called the **Reversal Property of Inequality**.
Examples: If $a > b$, then $b < a$.   If $a \geq b$, then $b \leq a$.

The **Transitive Property of Equality** states that if $a = b$ and $b = c$, then $a = c$.

The **Addition Property of Equality** states that if we add the same value to both sides of an equation, the equality remains. That is, if $a = b$, then $a + c = b + c$.

This extends to the other basic operations as well.
Subtraction Property of Equality: If $a = b$, then $a - c = b - c$.
Multiplication Property of Equality: If $a = b$, then $ac = bc$.
Division Property of Equality: If $a = b$, then $\dfrac{a}{c} = \dfrac{b}{c}$ (where $c \neq 0$).

Closure: A set is **closed** under an operation if, for <u>every pair</u> of elements, when the operation is performed on them, the result is an element of the same set.
Examples: (a) The set of integers is closed under addition because, whenever we add two integers, the result is always another integer.
(b) The set of integers is *not* closed under division because when we divide two integers we *may* get a result that is a fraction (decimal) and not an integer. For example, if we divide 1 by 2, the result is one half, which is not an integer.

The table below shows whether the given sets are closed under the specified operations. The set of whole numbers is often called the set of natural numbers. Note that division is *not* closed for any set that includes zero, since division by zero is undefined.

	Addition	Subtraction	Multiplication	Division
WHOLE NUMBERS	Y	N	Y	N
INTEGERS	Y	Y	Y	N
RATIONAL NUMBERS	Y	Y	Y	Y*
REAL NUMBERS	Y	Y	Y	Y*

* The sets of <u>non-zero</u> rational or real numbers only.

We can show that the set of **rational numbers is closed under multiplication**:

If $\frac{a}{b}$ and $\frac{c}{d}$ are rational numbers and a, b, c, and d are integers, then $\frac{a}{b} \times \frac{c}{d} = \frac{ac}{bd}$ by the rules for multiplying fractions. Since the set of integers is closed under multiplication, then ac and bd are integers, so $\frac{ac}{bd}$ is rational.

Similarly, we can show that the set of **rational numbers is closed under addition**:

If $\frac{a}{b}$ and $\frac{c}{d}$ are rational numbers and a, b, c, and d are integers, then $\frac{a}{b} + \frac{c}{d} = \frac{ad+bc}{bd}$ by the rules for adding fractions. Since the set of integers is closed under addition and multiplication, then $ad + bc$ and bd are integers, so $\frac{ad+bc}{bd}$ is rational.

MODEL PROBLEM 1:   *PROPERTIES OF REAL NUMBERS*

Justify the statement, "Subtraction is *not* associative."

Solution:

If subtraction were associative, then $a - (b - c)$ would equal $(a - b) - c$ for all real numbers a, b, and c. For example, $10 - (5 - 2)$ would equal $(10 - 5) - 2$. However, $10 - (5 - 2) = 7$ and $(10 - 5) - 2 = 3$. So, subtraction is not associative.

Explanation of steps:

When asked to justify that something is not true, it is usually best to offer a counterexample.

PRACTICE PROBLEMS

1. Which equation is an example of the use of the associative property of addition? (1) $x + 7 = 7 + x$ (2) $3(x + y) = 3x + 3y$ (3) $(x + y) + 3 = x + (y + 3)$ (4) $3 + (x + y) = (x + y) + 3$	2. The equation $3(4x) = (4x)3$ illustrates which property? (1) commutative (2) associative (3) distributive (4) multiplicative inverse
3. Which property is illustrated by the equation $(ab)c = a(bc)$?	4. Which property is illustrated by the equation $ax + ay = a(x + y)$?
5. Which statement illustrates the additive identity property? (1) $6 + 0 = 6$ (2) $-6 + 6 = 0$ (3) $4(6 + 3) = 4(6) + 4(3)$ (4) $(4 + 6) + 3 = 4 + (6 + 3)$	6. Which equation illustrates the multiplicative inverse property? (1) $a \cdot 1 = a$ (2) $a \cdot 0 = 0$ (3) $a\left(\frac{1}{a}\right) = 1$ (4) $(-a)(-a) = a^2$
7. What is the additive inverse of $\frac{2}{3}$?	8. What is the multiplicative inverse of $\frac{2}{3}$?
9. What is the additive inverse of the expression $a - b$?	10. What is the multiplicative inverse of the expression $-\frac{1}{ab}$?

11. Justify the statement, "Division is *not* commutative."

12. Is the set of whole numbers closed under subtraction? Justify your answer.

13. To find the product of x and 5, which property allows us to perform the following step?
$$x \cdot 5 = 5x$$

14. When adding 2 to the sum, $3 + x$, which property allows us to perform the first step below?
$$2 + (3 + x) =$$
$$(2 + 3) + x =$$
$$5 + x$$

15. Is the set of *non-zero* integers closed under division? Justify your answer.

16. Show that the set of *non-zero* rational numbers is closed under division.

MODEL PROBLEM 2: *APPLICATION OF THE DISTRIBUTIVE PROPERTY*

Distribute: $-4(1 - x)$

Solution: $-4(1 - x) = (-4)(1) + (-4)(-x) = -4 + 4x$

Explanation of steps:

The distributive property, $x(a + b) = xa + xb$, allows us to multiply the value outside the parentheses by each value inside the parentheses, and add the products.

[So, $-4(1 - x) = (-4)(1) + (-4)(-x)$]

PRACTICE PROBLEMS

17. Distribute: $5(x + 5)$	18. Distribute: $4(b - 4)$
19. Distribute: $-2(x - 1)$	20. Distribute: $-3(a - b)$
21. Simplify: $(1 + y)(-1)$	22. Simplify: $-(-a - 1)$
23. Apply the distributive property to: $rs + rt$	24. Apply the distributive property to: $2x + 10$

1.2　**Solve Linear Equations in One Variable**

KEY TERMS AND CONCEPTS

An **equation** is a statement that one expression is equal to another. It contains an = sign.

Example:　　$3x - 1 = x + 5$

Domain (replacement set): the set of numbers that can replace a variable. Usually, you can assume the domain is {real numbers}. However, if, for example, the variable represents the length of the side of a polygon, the domain should be {positive real numbers}.

Solution set: set of values from the domain that make an equation or inequality true.

Solution: each element of the solution set.

A **variable term** in an equation includes the variable as a factor (or the variable by itself). A variable term may include a numerical factor called a **coefficient**.

A **constant term** in an equation does not include a variable factor.

Example:　　$3x + 5 = 35$ has a variable term [$3x$, which has a coefficient of 3] and a constant term [5] on the left side, and a constant term [35] on the right side.

A **linear equation** is an equation in which each term is either a *constant term* or a *variable term* that includes only a *single variable to the first power* (ie, the variable can only have an exponent of 1, which is usually not written at all).

The goal when solving an equation is to **isolate the variable** (that is, transform it into the form, $x = some\ value$).

Like Terms: have the same exact variable parts (the numerical coefficients may differ). Like terms may be combined (added or subtracted); unlike terms may not.

Examples:　　Like terms:　　　$2x$ and $3x$　　　　$-4x^2y$ and x^2y

　　　　　　　Not like terms:　$2x$ and $3x^2$　　　$-4x^2y$ and x^2

To combine like terms:
1. Add or subtract the coefficients
2. Keep the variable part the same

Example:　　$2x + 5x - 2$ is equivalent to $7x - 2$, since $2x$ and $5x$ are like terms.

16

To solve a linear equation for one variable:

1. **SIMPLIFY:** Simplify each side of the equation to one or two terms.

    (a) Use the **distributive property** where possible to remove parentheses.

    (b) **Combine like terms** <u>on the same side of the equal sign</u> where possible.

2. **VARIABLE TERMS TO ONE SIDE:** If there are variable terms on both sides, eliminate a variable term from one side by adding its opposite to both sides. *Eliminate from which side? Here's a good rule of thumb...*

    (a) If one side has more terms, eliminate from that side.

    (b) Otherwise, eliminate the term with the smaller coefficient.

3. **ISOLATE THE VARIABLE:** Use the <u>reverse order of operations</u> to isolate the variable:

    (a) add the opposite (additive inverse) of the constant term to both sides.

    (b) divide both sides by (or multiply both sides by the reciprocal, or multiplicative inverse, of) the variable term's coefficient.

To check your solution:

Substitute your solution for the variable in the original equation. *It is usually best to use parentheses around the value when substituting.* Then, evaluate both sides of the equation to determine whether the solution makes the equation true.

CALCULATOR TIP

Checking a solution on the calculator:

1. Type your answer, then press [STO▸][X,T,Θ,*n*] to store your answer into the variable *x*, or press [STO▸][ALPHA] and a letter key to store your answer in a different variable, and press [ENTER].

2. Type in the equation, using [2nd][TEST][1] to enter the equal sign. Use [X,T,Θ,*n*] for *x* or [ALPHA] and a letter key for a different variable. Then, press [ENTER].

3. The calculator will display [1] If the equation is true for the given value of the variable, or [0] if it is false.

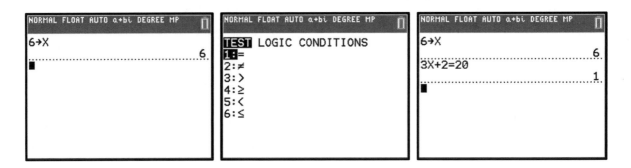

Note: In step 1 above, after pressing [ALPHA], you can press any of the letters associated with the [ALPHA] key to store the value in that variable. For examples, [MATH] for [A], [APPS] for [B], etc.

MODEL PROBLEM 1:   *EQUATIONS NEEDING TO BE SIMPLIFIED FIRST*

Solve: $5(x - 2) + 3x = 30$

Solution: **Explanation of steps:**

$$5(x - 2) + 3x = 30$$

(A)   Distribute *[$5(x - 2) = 5x - 10$]*

(A) $5x - 10 + 3x = 30$

(B)   Combine like terms *[$5x + 3x = 8x$]*

(B) $8x - 10 = 30$

(C)   Solve the two-step equation *[add 10 to both sides then divide both sides by 8].*

(C) $8x = 40$

           $x = 5$

Check by substituting: $5(5 - 2) + 3(5) = 30$

Evaluating the left side gives us $30 = 30$ ✓

Check on the calculator: 5 STO▸ X,T,Θ,*n* ENTER

(1 means true.)   5 (X,T,Θ,*n* − 2) + 3 X,T,Θ,*n* 2nd [TEST] 1 3 0 ENTER

PRACTICE PROBLEMS

1. Solve: $3(m - 2) = 18$	2. Solve: $4n - n = -12$
3. Solve: $2(x - 4) + 7 = 3$	4. Solve: $0.2(n - 6) = 2.8$
5. Solve: $-5 = -(y + 1) - y$	6. Solve: $15x - 3(3x + 4) = 6$

MODEL PROBLEM 2:   *EQUATIONS WITH VARIABLES ON BOTH SIDES*

Solve for x: $2(x - 3) - 3 = 8x + 3$

Solution: **Explanation of steps:**

$$2(x - 3) - 3 = 8x + 3$$

(A) $2x - 6 - 3 = 8x + 3$

$$2x - 9 = 8x + 3$$

(B) $-2x \qquad - 2x$

$$-9 = 6x + 3$$

(C) $-12 = 6x$

$$-2 = x$$

(A)   Simplify the left side by distributing *[2(x − 3) becomes 2x − 6]* and then by combining like terms *[−6 − 3 = −9]*.

(B)   Since there are variables on both sides, eliminate the variable term with the smaller coefficient *[2x, since 2 < 8]* by adding its opposite *[−2x]* to both sides *[8x − 2x = 6x]*.

(C)   Now solve the simpler equation *[by adding −3 to both sides, then dividing both sides by 6]*.

Check on the calculator: (-) 2 STO▸ X,T,Θ,*n* ENTER

(1 means true.)   2 (X,T,Θ,*n* − 3) − 3 2nd [TEST] 1 8 X,T,Θ,*n* + 3 ENTER

PRACTICE PROBLEMS

7. Solve for x: $3x + 8 = 5x$	8. Solve for g: $3 + 2g = 5g - 9$
9. What is the value of p in the equation $8p + 2 = 4p - 10$?	10. What is the value of p in the equation $5p - 1 = 2p + 20$?

11. Solve for y: $0.06y + 200 = 0.03y + 350$	12. Solve for x: $5 - 2x = -4x - 7$
13. What is the value of x in the equation $5(2x - 7) = 15x - 10$?	14. Solve for x: $5(x - 2) = 2(10 + x)$
15. Solve for x: $2(x - 4) = 4(2x + 1)$?	16. Solve for x: $3(x + 1) - 5x = 12 - (6x - 7)$
17. Solve for y: $-4(y - 3) = 5(2y - 6)$	18. Solve for x: $3(x - 2) - 2(x + 1) = 5(x - 4)$

1.3   Solve Linear Inequalities in One Variable

KEY TERMS AND CONCEPTS

An **inequality** is a statement that one expression is compared to, but not equal to, another. It contains one of the other relational symbols: $<, >, \leq, \geq,$ or $\neq$.

Example: $15 < 2x + 1$

Solving an inequality: Follow the same steps as in solving an equation EXCEPT when multiplying or dividing both sides by a negative number, REVERSE the inequality symbol.

Example: If $-3x \leq 15$, then dividing both sides by –3 gives us $x \geq -5$.

It may help to "flip" after solving: Once the variable is isolated, if it appears on the right side of the inequality, it is usually helpful to "flip" the entire inequality (switch the two sides and reverse the inequality symbol) so that the variable appears on the left side instead.

Example: The inequality $6 > y$ can be "flipped" to $y < 6$.

Graphing an inequality: Once a simple inequality is solved for a variable, it can be graphed on a number line using the following steps.

1. On the number line, find the value that the variable is being compared to.
2. If the inequality symbol is:
    a. **> or <**, draw an open circle $\bigcirc$ at that value, which means it is *not* in the solution set.
    b. **≥ or ≤**, draw a closed circle ● at that value, which means it is in the solution set.
3. If the variable is > or ≥ the value, shade an arrow to the right; otherwise, if the variable is < or ≤ the value, shade an arrow to the left. All the values represented by the shaded arrow, extending infinitely in that direction, are in the solution set.

Examples: (a) The number line below represents $x > 2$.

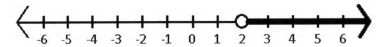

(b) The number line below represents $x \leq 3$.

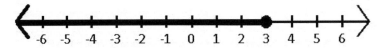

MODEL PROBLEM

Solve and graph the solution set: $7 > 5 - 2x$

Solution:

$7 > 5 - 2x$

(A) $\underline{-5 \quad -5}$

$\dfrac{2}{-2} > \dfrac{-2x}{-2}$

(B) $-1 < x$

(C) $x > -1$

(D)

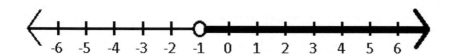

Explanation of steps:

(A)   Solve like an equation. *[Here, we subtract 5 from both sides, then divide both sides by –2.]*

(B)   If, in the process of solving, we multiply or divide both sides by a negative number, reverse the inequality symbol. *[Since we divided by–2, we reverse the symbol from > to <.]*

(C)   After solving, if the variable is on the right side, it is helpful to "flip" the entire inequality, including the inequality symbol, so that it appears on the left side.

(D)   Graph the result *[open circle, arrow to the greater side].*

PRACTICE PROBLEMS

1. Write an inequality that represents the graph below. 	2. Write an inequality that represents the graph below. 
3. Solve and graph the solution set: $\qquad 2x - 5 \leq 11$	4. Solve and graph the solution set: $\qquad -6y + 1 > 25$

23

5. Solve and graph the solution set: $$-4 > 2(r - 3)$$	6. Solve and graph the solution set: $$-\frac{4}{3}(x - 3) \le 12$$
7. Solve: $-6x - 17 \ge 8x + 25$	8. Solve: $-5(x - 7) < 15$
9. Which graph represents the solution set of $2x - 5 < 3$? (1) (2) (3) (4)	10. Solve: $3(2m - 1) \le 4m + 7$
11. Solve: $-4(2m - 6) + m > 3m + 4$	12. Solve: $-5(p + 1) \ge -p + 11$

1.4   **Compound Inequalities [CC]**

KEY TERMS AND CONCEPTS

A **compound inequality chain** has two inequality symbols with a variable in the middle.

Example: $-4 < x \leq 1$ means $\boxed{-4 < x}$ and $\boxed{x \leq 1}$

Solving a compound inequality chain: If the variable is not isolated, perform the inverse operations to eliminate everything around the variable, but do so to *all parts* of the inequality. Be sure to reverse the inequality symbols when multiplying or dividing by a negative number.

Example: Solve $0 < x - 1 < 5$ by adding 1 to all three parts, resulting in $1 < x < 6$.

It may help to "flip" after solving: Once the variable is isolated, if the inequality symbols are > or ≥, it is usually helpful to "flip" the entire compound inequality – making sure to reverse the symbols as well – so that the lower limit is on the left and the upper limit is on the right.

Example: $6 > x \geq 2$ can be "flipped" to $2 \leq x < 6$.

To graph a compound inequality chain: Once a compound inequality is solved and arranged so that only < or ≤ symbols are used, it can be graphed as follows:

1. On the number line, find the lower limit and draw an open (for <) or closed (for ≤) circle. Then find the upper limit and draw an open (for <) or closed (for ≤) circle.
2. Shade the number line between the lower and upper limits.

Example: $-1 \leq x < 2$ is graphed as

Compound inequality joined by "and": Two simple inequalities joined by "and" can be combined into a compound inequality chain. It may require solving and/or flipping.

Example: $x > 4$ *and* $x \leq 10$ can be combined into the one chain, $4 < x \leq 10$, by flipping the first inequality and then joining them at the *x*.

Compound inequality joined by "or": Two simple inqualities joined by "or" cannot be combined into a chain. Any solution to *either one or the other* inequality (*or both*) will solve the compound inequality. So, we can graph them on the number line, where they may overlap.

Examples: (a) The compound inequality $x \leq -4$ *or* $x > 3$ is graphed below.

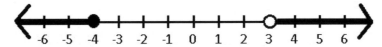

(b) Consider the compound inequality $x \leq -1$ *or* $x < 3$. Looking at the graphs of the simple inequalities separately, we can easily see that if $x \leq -1$, then certainly $x < 3$. So, the compound inequality is the overlap of the two simple inequalities, or simply $x < 3$.

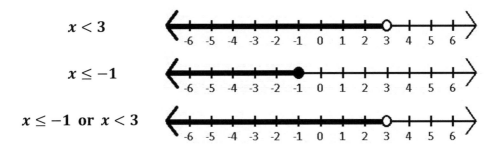

MODEL PROBLEM

Solve and graph the solution set: $-4 < r - 5 \leq -1$

Solution:

$$-4 < r - 5 \leq -1$$
(A) $+5 \quad\quad +5 \quad\ +5$
$$1 < r \leq 4$$

(B)

Explanation of steps:

(A)   Solve like any inequality by isolating the variable, but whatever operation is done to the middle part must be done to the other two. The rule still applies: when multiplying or dividing by a negative, reverse the inequality symbols.

(B)   Graph the result.

PRACTICE PROBLEMS

1. Write a compound inequality represented by the graph below. 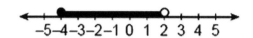	2. Write a compound inequality represented by the graph below. 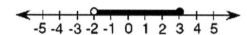
3. Write a compound inequality represented by the graph below. 	4. Write a compound inequality represented by the graph below. 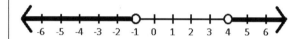
5. Graph $-1 < x < 3$ on the number line. 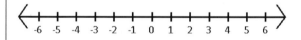	6. Solve and graph the solution set: $$3 \le 2x + 1 < 9$$
7. How many positive integers are in the solution set of $-2 < 3x + 4 \le 10$?	8. The statement $|-15| < x < |-20|$ is true when x is equal to (1) −16 (3) 17 (2) −14 (4) 21

1.5   <u>**Solve Equations with Fractions**</u>

KEY TERMS AND CONCEPTS

When an equation involves, we can solve the equation by **eliminating the fractions.** We can accomplish this by **multiplying each term** of the equation by the **least common multiple (LCM)** of the denominators, also called the **least common denominator (LCD).** This will eliminate the denominator of each term since it will divide evenly into the LCD. *(For this course, equations of this type will have no variables in the denominators.)*

Why can we multiply each term by the LCD? This is because we are actually multiplying both sides of the equation by the LCD (*multiplication property of equality*) and then distributing, without actually showing the distribution step.

Example: To solve $\dfrac{x}{4} - \dfrac{1}{2} = 2$,

$$\boxed{4\left(\dfrac{x}{4} - \dfrac{1}{2}\right) = 4(2)} \Rightarrow 4\left(\dfrac{x}{4}\right) - 4\left(\dfrac{1}{2}\right) = 4(2) \Rightarrow x - 2 = 8 \Rightarrow x = 10$$

you may skip this step

CALCULATOR TIP

To enter a fraction on the calculator:

- On the TI-83 models, fractions are entered as division; for example, $\frac{1}{2}$ is entered as

  $\boxed{1}\boxed{\div}\boxed{2}$. If there are multiple terms joined by addition or subtraction in the numerator or denominator, be sure to place the terms in parentheses.

- On the TI-84 models, fractions can be entered by pressing $\boxed{\text{ALPHA}}\boxed{\text{F1}}\boxed{1}$. Type the numerator, press $\boxed{\blacktriangleright}$, type the denominator, and press $\boxed{\blacktriangleright}$ again. Mixed fractions can also be entered using $\boxed{\text{ALPHA}}\boxed{\text{F1}}\boxed{2}$.

Example: The following TI-84 screenshots show how to check the solution above. Remember to press $\boxed{\text{MATH}}\boxed{\text{TEST}}\boxed{1}$ for the equal sign.

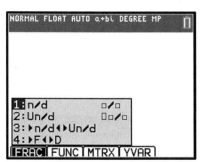 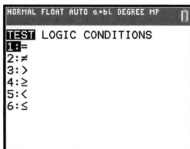 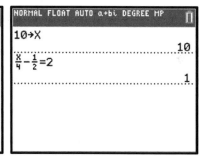

MODEL PROBLEM

Solve for x: $\dfrac{x+1}{4} - \dfrac{2x}{3} = \dfrac{x}{12}$

Solution:

(A) $\quad 12\left(\frac{x+1}{4}\right) - 12\left(\frac{2x}{3}\right) = 12\left(\frac{x}{12}\right)$

(B) $\quad\quad 3(x+1) - 4(2x) = x$

(C) $\quad\quad\quad\quad 3x + 3 - 8x = x$

$\quad\quad\quad\quad\quad\quad -5x + 3 = x$

$\quad\quad\quad\quad\quad\quad\quad\quad 3 = 6x$

$\quad\quad\quad\quad\quad\quad\quad\quad \frac{1}{2} = x$

Explanation of steps:

(A) Find the LCD *[12]*. Multiply each term by the LCD.

(B) Each denominator will divide evenly into the LCD, thereby eliminating the denominator.

(C) Solve the resulting equation.

PRACTICE PROBLEMS

1. Solve for *x*: $\dfrac{x}{16} + \dfrac{1}{4} = \dfrac{1}{2}$	2. Solve for *x*: $\dfrac{x}{2} + \dfrac{x}{6} = 2$
3. Solve for *x*: $\dfrac{2x}{3} + \dfrac{x}{6} = 5$	4. Solve for *x*: $\dfrac{3}{5}x + \dfrac{2}{5} = 4$
5. Solve for *x*: $\dfrac{3}{4}x + 2 = \dfrac{5}{4}x - 6$	6. Solve for *x*: $\dfrac{2}{3}x + \dfrac{1}{2} = \dfrac{5}{6}$
7. Solve for *x*: $\dfrac{3}{4}x = \dfrac{1}{3}x + 5$	8. Solve for *x*: $\dfrac{x}{3} + \dfrac{x+1}{2} = x$

9. Solve for x: $\dfrac{2x}{5} + \dfrac{1}{3} = \dfrac{7x-2}{15}$

10. Solve for x: $\dfrac{1}{7} + \dfrac{2x}{3} = \dfrac{15x-3}{21}$

11. Solve for x: $\dfrac{3}{4}(x+3) = 9$

12. Solve for x: $\dfrac{3}{5}(x+2) = x - 4$

13. Solve for x: $\dfrac{1}{2}(18 - 5x) = \dfrac{1}{3}(6 - 4x)$

14. Solve for x: $\dfrac{2}{3}\left(2x - \dfrac{1}{2}\right) = 13$

15. Solve for m: $\dfrac{m}{5} + \dfrac{3(m-1)}{2} = 2(m-3)$

1.6 Solve Literal Equations and Inequalities

KEY TERMS AND CONCEPTS

Literal equations and **literal inequalities** contain several variables or letters. To solve a literal equation or literal inequality for a specific variable, perform the same steps to isolate that variable as you would for any equation or inequality. In other words, solve for the specific variable by transforming the equation into one where the variable is written as equal to an expression **in terms of** the other variables.

Example: To solve $c = a + b$ for a, we can isolate a by subtracting b from both sides. This gives us $b = c - a$, an equation where b is written in terms of a and c.

If the specified variable appears in **more than one term** that cannot be combined, use the distributive property to factor it out before dividing both sides by the other factor.

Example: $mx + nx$ can be rewritten as $x(m + n)$ if you need to isolate x.

When solving a *literal inequality*, remember that the inequality symbol needs to switch whenever you multiply or divide both sides by a negative number.

Example: To solve $\frac{x}{a} > b$, we need to know whether a is positive or negative.

(We know $a \neq 0$ since a value of zero would make the fraction undefined.)

If $a > 0$, then $x > ab$, but if $a < 0$, then $x < ab$.

A formula is an equation made up of **dependent and independent variables**. The dependent variable's value is determined based on the freely chosen values of the independent variables. In a formula, the dependent variable is written *in terms of* the independent variables.

Example: In the formula for the area of a triangle, $A = \frac{1}{2}bh$, A is the dependent variable and b and h are the independent variables. A is dependent on b and h.

When we are asked to solve a formula for a different variable, the status of the variables in the resulting formula will change.

Example: If we solve the formula $A = \frac{1}{2}bh$ for h, the resulting formula is $h = \frac{2A}{b}$. In this new formula, h is the dependent variable and A and b are independent variables.

Terms and expressions may also be considered dependent on the variables they contain.

Example: In the formula, $m = 2xy + 4x - 2y + 5$, variables x and y are independent. In the expression on the right side, $2xy + 4x - 2y + 5$, the first and second terms are dependent on x and the first and third terms are dependent on y. The last term is constant and not dependent on any variables. The expression itself is dependent on both x and y. The variable m is also dependent on x and y.

MODEL PROBLEM 1:   *MULTI-STEP LITERAL EQUATIONS*

Solve for x in terms of a, b, c, and y: $ax + by = c$

Solution:

$$ax + by = c$$

(A) $\dfrac{-by \quad - by}{\quad}$

$$\dfrac{ax}{} = c - by$$

(B) $\dfrac{ax}{a} = \dfrac{c - by}{a}$

$$x = \dfrac{c - by}{a}$$

Explanation of steps:

(A)   Isolate the specified variable *[x]* by first eliminating terms that do not contain the variable. Add the opposite of any such term *[–by]* to both sides.

(B)   Eliminate any coefficient (numerical or literal) of the specified variable *[a]* by dividing both sides by it.

PRACTICE PROBLEMS

1.   Solve for p in terms of m:
 	
     $2m + 2p = 16$
	2. Solve for x in terms of b and K:
	
	     $bx - 2 = K$

3.   Solve for m in terms of c and d:
 	
     $c = 2m + d$
	4. Solve for x in terms of a, b, and c:
	
	     $bx - 3a = c$

5. Solve for w in terms of V, l, and h: $$V = lwh$$	6. Solve for h in terms of A and b: $$A = \frac{bh}{2}$$
7. If $abx - 5 = 0$, what is x in terms of a and b?	8. If $2y + 2w = x$, then what is w in terms of x and y?
9. Solve for x in terms of r, s, and t: $$s = \frac{2x + t}{r}$$	10. The formula for the volume of a pyramid is $V = \frac{1}{3}Bh$. What is h expressed in terms of B and V?
11. A formula used for calculating velocity is $v = \frac{1}{2}at^2$. What is a expressed in terms of v and t?	12. If $\frac{ey}{n} + k = t$, what is y in terms of e, n, k, and t?

MODEL PROBLEM 2:   *USING THE DISTRIBUTIVE PROPERTY*

Solve for x in terms of a, b, and c: $ax + bx = c$

Solution:

$$ax + bx = c$$

(A) $x(a + b) = c$

(B) $\dfrac{x(a + b)}{a + b} = \dfrac{c}{a + b}$

$x = \dfrac{c}{a + b}$

Explanation of steps:

(A)   If the variable we're trying to isolate *[x]* appears in more than one term on the same side of the equation, use the distributive property to factor it out. *[ax + bx = x(a + b)]*

(B)   Then, divide both sides by the other factor *[a + b]*.

PRACTICE PROBLEMS

13. Solve for x in terms of a and b: $3x - ax = b$	14. Solve for c in terms of a and b: $bc + ac = ab$
15. If $k = am + 3mx$, what is m in terms of a, k, and x?	16. Solve for x in terms of a and b: $2ax = -bx + 1$
17. If $ax + 3 = 7 - bx$, what is x expressed in terms of a and b?	18. If $z + y = x + xy^2$, what is x expressed in terms of y and z?

Chapter 2.   Verbal Problems

2.1   Translate Expressions

KEY TERMS AND CONCEPTS

To translate verbal expressions into algebraic expressions, look for phrases commonly used to represent operations:

Addition	**Subtraction**	**Multiplication**	**Division**
increased by	decreased by	multiplied by	divided by
sum	difference	product	quotient
plus	minus	times	
more than	*less than*		
added to	*subtracted from*		

Of course, this is not a comprehensive list. For example, just as we can express subtraction using the word, "decreased," we can also use a synonym, such as "diminished" or "reduced."

Order of operands: Generally, operands are written in the order they appear in the verbal expression, with the important exception of the phrases written in *italics* above.

Example: The following are written as $a - b$,   but the following are written as $b - a$

        a decreased by *b*   *a* less than *b*

        difference of *a* and *b*   *a* subtracted from *b*

        a minus *b*

Addition and multiplication are commutative, so the order of their operands shouldn't matter.

Note also: When we multiply a variable by a number, we generally write the number (called the numerical coefficient) first.

Example: "x times 5" is usually written $5x$ rather than $x \cdot 5$

Other common phrases:

Twice	means two times:	"twice x" is written $2x$
Fraction of	means fraction times:	"two-fifths of x" is written $\frac{2}{5}x$
The quantity	means parentheses:	"twice the quantity $x + 5$" is written $2(x + 5)$

The placement of **commas** may be important at times.

Example: "Product of x and y, decreased by 2"   means $xy - 2$

               "Product of x and y decreased by 2"   means $x(y - 2)$

Writing an expression "in terms of" a variable:

- Often in verbal expressions, a quantity is described by comparing it to another quantity.
- This latter quantity, to which it is being compared, will be represented by a variable.
- This variable quantity will often appear at the end of a verbal clause, and commonly after comparative words such as "than" or "as many as."
- Once the variable quantity is established, then the other quantities will be written as expressions containing, or in terms of, this variable.

Example: If "John's age is 5 less *than* Tom's age," let the variable t represent Tom's age. John's age is represented by an expression in terms of t, namely: $t - 5$.

Ratios: if a ratio is stated between two (or more) quantities, then use a variable to represent their common factor.

Example: If the numbers of boys and girls in a class are in the ratio 3:2, then express the number of boys as $3x$ and the number of girls as $2x$.

Consecutive integers are such that each integer is <u>1 larger than the previous</u>.

Examples: 4, 5, and 6 are three consecutive integers, as are –2, –1, and 0.

If x is the smallest of three consecutive integers, then the three numbers can be expressed as x, $x + 1$, and $x + 2$. The next consecutive integer after $x + 2$ is $x + 3$.

Consecutive even integers (for example, 6, 8, 10, and 12) and **consecutive odd integers** (for example, 5, 7, 9, and 11) are each <u>2 larger than the previous</u>.

So, If x is the smallest of four consecutive even integers, then the four numbers can be expressed as x, $x + 2$, $x + 4$, and $x + 6$. (The same expressions are used if x is the smallest of four consecutive *odd* integers.)

Monetary values: to find the value of coins or bills, multiply the number of each coin or bill by its denomination, and add the products.

Example: x dimes and $3x$ nickels have a total value of $(0.10)x + (0.05)3x$, or $0.25x$.

Total costs: to find the total cost of items purchased, multiply the number of each item by its price, and add the products.

Example: x apples at \$0.25 each and $(10 - x)$ oranges at \$0.40 each costs a total of $(0.25)x + (0.40)(10 - x)$, or after simplifying, $4.00 - 0.15x$.

Chain comparisons: In some cases, a quantity is written as an expression in terms of a variable, and then another quantity is written in terms of *this expression*. Use a variable for the quantity at the *end of the chain*, and then work backwards to express the others.

Example: Mark is 4 years younger than Samuel and Charles is three times as old as Mark. What is the sum of their ages written as an expression?

Mark is described in terms of Samuel and Charles is described in terms of Mark, so the chain is: Charles → Mark → Samuel.

Let s be Samuel's age.

If s is Samuel's age, Mark's age is $s - 4$, and Charles' age is $3(s - 4)$.

The sum of their ages is $s + (s - 4) + 3(s - 4)$, which simplifies to $5s - 16$.

MODEL PROBLEM 1:   *EXPRESSIONS IN TERMS OF ONE VARIABLE*

Abby, Barbie, and Carol are sisters. Abby's age is four times Carol's age and Barbie's age if 5 less than twice Carol's age. Write an expression, in terms of Carol's age, c, for the sum of their ages.

Solution:

Carol's age is c.   Abby's age is $4c$.   Barbie's age is $2c - 5$.

So the sum of their ages can be represented by $c + 4c + 2c - 5$, which simplifies to $7c - 5$.

Explanation of steps:

A common temptation is to create a separate variable for each quantity *[the three ages]*. But, since all other quantities *[Abby's and Barbie's ages]* are expressed using comparisons to a single value *[Carol's age]*, it is much better to use only one variable *[c]* and then write expressions for the others in terms of this variable.

PRACTICE PROBLEMS

1. Which verbal expression can be represented by $2(x-5)$? (1) 5 less than 2 times x (2) 2 multiplied by x less than 5 (3) twice the difference of x and 5 (4) the product of 2 and x, decreased by 5	2. Which verbal expression is represented by $\frac{1}{2}(n-3)$? (1) one-half n decreased by 3 (2) one-half n subtracted from 3 (3) the difference of one-half n and 3 (4) one-half the difference of n and 3
3. Write an expression for 5 less than the product of 7 and x.	4. Write an expression for twice the difference of x and 8.
5. The sum of Scott's age and Greg's age is 33 years. If Greg's age is represented by g, what is Scott's age in terms of g?	6. Tara buys two items that cost d dollars each. She gives the cashier $20, which is more than the total cost. Write an expression to represent the change she should receive.
7. John is four times as old as Ashley. If x represents Ashley's age, write an expression to represent how old John will be in 10 years.	8. If n represents the height of an object in inches, write an expression in terms of n to represent the height of the object in feet. (12 inches = 1 foot.)

9. If Jose's weekly allowance is d dollars, write an expression for his allowance, in dollars, for x weeks?

10. A skateboard and two helmets cost a total of d dollars. If each helmet cost h dollars, write an expression for the cost of the skateboard.

11. What is the perimeter of a regular pentagon with a side whose length is $x + 4$?

12. Angelina determined that her father's age is four less than three times her age. If x represents Angelina's age, write an expression for her father's age?

13. Marcy bought d dollars worth of stock. During the first year, the value of the stock tripled. The next year, the value of the stock decreased by $1200. Write an expression in terms of d to represent the value of the stock after two years.

14. Charles gets paid $280 per week plus 5% commission on all sales for selling gym memberships. If he sells n dollars worth of gym memberships in one week, write an expression for the amount of money he will earn that week.

MODEL PROBLEM 2:   *CONSECUTIVE INTEGERS*

Write an expression, in simplest terms, for the sum of three consecutive odd integers.

Solution:

$x + x + 2 + x + 4 = 3x + 6$

Explanation of steps:

Let a variable *[x]* represent the smallest of the integers. Write expressions involving this variable for each of the other integers *[x+2 and x+4]*. Express the sum and simplify the result by combining like terms.

PRACTICE PROBLEMS

15. If *y* is the smallest of four consecutive integers, write an expression, in simplest terms, for the sum of the four integers.	16. If the smallest of three consecutive even integers is $x + 3$, write the sum of the three integers in simplest terms.
17. The ages of three children are consecutive odd integers. If *x* represents the youngest child's age, write an expression, in simplest terms, for the sum of the children's ages.	18. Two numbers are consecutive integers. If *x* represents the smaller number, write an expression, in simplest terms, for the product of the numbers.

MODEL PROBLEM 3: *CHAIN COMPARISONS*

Ashanti and Maria went to the store to buy snacks for their back-to-school party. They bought bags of chips, pretzels, and nachos. They bought three times as many bags of pretzels as bags of chips, and two fewer bags of nachos than bags of pretzels. If x represents the number of bags of chips they bought, express, in terms of x, how many bags of snacks they bought in all.

Solution:

   (A)   Let x be the number of bags of chips bought.

   (B)   Then, $3x$ represents the bags of pretzels, and $3x - 2$ represents the bags of nachos.

   (C)   Altogether, they bought $x + 3x + 3x - 2$, or $7x - 2$, bags of snacks.

Explanation of steps:

   (A)   Create the comparison chain and let the variable represent the quantity at the end of the chain. *[Pretzels are expressed in terms of chips and nachos are expressed in terms of pretzels. So, the chain is Nachos → Pretzels → Chips. Let x represent the chips.]*

   (B)   By working backwards in the chain, express the other quantities in terms of this variable.

   (C)   Combine the expressions using the operation specified.

PRACTICE PROBLEMS

19. Camille is 7 years older than Donny, and Donny is 4 years younger than Tommy. Write an expression for the total ages of the three people, in simplest form.	20. The life span of a whale is 4 times than of a stork, which lives 70 years longer than a horse. Write an expression, in simplest form, for the total life spans of the three creatures.

21. Carl ate four more cookies than Alice. Bob ate twice as many cookies as Carl. Write an expression that represents the number of cookies Bob ate.

22. Two friends went to the store to buy snacks for a party. They bought bags of chips, pretzels, and nachos. They bought three times as many bags of pretzels as bags of chips, and two fewer bags of nachos than bags of pretzels. If x represents the number of bags of chips they bought, express, in terms of x, how many bags of snacks they bought in all.

2.2   <u>**Translate Equations**</u>

KEY TERMS AND CONCEPTS

An **equation** is simply a statement in which two expressions are set equal to each other.
So, to translate a verbal problem into an equation:

1. translate each quantity into an expression in terms of a variable
2. determine from the problem how the expressions form an equation

Examples: the sum of x and $2x$ is 42   becomes $x + 2x = 42$

               $4s$ is 15 more than s becomes $4s = s + 15$

Sometimes a **known formula** needs to be applied in order to write the equation.

Example: If a rectangle's length is $4x$, its width is x, and its area is 100, use the formula
               $A = lw$ to produce the equation, $100 = (4x)(x)$, or $100 = 4x^2$

MODEL PROBLEM

Write an equation to find three consecutive even integers whose sum is 84.

Solution:

(A)   Let x be the first even integer.

(B)   Therefore, $x + 2$ is the second even integer and $x + 4$ is the third even integer.

(C)   So, $x + (x + 2) + (x + 4) = 84$, or, simplifying the left side of the equation,
       $3x + 6 = 84$.

Explanation of steps:

(A)   Determine which quantity will be represented by the variable *[in a consecutive integers problem, x can represent the first in the sequence]*.

(B)   Express the other quantities as expressions in terms of this variable *[each consecutive even integer is two larger than the previous]*.

(C)   Arrange the expressions to form a correct equation *[the sum is 84]*.

PRACTICE PROBLEMS

1. If h represents a number, write an equation for the statement, "Sixty more than 9 times the number is 375"	2. Three times the sum of a number and four is equal to five times the number, decreased by two. If x represents the number, write an equation that could be used to find x.
3. The width of a rectangle is 4 less than half the length. If l represents the length, write an equation that could be used to find the width, w.	4. The width of a rectangle is 3 less than twice the length, x. If the area of the rectangle is 43 square feet, write an equation that could be used to find the length, in feet.
5. The radius of a circle is represented by $3x + 2$, and the length of the diameter is 22 centimeters. Write an equation to find the value of x, in centimeters.	6. Jerome purchased four more apples than oranges. Apples cost 30 cents each and oranges cost 50 cents each. Jerome spent a total of $3.60. Write an equation to find how many oranges he purchased.

7. Byron has $1.35 in nickels and dimes in his piggy bank. If he has six more dimes than nickels, write an equation that could be used to determine n, the number of nickels he has.	8. Rhonda has 72 coins in a jar. The jar contains only dimes and quarters. If the jar contains $14.70, write an equation that could be used to determine q, the number of quarters in the jar.
9. Write an equation that could be used to find two consecutive integers whose product is 20.	10. Write an equation that could be used to find three consecutive odd integers whose sum is –3.

2.3   <u>**Translate Inequalities**</u>

KEY TERMS AND CONCEPTS

Translate a verbal problem into an **inequality** the same way as you do for an equation, but instead of using an = sign for equality, use the appropriate **inequality symbol**:

$>$	"is more than"	"is greater than"
$<$	"is less than"	
$\geq$	"greater than or equal to" "at least"	"not less than"
$\leq$	"less than or equal to" "at most"	"not more than"

Caution: recognize the distinction in verbal problems between the phrases "more than" and "less than" for addition and subtraction and the phrases "is more than" and "is less than" for an inequality.

Example: 5 more than x $\rightarrow$ $x + 5$ 5 is more than x $\rightarrow$ $5 > x$

                5 less than x $\rightarrow$ $x - 5$ 5 is less than x $\rightarrow$ $5 < x$

MODEL PROBLEM

Barbara has $10 to buy milk and cookies for her child's party. If each pint of milk costs $0.55 and each cookie costs $0.15, and she wants to buy 6 times as many cookies as pints of milk, write an inequality that shows how much she can buy for at most $10.

Solution:

(A)   Let m = the number of pints of milk she buys; $6m$ = the number of cookies she buys.

(B) $0.55m + 0.15(6m) \leq 10.00$

Explanation of steps:

(A)   Write expressions in terms of a variable.

(B)   Create an appropriate inequality using the expressions.

PRACTICE PROBLEMS

1. If x represents a number, write an inequality to represent the statement, "Eight less than three times a number is greater than fifteen."	2. A sign in front of a roller coaster ride says that all riders must be at least 48 inches tall. If h represents the height of a rider in inches, write an inequality for the statement on this sign.
3. Allison is nine inches taller than Ben. The sum of their heights is less than 144 inches. Write an appropriate inequality to describe this situation.	4. Cyril is going to buy a coat and a hat. The coat costs 3 times as much as the hat. He cannot spend more than $120. Write an inequality to describe this situation.
5. Abe and Betty need to sell at least 90 magazine subscriptions between them. If Abe sells twice as many subscriptions as Betty, write an inequality that could be used to determine how many subscriptions, x, Betty needs to sell.	6. You need to purchase a apples and b bananas, and you can spend no more than $25. Apples cost 75 cents each and bananas cost $1.25 each. Write an inequality, in terms of a and b, to describe this situation.

7. The length of a rectangle is 15 and its width is *w*. The perimeter of the rectangle is, *at most*, 50. Write an inequality that could be used to find the longest possible width.	8. The length of a rectangle is three feet less than twice its width. The area of the rectangle is at most 30 square feet. If *w* represents the width of the rectangle, in feet, write an inequality that could be used to find the width.
9. Students measured their heights, *h*, in centimeters. The height of the shortest student was 155 cm, and the height of the tallest student was 190 cm. Write a *compound inequality* representing the range of heights.	10. Every day, a woman needs to eat at least 1500 but less than 1800 calories. Write a *compound inequality* representing the possible amount of calories she could eat.

11. A local high school needs to pay $250.00 for a hall where a school dance will be held. Each student attending the dance pays $0.75 and each guest pays $1.25. If 200 students attend the dance, write an inequality that could be used to determine the number of guests, *x*, needed to cover the cost of the hall.

2.4   <u>Linear Model in Two Variables</u>

KEY TERMS AND CONCEPTS

As we have seen, a *linear equation* is an equation in which each term is either a *constant term* or a *variable term*, and where each variable term includes only a *single variable to the first power* and an optional *numerical coefficient*. A linear equation can have any number of variables, but to be graphed on a two-dimensional coordinate grid (as we'll see in the next unit), it can have at most two variables.

If we use x and y as the two variables, any linear equation can be simplified into the form:

$$y = \Box x + \Box$$

where the boxes represent numerical values. On the right side of the equation above, the first term is the *variable term* (it includes the variable x) and the second term is the *constant term*.

Example: $y = 16x - 12$ (note that either numerical value can be negative)

We have already seen the word "each" used in a number of verbal expressions. Phrases such as "for each," "for every," or "per" are frequently used to represent the **variable term** in a linear expression. Often, the situation will also involve a "starting" or "one-time" value, which usually represents a **constant term**.

Example: Taxis in a certain city charge \$2.50 just to enter the taxi and \$1.50 <u>for each</u> mile driven. If we let m represent the number of miles, the cost is 2.50 + 1.50m.

The **isolated variable** in the equation is the value that the linear model is used to calculate.

Example: If c represents the cost of the taxi ride in the previous example, we can write the linear equation $c = 1.50m + 2.50$ to calculate the cost. (Note that the commutative property of addition allows us to switch the order of the two terms.)

A linear model may be written in **function notation**. For now, this only means that the isolated variable is written as a "function of" the other variable, using the name of the function (usually an upper or lower case letter) followed by the other variable in parentheses.

Example: The previous equation, $c = 1.50m + 2.50$, could have been written as $c(m) = 1.50m + 2.50$, meaning that c (the cost) is a "function of" m.

Functions will be more formally introduced later, in Chapter 9.

If a problem defines the rate "for each additional" unit, then one or more of the units are already included in the constant term and need to be subtracted from the variable in the variable term.

Example: Suppose the taxi charges $2.50 for the <u>first</u> mile and $1.50 <u>for each additional</u> mile. The equation is $c = 1.50(m - 1) + 2.50$ for whole numbers $m \geq 1$.

MODEL PROBLEM

Oberon Cell Phone Company advertises service for 3 cents per minute plus a monthly fee of $29.95. Write an equation to calculate the monthly cost, c, if n call minutes are used.

Solution: **Explanation:**

$c = 0.03n + 29.95$ The monthly fee is a one-time starting cost for the month, so it is the constant term. The cost "per" minute *[3 cents times n]* is the variable term. We are calculating the cost *[c]*.

PRACTICE PROBLEMS

1. Kim and Cyndi are starting a business tutoring students in math. They rent an office for $400 per month and charge their students $40 per hour. They write an equation for their profit (or loss) as $y = 40x - 400$. In this equation, what does the variable x represent?	2. A car rental company charges its customers a fixed rental fee plus 30 cents per mile driven. If a customer's cost is expressed as the function $C(x) = 0.30x + 100$, what does the variable x represent?
3. Essence of Yoga charges $80 per month with a $75 registration fee. Write an equation for the cost, c, of an x-month membership.	4. Andy deposits $100 in a bank account that earns $5 interest annually. Write a function, $P(y)$, for the balance in the account after y years.
5. Abbey starts with $20 and plays an arcade game that costs 50 cents per game. Write an equation for the amount of money, m, remaining after g games are played.	6. An airplane 30,000 feet above the ground begins descending at the constant rate of 2000 feet per minute. Write an function for the plane's altitude, $h(m)$, after m minutes.

7. A video rental company charges its customers $5 for the first day's rental and $2 for each additional day. Write an equation for the cost, c, of renting a video for n days, where $n \geq 1$.	8. An employee is paid $800 per week for the first 40 hours of work, plus overtime pay of $30 per hour for each hour over 40. Write a function for the employee's total wages, $w(h)$, for working h hours in a week ($h \geq 40$).

2.5   <u>Word Problems – Linear Equations</u>

KEY TERMS AND CONCEPTS

To solve a word problem using an equation:

1. Translate each quantity into an expression in terms of a variable
2. Determine from the problem how the expressions form an equation
3. Write the equation
4. Solve for the variable, and check your solution
5. Be sure to answer the question asked by the problem, and make sure your answer is reasonable!

How to check your solution: Substitute the solution for the variable into the original equation and evaluate both sides of the equation to make sure the solution makes the equation true.

When is an answer unreasonable?

For examples, if your answer is that the length of a side of a triangle is –4 inches, or that the number of people on a bus is 10.75, dismiss these as unreasonable and retrace your steps.

MODEL PROBLEM

Tamara has five less than four times as many friendship bracelets as Allison. If they have a total of 55 bracelets, how many bracelets does Tamara have?

Solution:

(A)   Let a = how many bracelets Allison has;

(B)   Tamara has $4a - 5$ bracelets.

$$a + 4a - 5 = 55$$

(C) $5a - 5 = 55$

$$5a = 60$$

$$a = 12$$

(D)   To check the solution:

$$a + 4a - 5 = 55$$

$$(12) + 4(12) - 5 = 55$$

$$12 + 48 - 5 = 55$$

$$55 = 55 \checkmark$$

(E)   If Allison has 12 bracelets, then Tamara has $4a - 5 = 4(12) - 5 = 43$ bracelets. This is reasonable: $12 + 43 = 55$. Tamara has 43 bracelets.

Explanation of steps:

(A)   Determine what the variable is.

(B)   Express other quantities *[Tamara's bracelets]* in terms of the variable, and write an appropriate equation *[the sum of a and 4a – 5 is 55]*.

(C)   Solve for the variable.

(D)   Check the solution *[a = 12]* by substituting it into the original equation *[substitute (12) for a]* and then evaluate each side to see if the equation is true.

(E)   Answer the question asked by the problem; sometimes the value of the variable does **not** answer the question *[a is the number that Allison has, but we need to say how many Tamara has, which is 4a – 5]*. Check that the answer is reasonable.

PRACTICE PROBLEMS

1. Jamie is 5 years older than her sister Amy. If the sum of their ages is 19, how old is Jamie?	2. Arielle has a collection of grasshoppers and crickets. She has 561 insects in all. The number of grasshoppers is twice the number of crickets. Find the number of *each* type of insect that she has.
3. Three times as many robins as cardinals visited a bird feeder. If a total of 20 robins and cardinals visited the feeder, how many were robins?	4. On the JV baseball team, the number of sophomores is four more than twice the number of freshmen. If there are 16 players combined on the team, how many of each grade level are there?
5. Every year, Jack buys pizzas to serve at a Super Bowl party for his friends. This year, he bought three more than twice the number of pizzas he bought last year. If he bought 15 pizzas this year, how many pizzas did he buy last year?	6. A DVD costs twice as much as a music CD. Omar buys 2 DVDs and 2 CDs and spends $45. How much does one CD cost?

7. Keisha has 28 video discs, which is 8 less than 4 times the number of video discs in Minnie's collection. How many video discs does Minnie own?	8. During a recent winter, the ratio of deer to foxes was 7 to 3 in one county of New York State. If there were 210 foxes in the county, what was the number of deer in the county?
9. A jar contains red and black marbles. The number of red marbles in the jar is three more than twice the number of black marbles. There are 42 marbles in all. How many red marbles are there?	10. Marilyn spent $17 at an amusement park for admission and rides. If she paid $5 for admission, and rides cost $3 each, what is the total number of rides that she went on?
11. A passenger pays $44.25 in taxi fare from the hotel to the airport. The taxi charged $2.25 for the first mile plus $3.50 for each additional mile. How many miles did the taxi travel?	12. The ages of three brothers are consecutive even integers. Three times the age of the youngest brother exceeds the oldest brother's age by 48 years. What is the age of the youngest brother?

13. There are 357 seniors in Harris High School. The ratio of boys to girls is 7:10. How many boys are in the senior class?

14. There were 100 more balcony tickets than main-floor tickets sold for a concert. The balcony tickets sold for $4 and the main-floor tickets sold for $12. The total amount of sales for both types of tickets was $3,056. Find the number of balcony tickets that were sold.

15. In his piggy bank, Neil has three times as many dimes as nickels and he has four more quarters than nickels. The coins total $4.60. How many of each coin does he have?

16. A craft shop sold 150 pillows. Small pillows were $6.50 each and large pillows were $9.00 each. If the total amount collected from the sale of these items was $1180.00, what is the total number of each size pillow that was sold?

2.6   **Word Problems – Inequalities**

KEY TERMS AND CONCEPTS

To solve a word problem using an inequality:

1. Translate each quantity into an expression in terms of a variable
2. Determine from the problem how the expressions form an inequality
3. Write and solve the inequality
4. Be sure to answer the question asked by the problem

MODEL PROBLEM

Thelma and Laura start a lawn-mowing business and buy a lawnmower for $225. They plan to charge $15 to mow one lawn. What is the *minimum* number of lawns they need to mow if they wish to earn a profit of *at least* $750?

Solution:

(A)   Let x represent the number of lawns they need to mow. Total profit is $15x - 225$.

(B) $15x - 225 \geq 750$

(C) $\underline{+225 + 225}$

$\dfrac{15x \geq 975}{}$

$15 15$

$x \geq 65$

(D)   They need to mow a minimum of 65 lawns.

Explanation of steps:

(A)   Translate each quantity into an expression in terms of a variable *[profit would be $15 per mowed lawn, less the $225 cost of the lawnmower, or 15x – 225]*.

(B)   Determine from the problem how the expressions form an inequality *[the profit must be at least – greater than or equal to – $750]*.

(C)   Write and solve the inequality.

(D)   Be sure to answer the question asked by the problem.

PRACTICE PROBLEMS

1. Find the smallest integer such that five less than twice the integer is greater than 23.	2. If five times a number is less than 55, what is the greatest possible integer value of the number?
3. The larger of two integers is 7 times the smaller. The sum of the integers is at most 60. What are the largest two integers that can make these statements true?	4. Tony's job pays him $155 a week. If he has already saved $375, what is the minimum number of weeks he needs to work in order to have enough money to buy a drone for $900?
5. Andy earns $5.95 per hour working after school. He needs at least $215 for his holiday shopping. How many hours must he work to reach his goal?	6. The cost per month of making n number of wooden toys is $3n + 30$. The income from selling n toys is $6n$. How many toys must the company make to make a profit (the income is greater than the cost)?

7. A music club has a registration fee of $13.95 and charges $0.49 to buy each song. Nelly has $50.00 to join the club and buy songs. What is the maximum number of songs she can buy?	8. A cell phone plan charges $0.07 per minute plus a monthly fee of $19.00. Tamara budgets $29.50 per month for total cell phone expenses. What is the maximum number of minutes she could use each month in order to stay within her budget?
9. Parking charges at Superior Parking Garage are $5.00 for the first hour and $1.50 for each additional 30 minutes. If Margo has $12.50, what is the maximum amount of time she will be able to park her car at the garage?	10. Members of the band boosters are planning to sell programs at football games. The cost to print the programs is $150 plus $0.50 per program. They plan to sell each program for $2. How many programs must they sell to make a profit of at least $500?

2.7   Conversions

KEY TERMS AND CONCEPTS

At times, the solution of a problem may require a conversion between units of measure, or between unit rates.

A **measurement equivalent** is an equation or approximation expressing the relationship between two different units of measure, and is used to convert between the two units.

Examples: 60 minutes = 1 hour

                            1.61 kilometers ≈ 1 mile

A **conversion fraction** is a fraction (*ratio*) which derives from a measurement equivalent. The numerator and denominator are equivalent measures, so the fraction is equal to 1. Therefore, you can multiply a value by a conversion fraction without changing its value.

Examples: $\dfrac{60\ mins}{1\ hr}$ $\dfrac{1\ hr}{60\ mins}$ $\dfrac{1.61\ km}{1\ mi}$ $\dfrac{1\ mi}{1.61\ km}$

To convert units of measure using measurement equivalents:

1. Write the given measurement.
2. Create a *conversion fraction* from one of the *measurement equivalents*, placing the unit of measure from which we need to change in the denominator. Write as a product and cancel the common unit of measure.
3. Repeat step 2 with any additional conversion fractions that are needed until only the desired unit of measure remains.
4. Multiply.
5. Simplify and write the answer, rounding if necessary.

Example: To convert 6 feet into inches, start by writing 6 feet. Then, use the conversion fraction $\dfrac{12\ inches}{1\ foot}$, making sure to keep the number of feet in the denominator. Cancel the common unit, feet, and multiply. This gives us $6 \times 12 = 72$ inches.

$$6\ \cancel{feet} \cdot \frac{12\ inches}{1\ \cancel{foot}} = 72\ inches$$

To convert unit rates using measurement equivalents:
1. Write the given rate in fraction form.
2. To change the unit in the numerator, create a *conversion fraction* from one of the *measurement equivalents*, placing this unit in the denominator. Write as a product and cancel out the common unit.
3. Similarly, to change the unit in the denominator, create another conversion fraction, but place this unit in the numerator. Write as a product and cancel out the common unit.
4. Multiply the fractions.
5. Simplify and write the answer, rounding if necessary.

Example: To convert 300 miles per hour into miles per minute,

$$\frac{300 \; miles}{1 \; \cancel{hour}} \cdot \frac{1 \; \cancel{hour}}{60 \; minutes} = \frac{300}{60} = 5 \; miles \; per \; minute$$

MODEL PROBLEM 1:   *CONVERTING UNITS OF MEASURE*

How many feet are in 3 furlongs?

> 8 furlongs = 1 mile
>
> 5280 feet = 1 mile

Solution:

(A)   (B)   (C)   (D)   (E)

$$3 \; \cancel{furlongs} \times \frac{1 \; \cancel{mile}}{8 \; \cancel{furlongs}} \times \frac{5280 \; feet}{1 \; \cancel{mile}} = \frac{(3)(1)(5280) \; feet}{(8)(1)} = 1,980 \; feet$$

Explanation of steps:

(A) Write the given measurement *[3 furlongs]*.

(B) Create a conversion fraction from one of the measurement equivalents, placing the unit of measure from which we need to change *[furlongs]* in the denominator. Write as a product and cancel the common unit of measure *[furlongs]*.

(C) Repeat step B with any additional conversion fractions that are needed *[we still need to change miles to feet]*, until only the desired unit of measure *[feet]* remains.

(D) Multiply.

(E) Simplify and write the answer, rounding if necessary.

PRACTICE PROBLEMS

1. Convert 20 inches into centimeters (*cm*), rounded to the *nearest centimeter*. 2.54 cm = 1 inch	2. Saul walked 8,900 feet from home to school. How far, to the *nearest tenth of a mile*, did he walk? 1 mile = 5,280 feet
3. A pet store manager needs to pack 1680 ounces of pet food into 5-pound bags. How many 5-pound bags of pet food can be packed? 1 pound = 16 ounces	4. Liz is baking cookies. A single batch uses ¾ teaspoon of vanilla. If Liz is mixing the ingredients for five batches at the same time, how many tablespoons of vanilla will she use? 3 teaspoons = 1 tablespoon

5. Little league baseball bats have barrels that measure 2.625 inches in diameter. What is the diameter of a bat in millimeters (*mm*), to the *nearest millimeter?*

  2.54 cm = 1 inch
  10 mm = 1 cm

6. The most common distance for a thoroughbred horse race is 6 furlongs. What is this distance in kilometers (*km*), to the *nearest hundredth of a kilometer?*

  8 furlongs = 1 mile
  1.61 km = 1 mile

7. Ribbon sells for $3.75 per yard. Find the cost, in dollars, for 48 inches of ribbon.

  12 inches = 1 foot
  3 feet = 1 yard

8. Convert 60 feet into meters, rounded to the *nearest tenth of a meter.*

  12 inches = 1 foot
  2.54 cm = 1 inch
  100 cm = 1 meter

MODEL PROBLEM 2:   *CONVERTING FROM ONE UNIT RATE TO ANOTHER*

A cheetah runs at a rate of 70 miles per hour. What is the cheetah's speed in feet per minute?

$$5280 \text{ feet} = 1 \text{ mile}$$
$$60 \text{ minutes} = 1 \text{ hour}$$

Solution:

$$
\overset{\text{(A)}}{\frac{70 \ \cancel{miles}}{1 \ \cancel{hour}}} \times \overset{\text{(B)}}{\frac{5280 \ ft}{1 \ \cancel{mile}}} \times \overset{\text{(C)}}{\frac{1 \ \cancel{hour}}{60 \ mins}} = \overset{\text{(D)}}{\frac{(70)(5280)(1) \ ft}{(1)(1)(60) \ mins}} \overset{\text{(E)}}{= 6{,}160 \ ft/min}
$$

Explanation of steps:

(A)   Write the given rate *[70 miles per hour]* in fraction form.

(B)   To change the unit in the numerator *[miles]*, create a conversion fraction from one of the measurement equivalents, placing this unit *[miles]* in the denominator. Write as a product and cancel out the common unit *[miles]*, leaving the desired unit *[feet, or ft]* in the numerator of the new fraction.

(C)   Similarly, to change the unit in the denominator *[hours]*, create another conversion fraction, but place this unit *[hours]* in the numerator. Write as a product and cancel out the common unit *[hours]*, leaving the desired unit *[minutes]* in the denominator.

(D)   Multiply the fractions.

(E)   Simplify and write the answer, rounding if necessary.

PRACTICE PROBLEMS

9. Roger ran a distance of 150 meters in 1½ minutes. What is his speed in meters per hour?	10. If the speed of sound is 344 meters per second, what is the approximate speed of sound, in meters per hour?

11. A Toyota Camry Hybrid automobile boasts a gas mileage of 43 miles per gallon. What is its gas mileage in kilometers (*km*) per liter, to the *nearest tenth*.

$$1.61 \text{ km} = 1 \text{ mile}$$
$$3.79 \text{ liters} = 1 \text{ gallon}$$

12. At a grocery store, a 2-liter bottle of soda costs $1.50 and a 1-gallon bottle costs $2.50. Which is a better buy? Justify your answer.

$$3.79 \text{ liters} = 1 \text{ gallon}$$

13. Nikita rode her bicycle a total of 8000 miles last year. To the *nearest yard*, Nikita rode an average of how many yards per day?

$$1 \text{ mile} = 1760 \text{ yards}$$
$$1 \text{ year} = 365 \text{ days}$$

14. If you travel 30 miles per hour, how many feet per second are you traveling?

$$5280 \text{ feet} = 1 \text{ mile}$$
$$60 \text{ minutes} = 1 \text{ hour}$$
$$60 \text{ seconds} = 1 \text{ minute}$$

15. A football player runs the length of a 100 yard football field in 11 seconds. How fast did he run in miles per hour, rounded to the *nearest tenth*?

   3 feet = 1 yard
   5280 feet = 1 mile
   60 minutes = 1 hour
   60 seconds = 1 minute

Chapter 3.   Linear Graphs

3.1   Determine Whether a Point is on a Line

KEY TERMS AND CONCEPTS

A **line** consists of a set of **points**, each of which can be represented by an **ordered pair** stating its x value and y value as (x, y). This set of points represents the **solution set** of a **linear equation** involving the two variables, x and y.

One way to graph a line is to by **creating a table**. The first column will contain some sample x values; I usually prefer to choose –2, –1, 0, 1, and 2. The second column is used to substitute the x value into the equation in order to solve for y. The resulting y values are written in the third column. The last column gives the corresponding ordered pairs of x and y values.

Example: We can graph $y = 3x + 1$ by using a table and drawing a line through the ordered pairs on a coordinate graph.

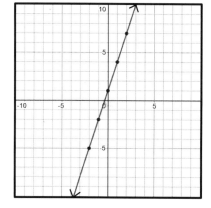

x	$y = 3x + 1$	y	(x, y)
–2	$y = 3(-2) + 1$	–5	$(-2, -5)$
–1	$y = 3(-1) + 1$	–2	$(-1, -2)$
0	$y = 3(0) + 1$	1	$(0,1)$
1	$y = 3(1) + 1$	4	$(1,4)$
2	$y = 3(2) + 1$	7	$(2,7)$

You can **determine whether a point is on a line** by substituting the x value and y value for the variables x and y in the equation and then checking if these values make the equation true.

Example: $(4,13)$ is on the line $y = 3x + 1$ because substituting 4 for x and 13 for y, we get $13 = 3(4) + 1$, which is true.

CALCULATOR TIP

This can also be done using the calculator.

Example: For the example above, enter [4][STO▸][X,T,Θ,n] and [1][3][STO▸][ALPHA][Y].

Then test by typing [ALPHA][Y] [2nd][TEST][1] [3][X,T,Θ,n][+][1].

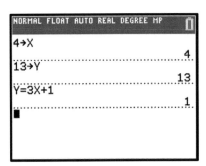

MODEL PROBLEM

Does the line whose equation is $2y + 6 = 4x$ contain the point $(1, -1)$?

Solution:

(A) $2y + 6 = 4x$ for $x = 1, y = -1$

(B) $2(-1) + 6 = 4(1)$?

(C) $4 = 4$, so yes, $(1, -1)$ is in the solution set.

Explanation of steps:

(A)   The first value in the ordered pair represents the value of x, the second is the value of y.

(B)   Substitute for x and y.

(C)   Evaluate both sides of the equation to determine if the equation is true.

PRACTICE PROBLEMS

1. Does the point $(3,7)$ lie on the line whose equation is $y = 3x - 2$?	2. Does the line whose equation is $y = \frac{1}{2}x + 5$ contain the point $(4,9)$?
3. Does the line whose equation is $y = 4x$ pass through the origin, $(0,0)$?	4. Does the point $(-2, -4)$ lie on the line whose equation is $2y - 3x = -2$?
5. Determine if the ordered pair $(-4, 3)$ is a solution of $4x - y = -13$.	6. Determine if the ordered pair $(-2, -4)$ is a solution of $5x - 2y = -2$.

7. Determine if the ordered pair $(-5, -1)$ is a solution of $2x - y = -11$.	8. Determine if the ordered pair $(3, -2)$ is a solution of $4x = 3y + 18$.
9. The graph of the equation $2x + 6y = 4$ passes through point $(x, -2)$. What is the value of x?	10. If $(k, 3)$ is a point on the line whose equation is $4x + y = -9$, what is the value of k?
11. Point $(k, -3)$ lies on the line whose equation is $x - 2y = -2$. What is the value of k?	12. Point $(5, k)$ lies on the line represented by the equation $2x + y = 9$. What is the value of k?

3.2   Lines Parallel to Axes

KEY TERMS AND CONCEPTS

If a linear equation has only one variable (that is, x or y is equal to a constant), then it represents a line that is parallel to one of the axes.

If y is equal to a constant, the line is parallel to the x-axis and crosses the y-axis at that constant.

Example: $y = 3$ represents a line parallel to the x-axis but 3 units above it. No matter what values we choose for x, the y value is always 3, as shown below.

x	$y = 3$	y	(x, y)
−2	$y = 3$	3	$(-2, 3)$
−1	$y = 3$	3	$(-1, 3)$
0	$y = 3$	3	$(0, 3)$
1	$y = 3$	3	$(1, 3)$
2	$y = 3$	3	$(2, 3)$

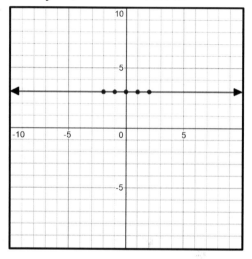

If x is equal to a constant, the line is parallel to the y-axis and crosses the x-axis at that constant.

Example: $x = -5$ represents a line parallel to the y-axis but 5 units to the left of it. The line contains the points $(-5, y)$ where y is any real number.

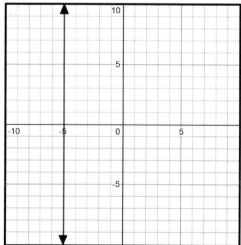

73

MODEL PROBLEM

Write the equation of a line parallel to the *x*-axis but 10 units below it.

Solution:

$y = -10$

Explanation of steps:

If a line is parallel to an axis, then the other variable is equal to a constant. *[A line parallel to the x-axis has y = constant; since it is 10 units below the axis, $y = -10$.]*

PRACTICE PROBLEMS

1. The graph of $y = -2$ is a line (1) parallel to the *x*-axis (2) parallel to the *y*-axis (3) passing through the origin (4) passing through the point $(-2,0)$	2. Which equation represents a line that is parallel to the *y*-axis and passes through the point (4,3)? (1) $x = 3$ (3) $y = 3$ (2) $x = 4$ (4) $y = 4$
3. Write the equation of the line parallel to the *y*-axis but 9 units to the right of it.	4. Write the equation of the line parallel to the *x*-axis but 1 unit above it.
5. Write the equation of the line that lies on the *y*-axis.	6. Write the equation of the line that lies on the *x*-axis.

7. At what point does the line whose equation is $x = 5$ intersect the x-axis, written as an ordered pair?

8. Graph the line whose equation is $x = 7$.

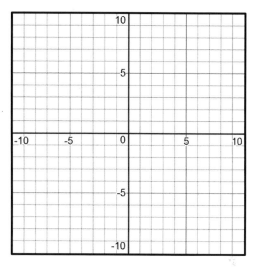

9. Graph the line whose equation is $y = -4$.

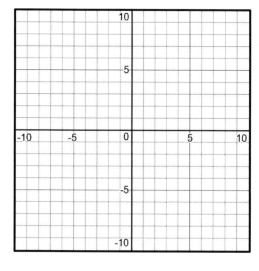

10. Graph the line whose equation is $y - 4 = -1$.

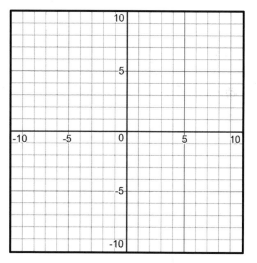

3.3   **Find Intercepts**

KEY TERMS AND CONCEPTS

The **y-intercept** is the value of y at the point where a graph intersects the y-axis and the **x-intercept** is the value of x at the point where the graph intersects the x-axis.

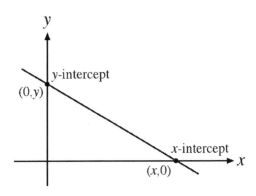

Algebraically, we can find the y-intercept by substituting 0 for x in the equation, and we can find the x-intercept by substituting 0 for y in the equation. This works because $x = 0$ all along the y-axis, and $y = 0$ all along the x-axis.

Example: For the equation $y = 2x - 1$, the y-intercept is $y = 2(0) - 1 = -1$. We can

find the x-intercept by solving for $0 = 2x - 1$, which gives us $x = \frac{1}{2}$.

Of course, if a line is parallel to an axis, it will never intersect that axis, so an intercept cannot be found for that axis' variable.

MODEL PROBLEM

What are the x-intercept and y-intercept of the line whose equation is $2x + 3y = 12$?

Solution:

(A)   (B)

$2(0) + 3y = 12$ $2x + 3(0) = 12$

$\quad\quad 3y = 12$ $\quad\quad 2x = 12$

$\quad\quad\quad y = 4$ $\quad\quad\quad x = 6$

(C) The y-intercept is 4 and the x-intercept is 6.

Explanation of steps:

(A) To find the y-intercept, substitute 0 for x in the equation and solve.

(B) To find the x-intercept, substitute 0 for y in the equation and solve.

(C) The resulting values of y and x are the intercepts.

PRACTICE PROBLEMS

1. State the x and y intercepts, both integers, of the graph below.

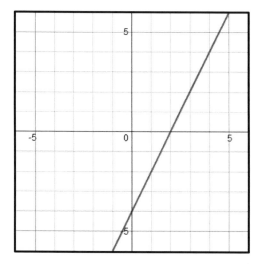

2. State the x and y intercepts, both integers, of the graph below.

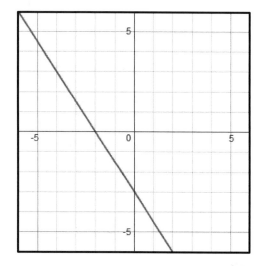

3. Find the x and y intercepts of the equation $3y + 2x = 6$.

4. Find the x and y intercepts of the equation $3x - 4y = 12$.

5. Find the x and y intercepts of the equation $y = -2x + 5$.

6. Find the x and y intercepts of the equation $9x - 6y + 5 = 0$.

3.4   <u>**Find Slope Given Two Points**</u>

KEY TERMS AND CONCEPTS

If you can imagine a person walking along a line *from left to right*, the **slope of the line** represents how steep the road is.

A **positive slope** would represent walking uphill and a **negative slope** would represent walking downhill. A **slope of zero** would mean the road is horizontal (parallel to the *x*-axis); it is neither uphill nor downhill. The person cannot walk from left to right along a vertical line (parallel to the *y*-axis), so we say that a vertical line has **no slope**. The larger the absolute value of the slope, the steeper the road: a slope of 3 is a steeper uphill climb than a slope of 1/3, and a slope of –3 is a steeper downhill descent than a slope of –1/3.

The slope is usually represented by the letter **_m_**. Given two points on a line, we can determine, either graphically or algebraically, the slope of the line.

Finding the slope graphically:

If we move from the left point to the right point, the slope $m = \dfrac{rise}{run}$.

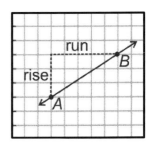

The **rise** is how many units we travel up (positive) or down (negative), and the **run** is how many units we travel to the right.

Example: From point A to point B on the graph at right,

the rise is 3 and the run is 5, so the slope is $\dfrac{3}{5}$.

Finding the slope algebraically:

We can think of the rise, or the number of *y*-value units we need to travel, as the **difference in the _y_-values**, and the run, or the number of *x*-value units we need to travel, as the **difference in the _x_-values**. If we name the coordinates of the two points (x_1, y_1) and (x_2, y_2), the slope formula can be written as: $m = \dfrac{y_2 - y_1}{x_2 - x_1}$

Example: The slope of the line through (1,3) and (2,6) is $m = \dfrac{y_2 - y_1}{x_2 - x_1} = \dfrac{6 - 3}{2 - 1} = \dfrac{3}{1} = 3.$

If the two points lie on a horizontal line (parallel to the *x*-axis), the slope is zero.

Example: (2,5) and (3,5) lie on the horizontal line $y = 5$. $m = \dfrac{y_2 - y_1}{x_2 - x_1} = \dfrac{5 - 5}{3 - 2} = \dfrac{0}{1} = 0.$

If the two points lie on a vertical line (parallel to the *y*-axis), there is no slope.

Example: (4,1) and (4,3) lie on the vertical line $x = 4$. To use the slope formula would result in a *denominator of zero*, which means that the slope is *undefined*.

MODEL PROBLEM 1:   *GRAPHICALLY*

What is the slope of the line passing through the points (2,4) and (6,6)?

Solution:

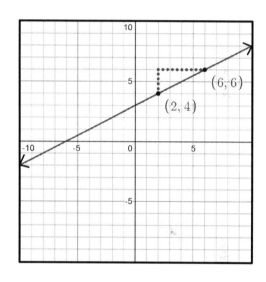

$$m = \frac{rise}{run} = \frac{2}{4} = \frac{1}{2}$$

Explanation of steps:

(A)   Using the graph, first trace how many units you need to travel up (+) or down (–), and call this the rise *[from $y = 4$ to $y = 6$ is 2 units]*.

(B)   Next, trace how many units you need to travel to the right, and call this the run *[from $x = 2$ to $x = 6$ is 4 units]*.

(C)   Write $\frac{rise}{run}$ as a fraction, and reduce.

79

PRACTICE PROBLEMS

1. What is the slope of the line passing through the points *A* and *B*, as shown on the graph below? 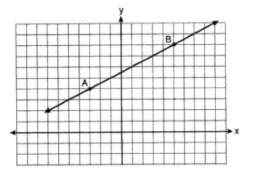	2. What is the slope of the line passing through the points *A* and *B*, as shown on the graph below? 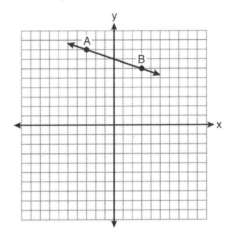
3. What is the slope of line ℓ in the accompanying diagram? 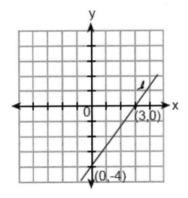	4. What is the slope of line ℓ in the accompanying diagram? 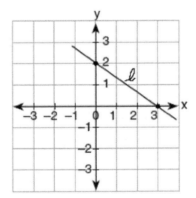

5. What is the slope of the line shown below?

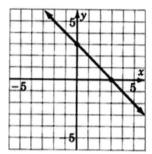

6. On a separate coordinate graph, draw a line through the points $(-4,-3)$ and $(1,2)$ and find the slope of the line.

MODEL PROBLEM 2:   *ALGEBRAICALLY*

What is the slope of the line passing through the points $(-3,4)$ and $(1,2)$?

Solution:

(A) $(x_1, y_1) = (-3,4)$ $(x_2, y_2) = (1,2)$

(B)   (C)   (D)   (E)

$$m = \frac{y_2 - y_1}{x_2 - x_1} = \frac{2-4}{1-(-3)} = \frac{-2}{4} = -\frac{1}{2}$$

Explanation of steps:

(A)   Label the coordinates of the two points. Each point has an x and y value, but the first point has subscripts of 1 and the second point has subscripts of 2.

(B)   Write the slope formula.

(C)   Substitute the coordinates as labeled.

(D)   Evaluate the numerator and denominator.

(E)   Simplify, if possible.

PRACTICE PROBLEMS

7. What is the slope of the line that passes through points (1,3) and (5,13)?	8. What is the slope of the line that passes through points $(3, -6)$ and (1,8)?
9. What is the slope of the line that passes through points (4,5) and $(0, -3)$?	10. What is the slope of the line that passes through $(-4, -2)$ and $(2, -2)$?

11. What is the slope of the line that passes through the points (2,5) and (7,3)?	12. What is the slope of the line that passes through the points (3,5) and $(-2, 2)$?

3.5   <u>Find Slope Given an Equation</u>

KEY TERMS AND CONCEPTS

The equation of a line is most commonly written in **slope-intercept form**: $y = mx + b$. In this form, m (the coefficient of x) is the **slope** of the line and b is the **y-intercept**. The y-intercept is the value of y at the point where the line intersects the y-axis.

Transforming an equation into slope-intercept form

If the equation is not already in slope-intercept form, you will need to transform the equation by solving for y in terms of x.

Examples: To transform the equations $y + 2x = 4$ and $3y = 2x - 9$,

$$y + 2x = 4 \qquad\qquad \frac{3y}{3} = \frac{2x - 9}{3}$$
$$\underline{-2x \quad - 2x} \qquad\qquad$$
$$y = -2x + 4 \qquad\qquad y = \frac{2}{3}x - 3$$

If two distinct lines have the **same slope**, they are **parallel**. So, to determine whether two lines are parallel, write each equation in *slope-intercept form* to determine whether the slopes are the same for both equations.

MODEL PROBLEM 1:   *TRANSFORMING AN EQUATION*

What is the slope of the line whose equation is $2y - 3x = x + 2$?

Solution:

(A) $2y - 3x = x + 2$
$$\underline{+3x \quad + 3x}$$
$$\frac{2y}{2} = \frac{4x + 2}{2}$$
$$y = 2x + 1$$

(B) Slope is 2

Explanation of steps:

(A) If the equation is not already in slope-intercept form, transform it by solving for y in terms of x. *[Add $3x$ to both sides, then divide each by 2.]*

(B) For an equation in slope-intercept form, the slope is the coefficient of x *[the slope is 2]*.

PRACTICE PROBLEMS

1. What is the slope of a line whose equation is $y = \frac{2}{5}x - 5$?	2. What is the slope of the line whose equation is $y - 3x = 1$?
3. What is the slope of the line whose equation is $2y = 5x + 4$?	4. What is the slope of the linear equation $5y - 10x = -15$?
5. What is the slope of the line represented by the equation $4x + 3y = 12$?	6. What is the slope of a line represented by the equation $2y = x - 4$?
7. What is the slope of the line whose equation is $3x - 2y = 12$?	8. What is the slope of the line whose equation is $3x - 4y - 16 = 0$?

MODEL PROBLEM 2:   *EQUATIONS OF PARALLEL LINES*

The equations of two distinct lines are $y = 3x - 6$ and $2y = 3x + 6$. Are the lines parallel?

Solution:

(A)   For $y = 3x - 6$, the slope $m = 3$.

Solving $2y = 3x + 6$ for y:

$$\frac{2y}{2} = \frac{3x + 6}{2}$$

$y = \frac{3}{2}x + 3$, so the slope $m = \frac{3}{2}$.

(B)   The lines are *not* parallel because the slopes are not equal.

Explanation of steps:

(A)   Write each equation in slope-intercept form to determine the slope of each line.

[The first equation is already in slope-intercept form, $y = mx + b$, so the slope m = 3.

The second equation needed to be transformed, resulting in a slope of $\frac{3}{2}$.]

(B)   If the slopes are equal, the lines are parallel.

[These slopes are 3 and $\frac{3}{2}$, so they are not parallel.]

PRACTICE PROBLEMS

9. Line ℓ has an equation of $y = -2x - 5$. Write the equation of a line that is parallel to line ℓ but has a y-intercept of 2.	10. Line ℓ has an equation of $y = \frac{1}{2}x + 2$. Write the equation of a line that is parallel to line ℓ but passes through the origin.

11. Which equation represents a line that is parallel to the line whose equation is $y = -3x - 7$?

(1) $y = -3x + 4$ (3) $y = \frac{1}{3}x + 5$

(2) $y = -\frac{1}{3}x - 7$ (4) $y = 3x - 2$

12. Which equation represents a line that is parallel to the line whose equation is $2x - 3y = 9$?

(1) $y = \frac{2}{3}x - 4$ (3) $y = \frac{3}{2}x - 4$

(2) $y = -\frac{2}{3}x + 4$ (4) $y = -\frac{3}{2}x + 4$

13. Which equation below represents a line that is parallel to the line, $y = -x + 4$?

$$2y + 2x = 6$$
$$2y - x = 6$$

14. Which equation below represents a line that is parallel to the line, $4x + 6y = 5$?

$$-3y = 2x + 5$$
$$-6y + 4x = 5$$

3.6   **Graph Linear Equations**

KEY TERMS AND CONCEPTS

Graphing an equation in slope-intercept form

Given an equation in the form $y = mx + b$, you can follow these steps to graph the line:

1. Use the y-intercept to plot the point $(0, b)$ on the y-axis.
2. Use the slope to determine at least two more points.
3. Draw a line through the points and label the line with the equation.

Example:

For the equation $y = 3x - 2$,

the slope $m = 3$ and the y-intercept $b = -2$.

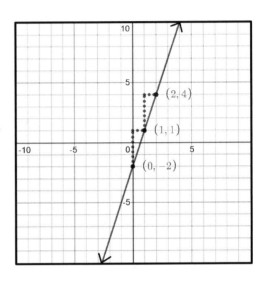

The y-intercept of -2 gives the starting point, $(0, -2)$.

Since the slope $m = 3 = \dfrac{3}{1} = \dfrac{rise}{run}$, use the rise of 3

and run of 1 to get two more points, $(1,1)$ and $(2,4)$.

It may help to remember that **b** tells us a point to *begin* graphing the line and the **m** tells us how to *move* to find other points on the line.

CALCULATOR TIP

We can also **graph the line using the calculator**:

1. Write the equation in slope-intercept form.

2. Enter the equation by pressing the [Y=] button, then type the right side of the equation. Use [X,T,Θ,*n*] to enter the variable *x*.

3. Press [GRAPH].

Example: For the equation $y = 3x - 2$, enter [Y=][3][X,T,Θ,*n*][−][2][ENTER] [GRAPH][ENTER].

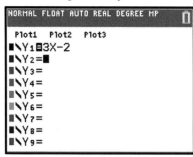 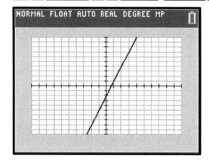

Note: After pressing the [Y=] button, if any of the Plots at the top of the screen are highlighted, use the arrow keys to move to them and press [ENTER] to turn them off.

The calculator's default zoom size, **ZStandard**, sets the grid size to 20 by 20 units centered at the origin. For graphs that may not display well in the standard grid size, you may need to adjust the **Window** size. Press [WINDOW] and enter values for [Xmin] and [Xmax], and also values for [Ymin] and [Ymax]. The values of [Xscl] and [Yscl] represent the difference between tick marks on each axis and can usually be left at 1. Then press [GRAPH].

Because the calculator screen is wider than it is tall, the cells in the grid are not squares in the ZStandard zoom size. Most of the time, you may want the zoom set to **ZSquare** by pressing [ZOOM][5]. This will graph your equation using square boxes on the grid, which will display the slopes of your lines more accurately, as shown below.

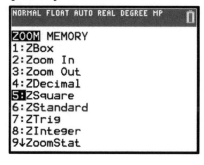 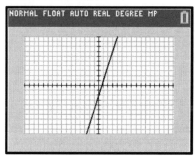

CALCULATOR TIP

To view a table of points on the line with the calculator:

Press [2nd][TABLE]. You can then scroll with the arrow keys [▲][▼] to see more points.

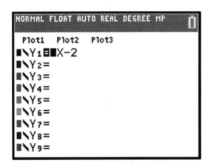 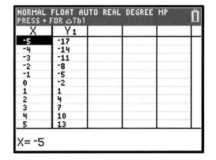

If you'd like to see both the graph and the table on the same screen, press [MODE], then scroll down and change from Full to G-T (or Graph-Table) mode.

Press [TRACE] and the [◄][►] keys to move the cursor along the line while the calculator scrolls to the corresponding points in the table. Or, press [2nd][TABLE] to switch to the table, then use the [▲][▼] keys to scroll through the table rows while the calculator moves to the corresponding points on the graph.

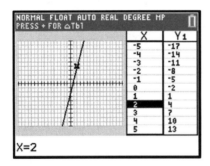 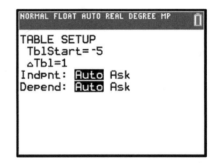

You can specify which values of x the calculator will use for its table. Press [2nd] [TBLSET], then enter values for TblStart and ΔTbl. For example, if you want the table to start at $x = -5$ with increments of 1, enter TblStart = –5 and ΔTbl = 1, as shown above right.

PRACTICE PROBLEMS

1. Graph the equation $y = x - 5$.

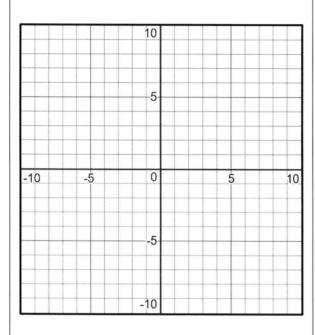

2. Graph the equation $y = -2x + 4$.

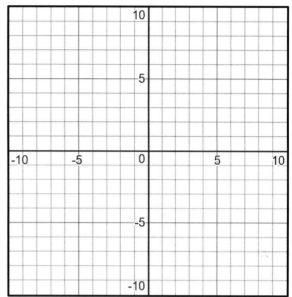

3. Graph the equation $y - 3x = 4$.

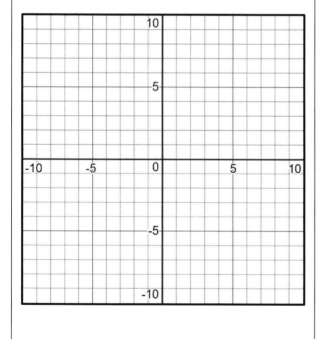

4. Graph the equation $2y + 2x = x - 2$.

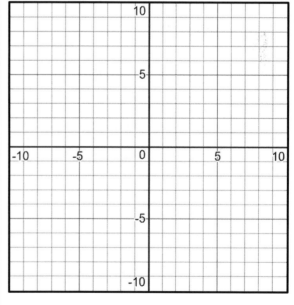

5. Which equation is represented by the graph?

    (1) $2y + x = 10$

    (2) $y - 2x = -5$

    (3) $-2y = 10x - 4$

    (4) $2y = -4x - 10$

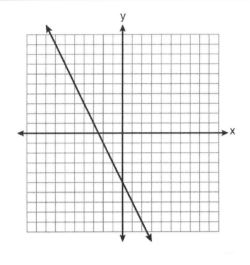

3.7   <u>**Write an Equation Given a Point and Slope**</u>

KEY TERMS AND CONCEPTS

If given the **slope** of a line and the coordinates of **one point**, substitute the slope for m and the coordinates of the point for x and y in the general **slope-intercept form**, $y = mx + b$. This will allow us to solve for b. Once m and b are known, the equation of the line may be written.

An alternative method uses the general **point-slope form** of a linear equation:

$y - y_1 = m(x - x_1)$ where m is the slope and (x_1, y_1) is a point on the line.

Using this form, we can substitute the given slope for m and the coordinates of the point for x_1 and y_1. If we want to transform the resulting equation into slope-intercept form, we need to solve for y in terms of x.

MODEL PROBLEM

Write the equation of the line through $(1, -3)$ with a slope of 2.

Solution:

(A) $y = mx + b$

(B) $-3 = 2(1) + b$

(C) $-3 = 2 + b$

   $-5 = b$

(D) $y = 2x - 5$

Explanation of steps:

(A)   Write the slope-intercept form of an equation.

(B)   Substitute the given values $[x = 1, y = -3, m = 2]$.

(C)   Solve for b.

(D)   Write the equation using the given slope m and the value of b.

PRACTICE PROBLEMS

1. Write an equation of a line through point $(1,4)$ with a slope of 2.	2. Write an equation of the line passing through point $(-6, 5)$ with a slope of 5.
3. Write an equation of a line that passes through $(-3,2)$ and has a slope of $\frac{1}{3}$.	4. Write an equation of the line passing through point $(8, -3)$ with a slope of $\frac{3}{4}$.
5. A line having a slope of $\frac{3}{4}$ passes through the point $(-8,4)$. Write the equation of this line in slope-intercept form.	6. Write an equation of the line that passes through the point $(3, -7)$ and has a slope of $-\frac{4}{3}$.

3.8   **Write an Equation Given Two Points**

KEY TERMS AND CONCEPTS

Given two points on a line, we can write the equation of the line in **slope-intercept form**. First, find the slope m. Then, substitute the slope and one of the point's coordinates into the general equation, $y = mx + b$, in order to solve for b. Once you have m and b, you can write the equation in slope-intercept form.

An alternative method uses the point-slope form of a linear equation. The general form of the point-slope equation is $y - y_1 = m(x - x_1)$. Find the slope m. Then substitute one of the point's coordinates for x_1 and y_1.

MODEL PROBLEM

Write an equation of the line that passes through $(3, -2)$ and $(6,4)$.

Solution:

(A) $m = \dfrac{y_2 - y_1}{x_2 - x_1} = \dfrac{4 - (-2)}{6 - 3} = \dfrac{6}{3} = 2$

(B) $y = mx + b$

(C) $4 = 2(6) + b$

(D) $4 = 12 + b$
$\quad\;\; -8 = b$

(E) $y = 2x - 8$

Explanation of steps:

(A) find the slope of the line

(B) write the general slope-intercept form of an equation

(C) substitute one point's coordinates *[(6,4)]* for x and y, and the slope *[2]* for m

(D) solve for b

(E) write the resulting equation using the calculated values of m and b

PRACTICE PROBLEMS

1. Write an equation of the line that passes through the points $(1,2)$ and $(5,6)$.	2. Write an equation of the line that passes through the points $(2,-1)$ and $(3,4)$.
3. Write an equation of the line that passes through the points $(-3,0)$ and $(3,-2)$.	4. Write an equation of the line that passes through the points $(-2,4)$ and $(2,4)$.
5. Write an equation, in point-slope form, of the line that passes through the points $(1,3)$ and $(8,5)$.	6. A line passes through the points $(5,4)$ and $(-5,0)$. (a) Write an equation of the line in slope-intercept form. (b) Write an equation of the line in point-slope form.

3.9   **Graph Inequalities**

KEY TERMS AND CONCEPTS

To graph a linear inequality, start by isolating (solving for) the variable y. Then, consider the graph of the equation that would result if the inequality symbol was replaced by an equal sign.

The points on this line are *included in the solution set* if the inequality symbol is ≤ or ≥, but *not included in the solution set* if the inequality symbol is < or >. To show inclusion (≤ or ≥), draw a **solid line**; otherwise, draw a **dashed line**.

Examples: A solid line is used to graph $y \geq 3x + 1$, but a dashed line is used to graph $y < 3x + 1$.

The line divides the plane into two parts. The part above the line includes all points where $y > mx + b$ and the part below the line includes all points where $y < mx + b$. So, if the inequality starts with $y >$ or $y \geq$, shade **above the line**; if it starts with $y <$ or $y \leq$, then shade **below the line**. Points in the shaded area are *included in the solution set*.

Examples: The graph of $y \geq 3x + 1$ is shaded above the line, but the graph of $y < 3x + 1$ is shaded below the line.

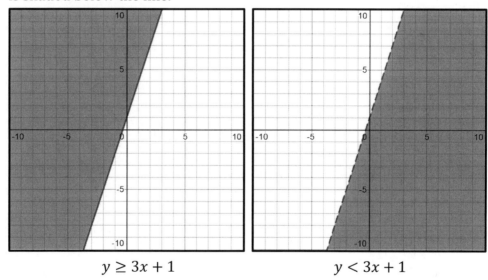

$y \geq 3x + 1$ $y < 3x + 1$

Special case: vertical lines

If the only variable in the inequality is x, solve for x and graph the corresponding vertical line (either solid or dashed according to the same rules). Then shade to the **right of the line** for $x >$ or $x \geq$, or to the **left of the line** for $x <$ or $x \leq$.

Example: The graph of $x \geq 5$ will have a solid vertical line at $x = 5$ and shading to the right of the line.

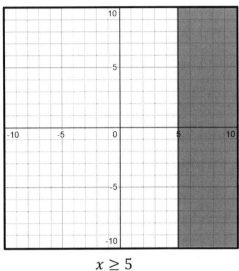

$$x \geq 5$$

CALCULATOR TIP

Inequalities can also be graphed on the calculator. Follow the same steps as entering an equation, but then change the symbol to the left of Y₁ from a line to a "shade above" or "shade below" symbol by moving to the line symbol and pressing ENTER repeatedly. (On some models, a popup will prompt you for the line type instead, as shown below.) You will still need to know whether to use a solid or dashed line when drawing your graph on paper, depending on the inequality symbol.

Example: The graph of $y \geq 3x - 2$ is graphed below.

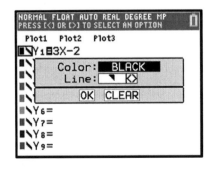

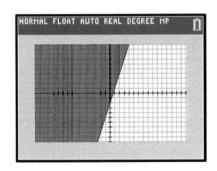

MODEL PROBLEM

Graph the inequality $-4y < 5x - 20$. Is the point (1,2) in the solution set?

Solution:

(A)   Solving for y,   (B)

$$\frac{-4y}{-4} < \frac{5x - 20}{-4}$$

$$y > -\frac{5}{4}x + 5$$

(C)   (1,2) is not in the solution set.

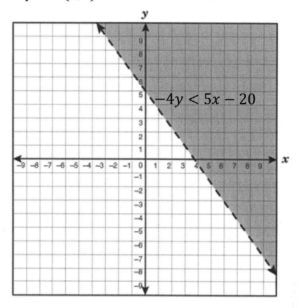

Explanation of steps:

(A)   Solve the inequality for y. *[Remember that multiplying or dividing both sides of an inequality by a negative value requires that you reverse the inequality symbol.]*

(B)   Use the y-intercept and slope to graph the line. Use a solid line for ≤ or ≥, or a dashed line for < or >. Shade above the line if y is > or ≥, or below the line is y is < or ≤. *[The > means dashed and shaded above.]*

(C)   If a point lies on a solid line or in a shaded area, it is in the solution set; otherwise, it is not. *[(1,2) lies in the unshaded area below the line, so it is not a solution.]*

You could also graph $y > -\frac{5}{4}x + 5$ on the calculator:

1.   Press Y= then the left arrow ◄ twice until the cursor is over the ⸗ symbol.

2.   Since the inequality starts with "$y >$" press the ENTER two times until the shade above ▜ symbol appears. Move the cursor back to the right, after the = sign.

3.   Enter the right side of the inequality, (-)5÷4 X,T,Θ,n +5 ENTER.
     [On the TI-84, you can enter the fraction using ALPHA F1 1 ► 4 ► instead.]

4.   Press GRAPH.

PRACTICE PROBLEMS

1.   Which graph represents the inequality $y > 3$?

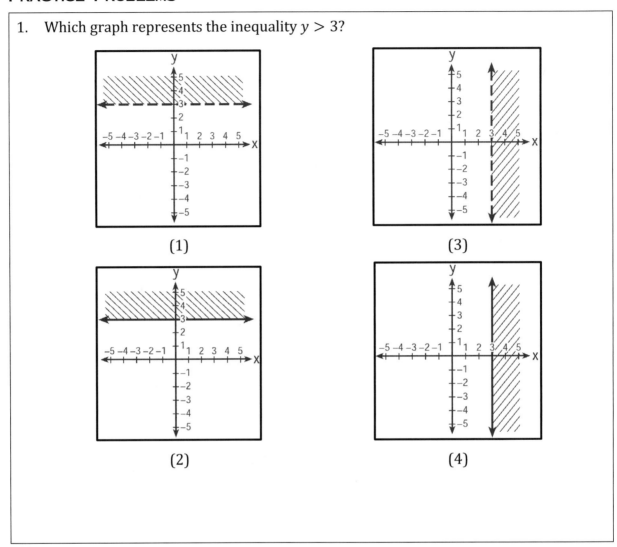

2. Which graph represents the inequality $y \geq x + 3$?

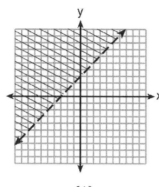

(1)

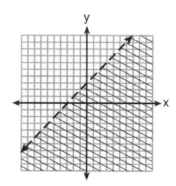

(3)

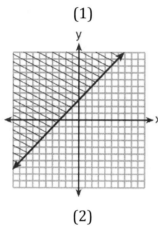

(2)

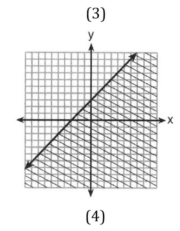

(4)

3. Which graph represents the solution of $2y + 6 > 4x$?

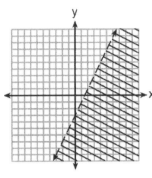

(1)

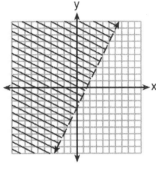

(3)

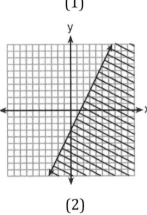

(2)

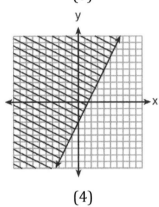

(4)

4. Write an inequality that is represented by the graph below.

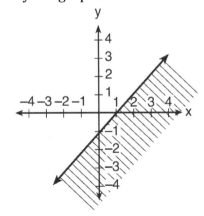

5. Write an inequality that is represented by the graph below.

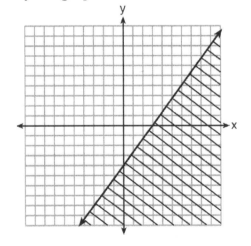

6.　Write an inequality that is represented by the graph below.

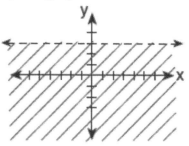

7.　Write an inequality that is represented by the graph below.

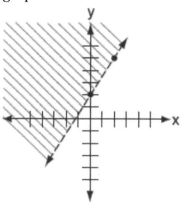

8.　Graph the inequality $y \geq 4$.

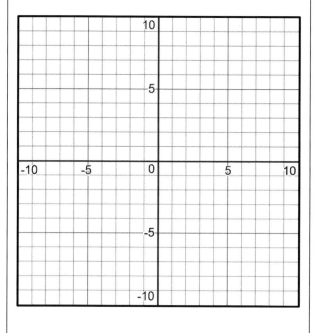

9.　Graph the inequality $x < -1$.

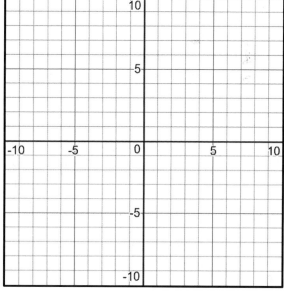

10. Graph the inequality $y > x - 2$.

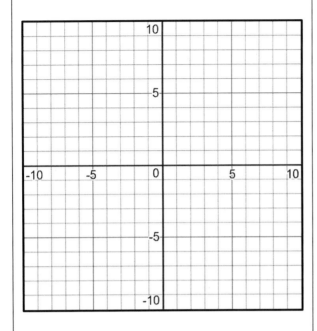

11. Graph the inequality $y \leq -\frac{2}{3}x + 5$.

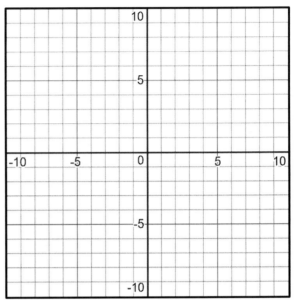

12. Graph the inequality $x + y \leq -3$.

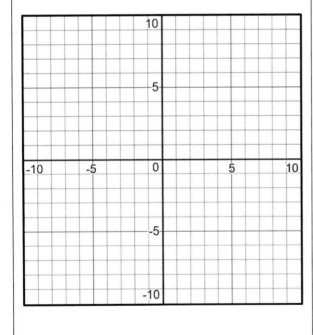

13. Graph the inequality $x - y \leq -1$.

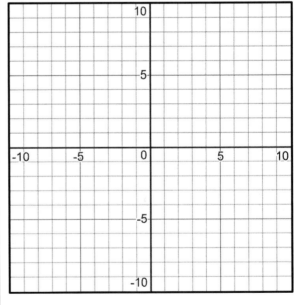

14. Graph the inequality $2y - 6x > 10$.

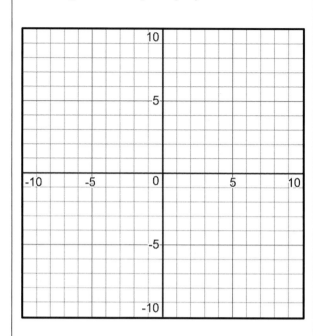

15. Graph the inequality $9 - x \geq 3y$.

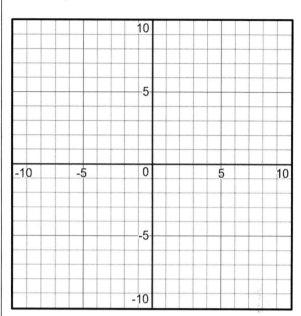

Chapter 4.   Linear Systems

4.1   Solve Linear Systems Algebraically

KEY TERMS AND CONCEPTS

A **linear system of equations** consists of two equations in two variables. A solution for a linear system is a set of one value for each variable that solves both equations at the same time. If the variables are x and y, the solution is an ordered pair which represents the point where the two equations' lines intersect on a coordinate plane.

There are two common methods used to solve linear systems algebraically: the addition method and the substitution method. In both methods, we aim to develop a new equation in which one of the two variables has been eliminated.

The **addition method (elimination method)** depends on the fact that if two equations are true, both the left and right sides of each equation can be added to create a new equation:

If $a = b$ and $c = d$, then $a + c = b + d$ or, written vertically ↘

$$\begin{array}{l} a=b \\ c=d \\ \hline a+c=b+d \end{array}$$

It also depends on the fact that we can multiply both sides of an equation by the same value and the equation remains true:

If $a = b$, then $ma = mb$

The goal in the addition method is to eliminate a variable by adding terms whose coefficients for that variable are additive inverses.

Example: $\begin{array}{l} 2x - y = 2 \\ \underline{x + y = 4} \\ 3x \quad\ = 6 \end{array}$ Adding $-y$ and $+y$ eliminates the variable y, allowing us to solve a simpler equation in one variable, $3x = 6$, or $x = 2$.

In the addition method, if two variable terms (in the same variable) are not already additive inverses, they can be made into additive inverses by multiplying one or both equations by values that will change the coefficients into inverses.

Example: $5a + b = 13$ $\times\, 3$ $15a + 3b = 39$ $+3b$ and $-3b$ are inverses

              $4a - 3b = 18$ → $\underline{4a - 3b = 18}$

                                $19a \quad\ \ = 57$

              Therefore, $a = \dfrac{57}{19} = 3.$

Once we know the value of one variable, we can substitute that value for the variable in either of the two original equations to solve for the other variable.

Example: In the above example, since we know $a = 3$, we can substitute 3 for a in

              either of the original equations to find b.

              $5(3) + b = 13$

              $15 + b = 13$

              $b = -2$

In the **substitution method**, an equation needs to have one of the variables expressed in terms of the other, or we will need to solve for one of the variables. Once we have a variable equal to an expression, we can substitute that expression for that variable in the other equation.

Example: $y = x + 1$

              $x + 2y = 17$ → $x + 2(x + 1) = 17$

              Now, solving the new equation for x gives us

              $x + 2(x + 1) = 17$

              $x + 2x + 2 = 17$

              $3x + 2 = 17$

              $3x = 15$

              $x = 5$

As with the addition method, once we know the value of one variable, we can substitute the known value into either original equation to solve for the other variable.

Example: For the above example, $y = x + 1$, so $y = 5 + 1 = 6$.

CALCULATOR TIP

We can check our algebraic solutions using the calculator's matrix feature:

1. Press [2nd][MATRIX] MATH [ALPHA] [B] to select the **rref** function (which stands for "reduced row echelon form").

2. Create a matrix with a size of 3 rows and 3 columns.

   - On the TI-84, press [ALPHA][F3], select 2 and 3 with the arrow keys, then select OK.

   - On the TI-83, press [2nd][MATRIX][1] and type 2 × 3 for 2 rows and 3 columns.

3. Each row of the matrix represents an equation. Enter the coefficients of the first variable in column 1, the coefficients of the second variable in column 2, and the constants in column 3.

   - On the TI-84, exit the matrix by pressing [▶]. Then, press [)][ENTER].

   - On the TI-83, press [2nd][QUIT][2nd][MATRIX][1][)][ENTER].

4. The resulting matrix will show the values of the variables, in order, in column 3.

Example: The screenshots below show how the calculator solves the system,

$$5a + b = 13$$

$$4a - 3b = 18$$

The solutions matrix shows that $a = 3$ and $b = -2$.

 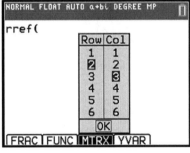 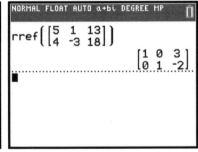

MODEL PROBLEM 1:   *ADDITION METHOD*

Solve the following system of equations using the addition method:

$$4a + 2b = 22$$
$$-4a + 3b = 3$$

Solution:

$$4a + 2b = 22$$
$$\underline{-4a + 3b = 3}$$

(A) $5b = 25$

(B) $b = 5$

(C) $4a + 2(5) = 22$

(D) $4a + 10 = 22$

           $4a = 12$

           $a = 3$

(E)   Solution: $a = 3$, $b = 5$

Explanation of steps:

(A)   If the coefficients for one of the variables are additive inverses *[4a and −4a]*, add the equations to derive a new equation without that variable.

(B)   Now that we have an equation with only one variable *[b]*, solve for that one variable.

(C)   Substitute this solution *[b=5]* into either one of the original equations.

(D)   Solve for the other variable *[a]*.

(E)   Write the solution by stating the values of both variables.

PRACTICE PROBLEMS

1. Solve the following system of equations for x and y algebraically and check your solutions on the calculator: $$3x - y = 8$$ $$x + y = 4$$	2. Solve the following system of equations for x and y algebraically and check your solutions on the calculator: $$2x - 3y = 19$$ $$3x + 3y = 21$$
3. Solve the following system of equations for x and y algebraically and check your solutions on the calculator: $$3x + 2y = 12$$ $$5x - 2y = 4$$	4. Solve the following system of equations for x and y algebraically and check your solutions on the calculator: $$2x - 5y = 11$$ $$-2x + 3y = -9$$
5. Solve the following system of equations for x and y algebraically and check your solutions on the calculator: $$2x - 4y = 12$$ $$-2x + y = -9$$	6. Solve the following system of equations for x and y algebraically and check your solutions on the calculator: $$3x + y = 0$$ $$-x - y = -4$$

MODEL PROBLEM 2:   *ADDITION METHOD WITH MULTIPLIERS*

Solve the following system of equations using the addition method:

$$5x + 8y = 1$$
$$3x + 4y = -1$$

Solution:

	(A)	(B)	(C)
$5x + 8y = 1$	$\rightarrow$	$5x + 8y = 1$	$5(-3) + 8y = 1$
$3x + 4y = -1$	$\times (-2)$	$\underline{-6x - 8y = 2}$	$-15 + 8y = 1$
		$-x \qquad = 3$	$8y = 16$
		$x = -3$	$y = 2$

(D) Solution: $(-3, 2)$

Explanation of steps:

(A)   If neither the x terms nor the y terms are additive inverses of each other, multiply one (or each) of the equations by a value to turn them into inverses *[to change the "y" terms into inverses, 8y and –8y, we can multiply the second equation by –2]*.

(B)   Adding the equations eliminates the inverses and will now give us a new equation in one variable. Solve for that variable.

(C)   Then, substitute the solution *[x = –3]* into either one of the original equations *[the first equation was used here]*, allowing you to solve for the other variable *[y = 2]*.

(D)   The solution for variables x and y may be written as an ordered pair, (x,y).

PRACTICE PROBLEMS

7. Solve the following system of equations for x and y algebraically and check your solutions on the calculator: $3x + 2y = 4$ $-2x + 2y = 24$	8. What is the value of y in the following system of equations? $2x + 3y = 6$ $2x + y = -2$
9. Solve the following system of equations for x and y algebraically and check your solutions on the calculator: $-3x + 4y = 11$ $6x - 5y = -16$	10. Solve the following system of equations for x and y algebraically and check your solutions on the calculator: $2x + 3y = 7$ $x + y = 3$

11. Solve the following system of equations for x and y algebraically and check your solutions on the calculator: $$2x + y = 8$$ $$x - 3y = -3$$	12. Solve the following system of equations for x and y algebraically and check your solutions on the calculator: $$x + 2y = 9$$ $$x - y = 3$$
13. Solve the following system of equations for x and y algebraically and check your solutions on the calculator: $$3x + 2y = 4$$ $$4x + 3y = 7$$	14. Solve the following system of equations for x and y algebraically and check your solutions on the calculator: $$3x + 4y = 9$$ $$5x + 6y = 21$$

MODEL PROBLEM 3: *SUBSTITUTION METHOD*

Solve the following system of equations using the substitution method:

$$3x - y = 16$$
$$y = x - 8$$

Solution:

(A) $3x - (x - 8) = 16$

(B) $3x - x + 8 = 16$

$\quad 2x + 8 = 16$

$\quad\quad 2x = 8$

$\quad\quad\ x = 4$

(C) $y = (4) - 8$

$\quad y = -4$

(D) Solution: $(4, -4)$

Explanation of steps:

(A) If one equation already has one of the variables isolated, as in *variable = expression*, substitute this expression for this variable in the other equation. *[y = x − 8 already has y expressed in terms of x, so substitute the expression x − 8 for the y in the first equation:* $3x - y = 16$ *becomes* $3x - \underline{(x - 8)} = 16$.] It is always safest to use parentheses around the expression whenever you perform a substitution.

(B) Solve the equation for one variable.

(C) Substitute the solution found in step (B) into either original equation *[substitute 4 for x]*.

(D) Solve the equation for the other variable.

(E) State the solution.

PRACTICE PROBLEMS

15. Solve the following system of equations for x and y:	16. Solve the following system of equations for x and y:
$\quad\quad y = 4x - 10$ $\quad\quad y = 5 - x$	$\quad\quad x = y - 2$ $\quad\quad y = 10 - 3x$

17. Solve the following system of equations for x and y: $$y = 9 - 2x$$ $$3y - 2x = 11$$	18. Using the substitution method, solve the following system of equations for x and y: $$7x + 3y = 68$$ $$x - 4y = -8$$
19. Solve the following system of equations algebraically: $$2a + 3b = 12$$ $$a = \frac{1}{2}b - 6$$	20. Solve the following system of equations algebraically: $$c + 3d = 8$$ $$c = 4d - 6$$

21. To solve the following system of equations by the substitution method, which equivalent equation could be used?

$$2x - y = 5$$
$$3x + 2y = -3$$

(1) $3x + 2(2x - 5) = -3$ 　　　(3) $3\left(y + \frac{5}{2}\right) + 2y = -3$

(2) $3x + 2(5 - 2x) = -3$ 　　　(4) $3\left(\frac{5}{2} - y\right) + 2y = -3$

4.2   <u>Solve Linear Systems Graphically</u>

KEY TERMS AND CONCEPTS

To solve a system of linear equations **graphically**, simply graph the two equations as lines in the same coordinate plane. The point (if any) where the two lines **intersect** is the solution. This is because the point of intersection is the only point that satisfies *both* equations.

Example: The lines $y = -x + 5$ and $y = 2x - 4$ intersect at (3,2).

                  Therefore, the solution for the system of equations is $x = 3$ and $y = 2$.

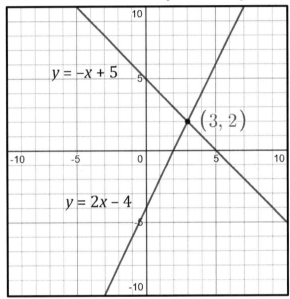

If the two lines are parallel, they never intersect, and so there is no solution. If the two lines are identical (coincide), then there are infinitely many solutions.

Whenever you graph two lines on the same set of axes, you should label both of them with their equations, as shown above.

▦▢ CALCULATOR TIP

Using a calculator, you can solve a system of equations by graphing both equations and then using the intersect feature.

Example:　To solve the system, $y = -x + 5$ and $y = 2x - 4$, graphically,

Press　[Y=] [(-)] [X,T,Θ,n] [+] [5] [ENTER]

[2] [X,T,Θ,n] [−] [4] [ENTER]

[2nd] [CALC] [5] to select intersect

First curve? [ENTER]　Second curve? [ENTER]　Guess? [ENTER]

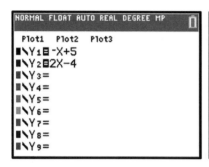
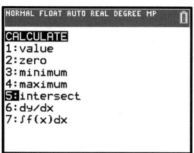
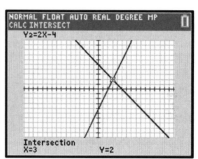

MODEL PROBLEM

Solve the following system of equations graphically:

$$x - y = -1$$
$$y = -3x + 9$$

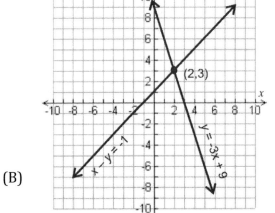

Solution:

(A) $x - y = -1$

$$\underline{-x \qquad\;\; -x}$$

$$\underline{-y = -x - 1}$$

$$-1 \qquad -1$$

$$y = x + 1 \qquad\qquad \text{(B)}$$

(C)   Solution: (2,3)

Explanation of steps:

(A)   If either equation is not already in slope-intercept form, transform the equation by solving for y in terms of x.

(B)   Graph both equations on the same coordinate plane, labeling each line.

(C)   The point of intersection is the solution to the system of equations.
      [A solution of (2,3) means $x = 2$, $y = 3$ solves both equations simultaneously.]

PRACTICE PROBLEMS

1. A system of equations is graphed below.

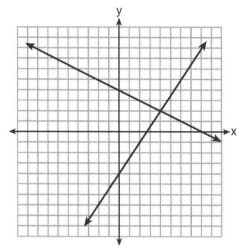

   The solution of this system is
   (1)   (0,4)   (3)   (4,2)
   (2)   (2,4)   (4)   (8,0)

2. A system of equations is graphed below.

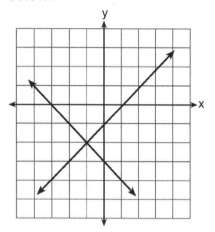

   The solution of this system is
   (1)   (1,0) and (−3,0)
   (2)   (0,−3) and (0,−1)
   (3)   (−1,−2)
   (4)   (−2,−1)

3. If the lines whose equations are $x = -2$ and $y = 3$ were graphed on the same set of coordinate axes, what would be their point of intersection?

4. Solve the system of equations graphically:
$$y = 3x - 2$$
$$y = -x - 6$$

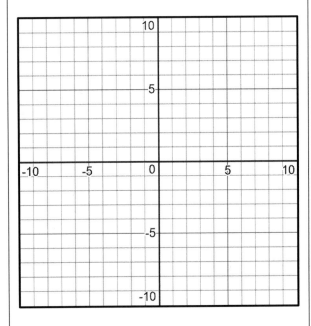

5. Solve the system of equations graphically:
$$x + y = 2$$
$$x - y = 4$$

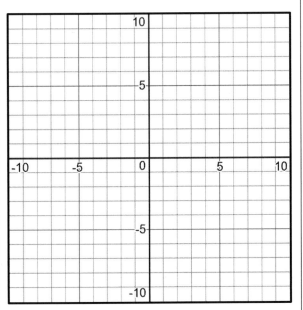

6. Solve the system of equations graphically:
$$3x - 5y = 15$$
$$y = 2x + 4$$

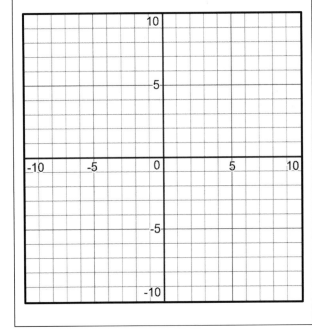

7. Solve the system of equations graphically:
$$y = \frac{2}{3}x + 5$$
$$x + 3y = -3$$

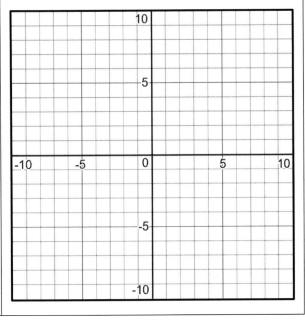

8. Solve the system of equations graphically:

$$4x - 2y = 10$$
$$y = -2x - 1$$

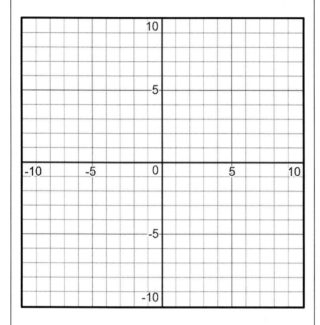

9. Solve the system of equations graphically:

$$y = 4x - 1$$
$$2x + y = 5$$

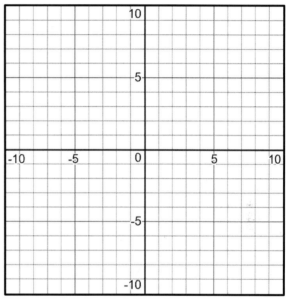

4.3   <u>Solutions to Systems of Inequalities</u>

KEY TERMS AND CONCEPTS

If given a system of two inequalities, you may determine whether an ordered pair is in the solution set by substitution. Simply substitute the x- and y-coordinates of the ordered pair for the variables, x and y, in both inequalities. Then check if both inequalities are true.

MODEL PROBLEM

Which ordered pair is in the solution set of the following system of linear inequalities?

$$y + 2 > 3x$$
$$-2y \geq x - 2$$

(1) $(5,2)$ (2) $(-5,-2)$ (3) $(-2,5)$ (4) $(2,-5)$

Solution:

(A)

$(5,2)$	$(-5,-2)$	$(-2,5)$	$(2,-5)$
$y + 2 > 3x$ $(2) + 2 > 3(5)?$ $4 > 15?$ *false*	$y + 2 > 3x$ $(-2) + 2 > 3(-5)?$ $0 > -15?$ *true* $-2y \geq x - 2$ $-2(-2) \geq (-5) - 2?$ $4 \geq -7?$ *true*	$y + 2 > 3x$ $(5) + 2 > 3(-2)?$ $7 > -6?$ *true* $-2y \geq x - 2$ $-2(5) \geq (-2) - 2?$ $-10 \geq -4?$ *false*	$y + 2 > 3x$ $(-5) + 2 > 3(2)?$ $-3 > 6?$ *false*
NO	YES	NO	NO

(B)   The ordered pair $(-5, -2)$ is a solution.

Explanation of steps:

(A)   For each ordered pair, substitute the coordinates for the variables x and y in the inequalities. Check whether each inequality is true for these values. If either is *false*, the ordered pair is not a solution and you may go on to check the next ordered pair.

(B)   The ordered pair is in the solution set if it makes both inequalities *true*.

▥▤ CALCULATOR TIP

Checking can be done using a calculator instead. To check if (5,2) is a solution:

5 [STO▸] [X,T,Θ,n] [ENTER]   2 [STO▸] [ALPHA] [Y] [ENTER]

[ALPHA] [Y] [+] [2] [2nd] [TEST] [3] [3] [X,T,Θ,n] [ENTER]

Result is 0 for false, so (5,2) is *not* a solution.

PRACTICE PROBLEMS

1. Which ordered pair is in the solution set of the following system of inequalities?

$$y < 2x + 1$$
$$y \leq -3x + 4$$

   (1) (1,1)   (3) (1,3)

   (2) (1,2)   (4) none of these

2. Which ordered pair is in the solution set of the following system of inequalities?

$$y \geq x + 7$$
$$2x + y \leq -5$$

   (1) (0,9)   (3) (9,0)

   (2) (0,−9)   (4) (−9,0)

3. Which ordered pair is in the solution set of the following system of inequalities?

$$y < \frac{1}{2}x + 4$$

$$y \geq -x + 1$$

(1) $(-5, 3)$ (3) $(3, -5)$

(2) $(0, 4)$ (4) $(4, 0)$

4. Which ordered pair is in the solution set of the following system of inequalities?

$$y < 2x + 2$$

$$y \geq -x - 1$$

(1) $(0, 3)$ (3) $(-1, 0)$

(2) $(2, 0)$ (4) $(-1, -4)$

5. Which ordered pair is in the solution set of the following system of inequalities?

$$y \le \frac{1}{2}x + 13$$
$$4x + 2y > 3$$

(1) $(-4,1)$ (3) $(1,-4)$

(2) $(-2,2)$ (4) $(2,-2)$

6. Which ordered pair is in the solution set of the following system of inequalities?

$$y \le 3x + 1$$
$$x - y > 1?$$

(1) $(-1,-2)$ (3) $(1,2)$

(2) $(2,-1)$ (4) $(-1,2)$

4.4   <u>**Solve Systems of Inequalities Graphically**</u>

KEY TERMS AND CONCEPTS

To solve a system of inequalities, graph both inequalities on the same coordinate plane. Be sure to label both inequalities. The graph of each inequality will have a shaded region representing the solution set for that inequality. The region where the two shaded regions **overlap** (the region that is shaded twice or darker), including any points on a **solid line** (but *not* a dashed line) bordering the region, represents the solution set of the system. Any point in the solution set would solve *both* inequalities. The point of intersection of the two lines is a solution only if *both* lines are solid.

MODEL PROBLEM 1:   *GRAPHING*

Graph the following system of inequalities and label the solution set S:

$$y + 2 > 3x$$
$$-2y \geq x - 2$$

Solution:

(A) $y + 2 > 3x$ $-2y \geq x - 2$

   $\underline{-2 \quad -2}$ $\underline{-2 \qquad -2}$

   $y > 3x - 2$ $y \leq -\frac{1}{2}x + 1$

(B)

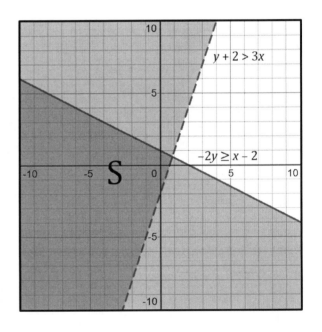

Explanation of steps:

   (A)   If either inequality is not already in slope-intercept form, solve the inequality for y. Remember to reverse the inequality symbol if both sides of an inequality are multiplied or divided by a negative value. *[In the second inequality, $\geq$ becomes $\leq$.]*

   (B)   Graph both inequalities on the same set of axes. Remember to use a solid line for inequalities with $\leq$ or $\geq$ symbols but a dashed line for those with $<$ or $>$ symbols. Label the double-shaded region "S" to represent the solution set.

PRACTICE PROBLEMS

1. Graph the following system and label the solution set S:

$$y \leq -x + 2$$
$$y < -1$$

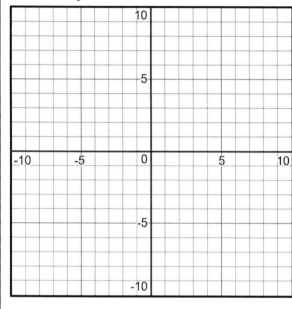

2. Graph the following system and label the solution set S:

$$y \geq 2x + 1$$
$$y \leq -x + 4$$

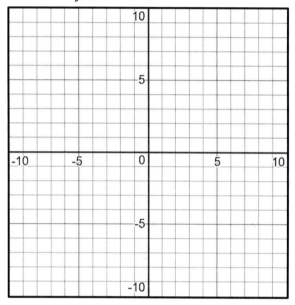

3. Graph the following system and label the solution set S:

$$y < x - 2$$
$$2x + y \geq 1$$

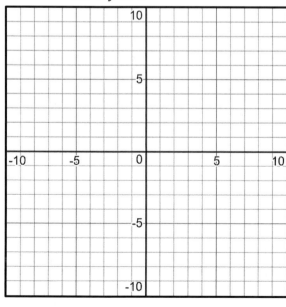

4. Graph the following system and label the solution set S:

$$2x + y \geq 3$$
$$x - 3y < -6$$

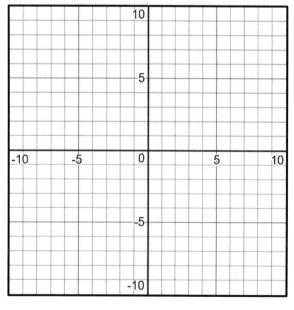

5. Graph the following systems of inequalities on the set of axes shown below and label the solution set S:

$$y > -x + 2$$
$$y \leq \frac{2}{3}x + 5$$

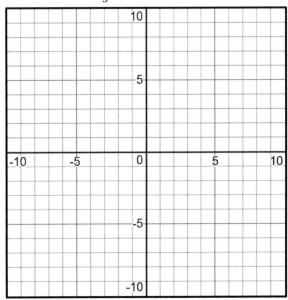

6. Graph the following systems of inequalities on the set of axes shown below and label the solution set S:

$$2x + 3y < -3$$
$$y - 4x \geq 2$$

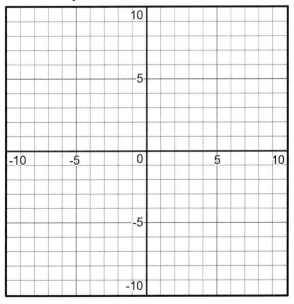

7. Graph the system of inequalities and state the coordinates of a point in the solution set.

$$2x - y \geq 6$$
$$x > 2$$

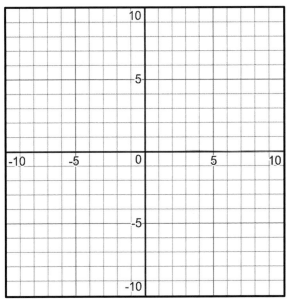

8. Graph the system of inequalities and state the coordinates of a point in the solution set.

$$y < 2x + 1$$
$$y \geq -\frac{1}{3}x + 4$$

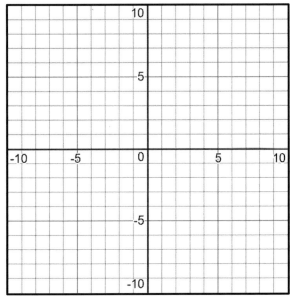

9. Graph $y < x$ and $x > 5$ on the axes below and state the coordinates of a point in the solution set.

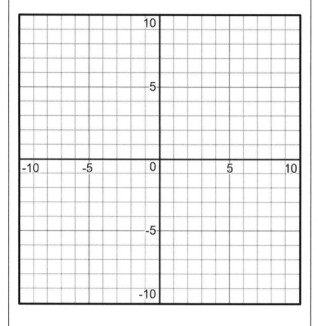

10. Graph the system of inequalities and state the coordinates of a point in the solution set.

$$y + 3 < 2x$$
$$-2y \le 6x - 10$$

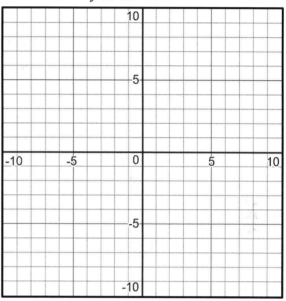

11. Graph the system of inequalities and state the coordinates of a point in the solution set.

$$3x + y < 7$$
$$y \ge \frac{2}{3}x - 4$$

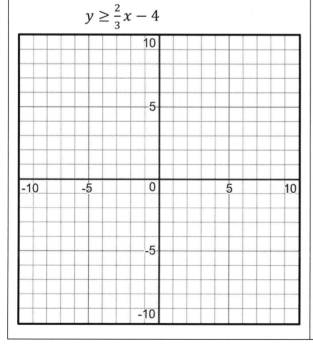

12. Graph the system of inequalities.

$$y + x \ge 3$$
$$5x - 2y > 10$$

State a point that satisfies $y + x \ge 3$, but does *not* satisfy $5x - 2y > 10$.

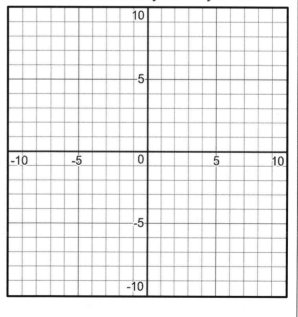

MODEL PROBLEM 2:   *SOLUTIONS*

Which ordered pair is in the solution set of the system of linear inequalities graphed at right?

     (1) (5,2)   (3) (−2,5)

     (2) (−5,−2)   (4) (2,−5)

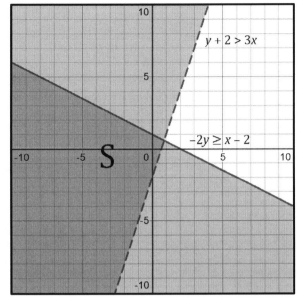

Solution:

The answer is (2). The ordered pair (−5,−2) is in the solution set.

Explanation of steps:

Plot each point to determine whether it lies within the double-shaded or darker region. *[(5,2) is in the unshaded region. Both (−2,5) and (2,−5) are in single-shaded regions.]*

PRACTICE PROBLEMS

13. Is (5,1) in the solution set of the system of inequalities graphed below?	14. Is (−1,−8) in the solution set of the system of inequalities graphed below?
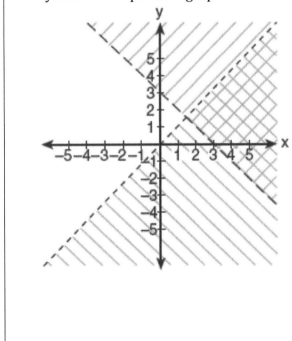	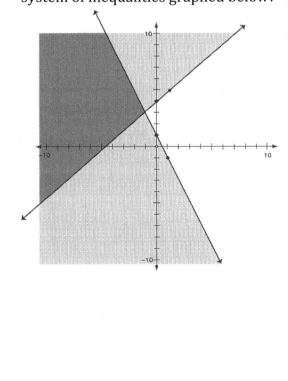

15. Which ordered pair is in the solution set of the system of inequalities shown in the graph below?

   (1)   (1, −4)   (3)   (5,3)

   (2)   (−5,7)   (4)   (−7, −2)

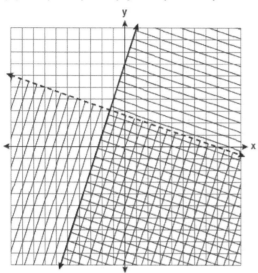

16. Which ordered pair is in the solution set of the system of inequalities shown in the graph below?

   (1)   (−2, −1)   (3)   (−2, −4)

   (2)   (−2,2)   (4)   (2, −2)

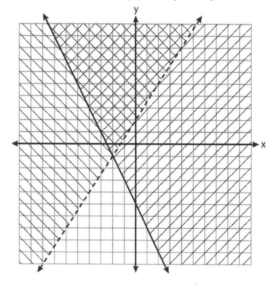

4.5   Word Problems – Linear Systems

KEY TERMS AND CONCEPTS

Sometimes, the circumstances described by a word problem may lead more naturally to the use of **two variables** instead of one. If this is the case, we can find a solution by writing **two equations** in terms of the variables. We can solve for the two variables by using one of the methods learned – addition or substitution – for solving a system of equations.

MODEL PROBLEM

Brenda's school is selling tickets to a spring musical. On the first day of ticket sales the school sold 3 senior citizen tickets and 9 child tickets for a total of $75. On the second day the school sold 8 senior citizen tickets and 5 child tickets for a total of $67. What is the price of each senior citizen ticket and each child ticket?

Solution:

(A)   Let s represent the cost of one *senior citizen* ticket.
      Let c represent the cost of one *child* ticket.

(B)

$$3s + 9c = 75$$
$$8s + 5c = 67$$

(C)

$$\times 8$$
$$\times (-3)$$

$$24s + 72c = 600$$
$$\underline{-24s - 15c = -201}$$
$$\frac{57c}{57} = \frac{399}{57}$$
$$c = 7$$

(D)

$$3s + 9(7) = 75$$
$$3s + 63 = 75$$
$$3s = 12$$
$$s = 4$$

(E)   Senior citizen tickets cost $4 each and child tickets cost $7 each.

Explanation of steps:

(A)   Write what each variable represents.

(B)   Write equations using the given information.

(C)   Solve the system of equations for one of the variables using either the addition method or the substitution method. *[Using the addition method, we need to create additive inverses. To make additive inverses of the s terms, we can multiply the first equation by 8 and the second equation by –3. Then, adding the equations eliminates the s terms, allowing us to solve the resulting equation for c.]*

(D)   Substitute the value of one variable into either original equation in order to solve for the other variable. *[Substituting 7 for c in the first equation allows us to solve for s.]*

(E)   Write your answer to the specific question posed by the word problem.

PRACTICE PROBLEMS

1. The difference of two numbers is 5. Their sum is 59. Find the numbers.	2. The sum of two numbers is 47, and their difference is 15. What is the larger number?
3. Justin went to the movie theater and bought one bag of popcorn and two cookies for $5.00. Martin went to the same theater and bought one bag of popcorn and four cookies for $6.00. How much does one cookie cost?	4. Alexandra purchases two doughnuts and three cookies at a doughnut shop and is charged $3.30. Briana purchases five doughnuts and two cookies at the same shop for $4.95. Find the cost of one doughnut and find the cost of one cookie.
5. Tanisha and Rachel had lunch at the mall. Tanisha ordered three slices of pizza and two colas. Rachel ordered two slices of pizza and three colas. Tanisha's bill was $6.00, and Rachel's bill was $5.25. What was the price of one slice of pizza? What was the price of one cola?	6. Ramón rented a sprayer and a generator. On his first job, he used each piece of equipment for 6 hours at a total cost of $90. On his second job, he used the sprayer for 4 hours and the generator for 8 hours at a total cost of $100. What was the hourly cost of *each* piece of equipment?

7. Kristin spent $131 on shirts. Fancy shirts cost $28 and plain shirts cost $15. If she bought a total of 7 shirts then how many of each kind did she buy?

8. The cost of three notebooks and four pencils is $8.50. The cost of five notebooks and eight pencils is $14.50. Determine the cost of one notebook and the cost of one pencil.

9. Last week, a fruit market sold a total of 108 apples and oranges. This week, five times the number of apples and three times the number of oranges were sold. A total of 452 apples and oranges were sold this week. Determine how many apples and how many oranges were sold last week.

10. The sum of the digits of a certain two-digit number is 7. Reversing its digits increases the number by 9. What is the number?

4.6   Word Problems – Systems of Inequalities

KEY TERMS AND CONCEPTS

There are times when a verbal problem requires more than one variable in one inequality. If the situation calls for it, use two variables and set up a system of two inequalitites. Be sure to label exactly what each variable represents.

Example: Don't write p = pencil. Instead, write p = number of pencils, or p = cost of a pencil in cents, or p = weight of a pencil in ounces, depending on the problem.

MODEL PROBLEM

A home-based company produces both hand-knitted scarves and sweaters. The scarves take 2 hours of labor to produce, and the sweaters take 14 hours. The labor available is limited to 40 hours per week, and the total production capacity is 5 items per week. Write a system of inequalities representing this situation, where x is the number of scarves and y is the number of sweaters.

Solution:

(A) x = number of scarves
     y = number of sweaters
(B) $2x + 14y \leq 40$
(C) $x + y \leq 5$

Explanation of steps:

(A) Clearly label the variables used.
(B) Write the first inequality based on given information *[constraint on total hours]*.
(C) Write the second inequality based on given information *[constraint on number of items]*.

PRACTICE PROBLEMS

1. You can work at most 20 hours next week. You need to earn at least $92 to cover you weekly expenses. Your dog-walking job pays $7.50 per hour and your job as a car wash attendant pays $6 per hour. Write a system of linear inequalities to model the situation.

2. Marsha is buying plants and soil for her garden. The soil cost $4 per bag, and the plants cost $10 each. She wants to buy at least 5 plants and can spend no more than $100. Write a system of linear inequalities to model the situation.

3. John is packing books into boxes. Each box can hold either 15 small books or 8 large books. He needs to pack at least 35 boxes and at least 350 books. Write a system of linear inequalities to model the situation.

4. During a family trip, you share the driving with your dad. At most, you are allowed to drive for three hours. While driving, your maximum speed is 55 miles per hour.

a) Write a system of inequalities describing the possible numbers of hours t and distance d you may have to drive.

b) Is it possible for you to have driven 160 miles?

5. FlyGlyde is a company that manufactures drones and hoverboards. FlyGlyde's daily production of drones cannot exceed 10, and its daily production of hoverboards must be less than or equal to 12. The combined number of drones and hoverboards cannot be more than 16.

If x is the number of drones and y is the number of hoverboards, graph on the accompanying set of axes the region that contains the number of drones and hoverboards FlyGlyde can manufacture daily.

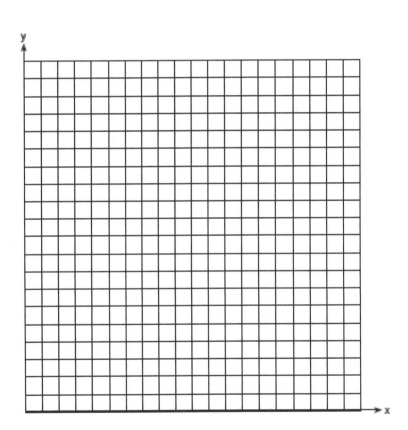

Chapter 5.   Polynomials

5.1   Polynomial Expressions

KEY TERMS AND CONCEPTS

A **term** is a number, a variable, or any product or quotient of numbers and variables.

A **monomial** is a single term without any variables in the denominator, such as $-2xy$.

A **polynomial** is a monomial or a sum of monomials.

Example: $x^2 + y - 2xy$ is a polynomial with 3 terms: x^2, y, and $-2xy$.

A **binomial** is a polynomial of 2 unlike terms, and a **trinomial** is a polynomial of 3 unlike terms.

Examples: $2x^2 + 5$ is a binomial and $2x^2 - 3x + 5$ is a trinomial.

A **constant term** is a term with no variable part.

Example: In the expression $2x^2 - 3 + x + 5$, the constant terms are -3 and 5.

The **degree of a term** is the sum of its variables' exponents. A constant term has a degree of 0.

Examples: $8x^2$ has a degree of 2, $4x^3$ has a degree of 3, and $2x$ has a degree of 1.

The term $12x^2y^3z$ has a degree of 6 (add $2 + 3 + 1$).

The **degree of a polynomial** is the largest degree of its terms.

Example: The degree of $9x^2 + x^4 - x$ is 4, since x^4 has the highest degree of 4.

To write a polynomial in standard form:

1. Combine all like terms (*simplify*)
2. Write terms in descending order (*exponents of a variable decrease*)

Example: $2a - 3a^2 + 4 + 9a$ → $11a - 3a^2 + 4$ → $-3a^2 + 11a + 4$

The **leading coefficient** of a polynomial is the coefficient of the term with the highest degree. When written in standard form, this is the coefficient of the first term of the polynomial.

Example: The leading coefficient of $-3a^2 + 11a + 4$ is -3.

MODEL PROBLEM

Write $2x + 3 - 4x^2 - x + 1$ in standard form.

Solution:

$-4x^2 + x + 4$

Explanation of steps:

Combine like terms *[$2x - x = x$ and $3 + 1 = 4$]*, then write terms in descending order *[the x^2 term, then the x term, then the constant]*.

PRACTICE PROBLEMS

1.	2.
a) How many terms does the polynomial $3x^4 - 2x^3 - 1$ have?	a) Write $x - 2 + x^2 - 3x + 5$ in standard form.
b) What is the degree of this polynomial?	b) What is the degree of this polynomial?
c) What is its leading coefficient?	c) What is its leading coefficient?
d) What is its constant term?	d) What is its constant term?

3. Write the expression $2x - 5x^3 - 2x(x + 5) + 15 - x^2$ as a polynomial in standard form.

5.2   **Add and Subtract Polynomials**

KEY TERMS AND CONCEPTS

To add polynomials: Join the polynomials and simplify into standard form.

Example: $(x^2 + 5x - 24) + (2x^2 + 10) =$
$x^2 + 5x - 24 + 2x^2 + 10 =$
$3x^2 + 5x - 14$

To subtract polynomials: Negate all the signs of the second polynomial and then add.

Example: $(2x^2 - 5x + 4) - (x^2 + 6x - 5) =$
$2x^2 - 5x + 4 - x^2 - 6x + 5 =$
$x^2 - 11x + 9$

You may find it easier to arrange the polynomials vertically before adding or subtracting. Just be sure to line up the terms that have the same degree.

Examples: The above problems could be written as shown below.

$$\begin{array}{r} x^2 + 5x - 24 \\ 2x^2 \qquad + 10 \\ \hline 3x^2 + 5x - 14 \end{array} \qquad \begin{array}{r} 2x^2 - 5x + 4 \\ -(x^2 + 6x - 5) \\ \hline x^2 - 11x + 9 \end{array}$$

When we add or subtract polynomials, the result is always a polynomial. Therefore, we can say that the set of polynomials is **closed** under addition and subtraction.

MODEL PROBLEM

Subtract $-4x^2 - 12x + 5$ from $x^2 + 9x - 5$ and write the result in standard form.

Solution:

(A) $(x^2 + 9x - 5) - (-4x^2 - 12x + 5) =$
(B) $x^2 + 9x - 5 + 4x^2 + 12x - 5 =$
(C) $5x^2 + 21x - 10$

Explanation of steps:

(A)   Set up the problem. *[Remember the rule: "Subtract x from y" means y − x.]*

(B)   In subtraction, negate all the terms in the second polynomial and then add.

(C)   Combine like terms and express in standard form.

PRACTICE PROBLEMS

1. Write the sum of $8x^2 - x + 4$ and $x - 5$ in standard form.	2. Write the sum of $3x^2 + x + 8$ and $x^2 - 9$ in standard form.
3. Write the sum of $4x^3 + 6x^2 + 2x - 3$ and $3x^3 + 3x^2 - 5x - 5$ in standard form.	4. What is the sum of $-3x^2 - 7x + 9$ and $-5x^2 + 6x - 4$ in standard form?
5. Add $3x^2 + 5x - 6$ and $-x^2 + 3x + 9$.	6. Add $8n^2 - 3n + 10$ and $-3n^2 - 6n - 7$.
7. Write in standard form: $(3x^2 + 2xy + 7) - (6x^2 - 4xy + 3)$	8. What is the result when $3a^2 - 2a + 5$ is subtracted from $a^2 + a - 1$?

9. What is the difference when $2x^2 - x + 6$ is subtracted from $x^2 - 3x - 2$?	10. Subtract $3x^2 + 4x - 1$ from $x^2 + 1$ and write the result in standard form.
11. Subtract $4x^2 + 7x - 5$ from $9x^2 - 2x + 3$. Write the result in standard form.	12. Subtract $5x^2 - 7x - 6$ from $9x^2 + 3x - 4$. Express the answer in standard form.
13. Subtract $2x^2 - 5x + 8$ from $6x^2 + 3x - 2$ and express the answer as a trinomial in standard form.	14. What is the result when $6x^2 - 13x + 12$ is subtracted from $-3x^2 + 6x + 7$?
15. What is the difference when $x^2 + 3x - 4$ is subtracted from $x^3 + 3x^2 - 2x$?	16. What is the difference when $5x + 4$ is subtracted from $5x - 4$?

5.3   **Multiply Polynomials**

KEY TERMS AND CONCEPTS

Factors are any parts of an expression that are multiplied to produce a product.

Examples: (a) In $2 \cdot 3$, both 2 and 3 are factors.

(b) In $2x^2y$, the factors are 2, x^2 and y.

(c) In $3(x + 1)$, both 3 and $(x + 1)$ are factors.

(d) The expression $(a - 2)(a + 3)$ has two binomial factors.

Multiplying a Monomial by a Polynomial: Apply the Distributive Property.

Examples: (a) $3(x^2 + x)$ → $3x^2 + 3x$

(b) $-(2m^4 - n^2)$ → $-2m^4 + n^2$

(c) $5a(a^3 - 3a + 1)$ → $5a^4 - 15a^2 + 5a$

Multiplying Binomials

Method 1: Distribution – Multiply term 1 by the second binomial, then term 2 by the second binomial

$$(a - 2)(a + 3) = a(a + 3) - 2(a + 3) =$$
$$a^2 + 3a - 2a - 6 =$$
$$a^2 + a - 6$$

Method 2: Vertically – Multiply terms like they were digits in whole number multiplication

$$
\begin{array}{r}
a-2 \\
\times \quad a+3 \\
\hline
3a-6 \\
a^2 - 2a \\
\hline
a^2 + a - 6
\end{array}
$$

← multiply $a - 2$ times $+3$

← shift left, then multiply $a - 2$ times a

← add like terms

Method 3: Rectangle diagram (Box Method) – Write the terms of each factor outside the side of a rectangle, find the algebraic areas of each inner rectangle, and add the inner areas

$(a-2)(a+3)$

	a	-2
a	a^2	$-2a$
3	$3a$	-6

$a^2 + 3a - 2a - 6 =$
$a^2 + a - 6$

Method 4: "FOIL" – Multiply these pairs of terms: Firsts, Outers, Inners, Lasts

$(a-2)(a+3) =$

F   O   I   L
$a^2 + 3a - 2a - 6 =$
$a^2 + a - 6$

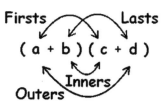

Squaring a Binomial: multiply the binomial by itself.
Example: $(x-3)^2 = (x-3)(x-3) = x^2 - 3x - 3x + 9 = x^2 - 6x + 9$

Multiplying a Binomial by a Trinomial
Expand one of the methods above except Method 4 (FOIL). Note that the "FOIL" method only works for multiplying two binomials.

Method 1: Distribution – Multiply term 1 by the trinomial, then term 2 by the trinomial.

$(a+2)(2a^2 - 5a + 3) = a(2a^2 - 5a + 3) + 2(2a^2 - 5a + 3) =$
$2a^3 - 5a^2 + 3a + 4a^2 - 10a + 6 =$
$2a^3 - a^2 - 7a + 6$

Method 2: Vertically – Multiply terms like they were digits in whole number multiplication

$$
\begin{array}{r}
a+2 \\
\times \quad 2a^2 - 5a + 3 \\
\hline
3a + 6 \\
-5a^2 - 10a \\
2a^3 + 4a^2 \\
\hline
2a^3 - a^2 - 7a + 6
\end{array}
$$

← multiply $a + 2$ times $+3$

← shift left, then multiply $a + 2$ times $-5a$

← shift left, then multiply $a + 2$ times $2a^2$

← add like terms

Method 3: Rectangle diagram (Box Method) – Write the terms of each factor outside a side of a rectangle, find the algebraic areas of each inner rectangle, and add the inner areas

$(a + 2)(2a^2 - 5a + 3)$

	a	2
$2a^2$	$2a^3$	$4a^2$
$-5a$	$-5a^2$	$-10a$
3	$3a$	6

$$
\boxed{\begin{array}{c} 2a^3 - 5a^2 + 3a + 4a^2 - 10a + 6 = \\ 2a^3 - a^2 - 7a + 6 \end{array}}
$$

When we multiply polynomials, the result is always a polynomial. Therefore, we can say that the set of polynomials is **closed** under multiplication. This is not true when we divide polynomials, since we may end up with an algebraic fraction (rational expression) that is not a polynomial.

MODEL PROBLEM

Write the product of $x + 8$ and $x - 2$ as a polynomial in standard form.

Solution:	**Explanation of steps:**
(A) $(x + 8)(x - 2) =$	(A) Set up the problem.
(B) $x(x - 2) + 8(x - 2) =$	(B) Multiply term 1 *[x]* by the second binomial, then term 2 *[8]* by the second binomial.
(C) $x^2 - 2x + 8x - 16 =$	(C) Distribute.
(D) $x^2 + 6x - 16$	(D) Combine like terms and express in standard form.

PRACTICE PROBLEMS

1. Multiply: $7x(1 - x^3)$	2. What is the product of $2r^2 - 5$ and $3r$?
3. What is the product of $-3x^2y$ and $(5xy^2 + xy)$?	4. The length of a rectangle is represented by $x^2 + 3x + 2$, and the width is represented by $4x$. Express the area of the rectangle as a trinomial.
5. The length of a rectangular room is 7 less than three times the width, w, of the room. Write an expression, in simplest form, for the area of the room.	6. What is the product of $(c + 8)$ and $(c - 5)$?
7. What is the product of $(3x + 2)$ and $(x - 7)$?	8. Express $(x - 7)(2x + 3)$ as a trinomial.

9. Use the following diagram to expand $(a + b)^2$ into an equivalent polynomial.

	a	b
a	a^2	ab
b	ab	b^2

10. Simplify the expression $(x - 6)^2$.

11. Create a rectangle diagram for $(x + 3)(x - y - 1)$.

12. Which of the following expressions is *not* equivalent to $(a + b)(x + y)$?

    (1) $(a + b)x + (a + b)y$

    (2) $a(x + y) + b(x + y)$

    (3) $ax + by$

    (4) $ax + bx + ay + by$

13. Multiply $(x - 1)(2x^2 + x - 2)$ and write the product in standard form.

14. Multiply $(x^2 + 2)(x^2 - 2x + 1)$ and write the product in standard form.

5.4   **Divide a Polynomial by a Monomial**

KEY TERMS AND CONCEPTS

When **dividing a polynomial by a monomial**, we may be able to simplify by dividing each term of the polynomial in the numerator by the monomial in the denominator. For each new fraction, divide the coefficients and subtract exponents of the same base. The result should have as many terms as the original polynomial.

Example: $$\frac{15x^2 + 20x}{5x} = \frac{15x^2}{5x} + \frac{20x}{5x} = 3x + 4$$

Note: In Algebra II, we will learn how to divide by a polynomial of more than one term.

MODEL PROBLEM

Divide $21a^2b - 3ab$ by $3ab$.

Solution:

$$\overset{\text{(A)}}{\frac{21a^2b - 3ab}{3ab}} = \overset{\text{(B)}}{\frac{21a^2b}{3ab} - \frac{3ab}{3ab}} = \overset{\text{(C)}}{7a - 1}$$

Explanation of steps:

(A) Write the division as an algebraic fraction.

(B) Split the expression into separate fractions, each with one term of the numerator written over the same denominator. Be sure to keep the correct operation between the terms (addition or subtraction).

(C) If each term of the numerator is divisible by the monomial in the denominator, simplify by dividing. For the variable parts, subtract exponents of the same base. *[$21a^2b \div 3ab = 7a$ and $3ab \div 3ab = 1$.]*

PRACTICE PROBLEMS

1. Divide: $\dfrac{2x + 4}{2}$

2. Write $\dfrac{x^2 + 2x}{x}$ in simplest form.

3. Divide: $\dfrac{14ab + 28b}{14b}$

4. Simplify: $\dfrac{6x^3 + 9x^2 + 3x}{3x}$

5. Simplify: $\dfrac{12x^3 - 6x^2 + 2x}{2x}$

6. What is the quotient when $16x^3 - 12x^2 + 4x$ is divided by $4x$?

7. Divide: $\dfrac{2x^6 - 18x^4 + 2x^2}{2x^2}$

8. Divide: $\dfrac{8x^5 - 2x^4 + 4x^3 - 6x^2}{2x^2}$

9. Simplify: $\dfrac{45a^4b^3 - 90a^3b}{15a^2b}$

10. Divide $24x^2y^6 - 16x^6y^2 + 4xy^2$ by $4xy^2$.

Chapter 6.   Irrational Numbers

6.1   <u>Simplify Radicals</u>

KEY TERMS AND CONCEPTS

$\sqrt{x}$ represents the principal square root of x, or the non-negative value that, when multiplied by itself, is equal to x. The $\sqrt{}$ symbol is called a **radical sign**, and the quantity under the radical sign is called the **radicand**. A **radical** is a term containing a radical sign.

Example: $\sqrt{36} = 6$ (36 is the radicand.)

▦▯ CALCULATOR TIP

To find the square root of a number on the calculator, press [2nd][√], then type the radicand, then press [▸][ENTER].

[On the TI-83, the symbols "$\sqrt{}($" appear; after typing the radicand, press [)][ENTER] instead.]

Example: Find $\sqrt{36}$ by entering [2nd][√][3][6][▸][ENTER]

      [or [2nd][√][3][6][▸][ENTER] on the TI-83].

Since a positive number has a **negative square root** as well, we represent the negative square root by placing a negative sign before the radical. To indicate both the positive and negative roots, we use the **± symbol** before the radical.

Examples: $\sqrt{36} = 6$ $-\sqrt{36} = -6$ since $(-6)(-6) = 36$ $\pm\sqrt{36} = \{-6, 6\}$

It is important to recognize that **squaring** and taking a **square root** are reverse operations. Therefore, $\sqrt{x^2} = x$ and $\left(\sqrt{y}\right)^2 = y$.

Examples: $\sqrt{3^2} = \sqrt{9} = 3$ and $\left(\sqrt{25}\right)^2 = 5^2 = 25$.

▦▯ CALCULATOR TIP

You can square a number on the calculator using the [x^2] key. To raise a number to a power other than 2, you can use the [^] key.

Examples: Find 5^2 by entering [5][x^2][ENTER], or find 5^4 by entering [5][^][4][ENTER].

Two more important rules are: $\sqrt{ab} = \sqrt{a}\sqrt{b}$ and $\sqrt{\dfrac{a}{b}} = \dfrac{\sqrt{a}}{\sqrt{b}}$ (for $b \neq 0$).

Examples: $\sqrt{36} = \sqrt{9 \cdot 4} = \sqrt{9}\sqrt{4} = 3 \cdot 2 = 6$ and $\sqrt{\dfrac{4}{9}} = \dfrac{\sqrt{4}}{\sqrt{9}} = \dfrac{2}{3}$.

To simplify a radical into simplest radical form:

1. Write the prime factorization of the radicand.
2. Group all pairs of factors, representing squares.
3. Remove the squares (pairs of factors) from the radicand by replacing them with their square roots (single factors outside the radical sign).
4. Multiply all factors outside the radicand, and all factors remaining inside the radicand.

Examples: $\sqrt{75} = \sqrt{3 \cdot \boxed{5 \cdot 5}} = 5\sqrt{3}$

$\sqrt{288} = \sqrt{\boxed{2 \cdot 2} \cdot \boxed{2 \cdot 2} \cdot 2 \cdot \boxed{3 \cdot 3}} = 2 \cdot 2 \cdot 3 \cdot \sqrt{2} = 12\sqrt{2}$

MODEL PROBLEM

Simplify $8\sqrt{90}$

Solution:

$$\begin{array}{cccc} (A) & (B) & (C) & (D) \end{array}$$

$$8\sqrt{90} = 8\sqrt{2 \cdot \boxed{3 \cdot 3} \cdot 5} = 8 \cdot 3\sqrt{2 \cdot 5} = 24\sqrt{10}$$

Explanation of steps:

(A) Write the prime factorization of the radicand.
(B) Group all pairs of factors, representing squares.
(C) Remove the squares (pairs of factors) from the radicand by replacing them with their square roots (single factors) outside the radical sign.
(D) Multiply all factors outside the radicand, and all factors remaining inside the radicand.

PRACTICE PROBLEMS

1. Simplify $\sqrt{12}$.	2. Simplify $\sqrt{50}$.
3. Simplify $\sqrt{32}$.	4. Express $4\sqrt{75}$ in simplest radical form.
5. Simplify $5\sqrt{20}$.	6. Simplify $3\sqrt{45}$.
7. Simplify $5\sqrt{72}$.	8. Simplify $2\sqrt{128}$.

9. Simplify $-3\sqrt{48}$.

10. Simplify $-\sqrt{98}$.

11. Express $2\sqrt{108}$ in simplest radical form.

12. Express $3\sqrt{250}$ in simplest radical form.

13. Simplify $\dfrac{\sqrt{32}}{4}$.

14. Simplify $\dfrac{7\sqrt{18}}{3}$.

6.2   <u>Operations with Radicals [NG]</u>

KEY TERMS AND CONCEPTS

Radicals may be combined by addition or subtraction only if, when expressed in simplest radical form, they are like radicals. **Like radicals** have the **same radicand**. (*Note:* they must also have the same index, but we are only concerned with square roots here.)

Sometimes unlike radicals may be simplified into like radicals.

Example: $\sqrt{12}$ and $\sqrt{75}$ can be simplified into $2\sqrt{3}$ and $5\sqrt{3}$, which are like radicals.

Combine like radicals just as you would combine like terms: add or subtract the coefficients and keep the radicand unchanged.

Example: $2\sqrt{3} + 5\sqrt{3} - \sqrt{3} = (2 + 5 - 1)\sqrt{3} = 6\sqrt{3}$

To multiply radicals, separately find the product of their coefficients and the product of their radicands, then simplify if possible.

Example: $\left(5\sqrt{3}\right)\left(2\sqrt{7}\right) = 10\sqrt{21}$

To divide radicals, separately find the quotient of their coefficients and the quotient of their radicands, then simplify if possible.

Example: $\dfrac{6\sqrt{72}}{3\sqrt{8}} = 2\sqrt{9} = 2 \cdot 3 = 6$

Sometimes, multiple operations involving radicals need to be performed.

Example: Simplify $\sqrt{2}\left(\sqrt{10} + 4\right)$ using the distributive property.

$\sqrt{2}\left(\sqrt{10} + 4\right) = \sqrt{20} + 4\sqrt{2} = 2\sqrt{5} + 4\sqrt{2}$

MODEL PROBLEM 1:   *ADDING OR SUBTRACTING RADICALS*

Express the sum $3\sqrt{8} + 2\sqrt{2}$ in simplest radical form.

Solution:

(A) $3\sqrt{8}$ can be simplified as follows: $3\sqrt{\boxed{2\cdot2}\cdot2} = 3\cdot2\sqrt{2} = 6\sqrt{2}$.

(B)   So, $3\sqrt{8} + 2\sqrt{2} = 6\sqrt{2} + 2\sqrt{2} = 8\sqrt{2}$.

Explanation of steps:

(A)   Express each term in simplest radical form.

(B)   Combine like radicals by adding or subtracting their coefficients.

PRACTICE PROBLEMS

1. Add $\sqrt{75} + \sqrt{3}$.	2. Add $\sqrt{27} + \sqrt{12}$.
3. Find the sum of $\sqrt{50}$ and $\sqrt{32}$ in simplest radical form.	4. Find the sum of $\sqrt{27}$ and $\sqrt{108}$ in simplest radical form.
5. Write the sum $\sqrt{28} + \sqrt{63}$ in simplest radical form.	6. Write the sum $\sqrt{150} + \sqrt{24}$ in simplest radical form.

7. What is $3\sqrt{2} + \sqrt{8}$ expressed in simplest radical form?

8. What is $\sqrt{72} - 3\sqrt{2}$ expressed in simplest radical form?

9. Add $5\sqrt{7} + 3\sqrt{28}$.

10. Subtract $2\sqrt{50} - \sqrt{2}$.

11. Write the expression $6\sqrt{50} + 6\sqrt{2}$ in simplest radical form.

12. Express $\sqrt{25} - 2\sqrt{3} + \sqrt{27} + 2\sqrt{9}$ in simplest radical form.

MODEL PROBLEM 2:   *MULTIPLYING RADICALS*

Express the product $(5\sqrt{8})(7\sqrt{3})$ in simplest radical form.

Solution:

(A) $(5\sqrt{8})(7\sqrt{3}) = 35\sqrt{24}$

(B)   Simplifying, we get $35\sqrt{24} = 35\sqrt{\boxed{2 \cdot 2} \cdot 2 \cdot 3} = 35 \cdot 2\sqrt{2 \cdot 3} = 70\sqrt{6}$

Explanation of steps:

(A)   Find the product of the coefficients *[5 × 7 = 35]*.
      Find the product of the radicands *[8 × 3 = 24]*.
(B)   Express in simplest radical form.

PRACTICE PROBLEMS

13. Express $\sqrt{6} \cdot \sqrt{15}$ in simplest form.	14. What is the product of $4\sqrt{2}$ and $2\sqrt{6}$?
15. Express in simplest form: $\sqrt{90} \cdot \sqrt{40} - \sqrt{8} \cdot \sqrt{18}$	16. Express the product $3\sqrt{20}(2\sqrt{5} - 7)$ in simplest radical form.

17. Express $3\sqrt{7}\left(\sqrt{14} + 4\sqrt{56}\right)$ in simplest radical form.

18. Express the product of $\left(3 + \sqrt{5}\right)$ and $\left(3 - \sqrt{5}\right)$ in simplest form.

19. Express $y\sqrt{3} - \left(\sqrt{32} + y\sqrt{27}\right)$ in simplest radical form.

20. The length of a rectangle is $\left(3\sqrt{8} + 2\right)$ and the width is $\left(2\sqrt{2} + 1\right)$.

a) Express the perimeter of the rectangle in simplest radical form.

b) Express the area of the rectangle in simplest radical form.

MODEL PROBLEM 3:   _DIVIDING RADICALS_

Express $\dfrac{9\sqrt{20}}{3\sqrt{5}}$ in simplest radical form.

Solution:

$$\frac{9\sqrt{20}}{3\sqrt{5}} = 3\sqrt{4} = 3 \cdot 2 = 6$$

Explanation of steps:

(A)   Find the quotient of the coefficients $[9 \div 3 = 3]$.

      Find the quotient of the radicands $[20 \div 5 = 4]$.

(B)   Express in simplest radical form.

PRACTICE PROBLEMS

21. Express $\dfrac{\sqrt{65}}{\sqrt{5}}$ in simplest form.	22. Express in simplest form: $\dfrac{20\sqrt{100}}{4\sqrt{2}}$
23. Express $\dfrac{\sqrt{84}}{\sqrt{3}}$ in simplest radical form.	24. Express $\dfrac{6\sqrt{20}}{3\sqrt{5}}$ in simplest radical form.

25. Express $\dfrac{3\sqrt{75} + \sqrt{27}}{3}$ in simplest radical form.

26. Express $\dfrac{16\sqrt{21}}{2\sqrt{7}} - 5\sqrt{12}$ in simplest radical form.

27. Express in simplest form:
$$\frac{\sqrt{48} - 5\sqrt{27} + 2\sqrt{75}}{\sqrt{3}}$$

28. Express in simplest form:
$$\frac{\sqrt{27} + \sqrt{75}}{\sqrt{12}}$$

6.3   **Rationalizing Denominators [NG]**

KEY TERMS AND CONCEPTS

When working with algebraic fractions involving square roots, we prefer to change it to an equivalent fraction that does not include any square roots in the denominator. Eliminating radicals from the denominator is called **rationalizing the denominator**. Whenever we simplify fractions, we should rationalize their denominators.

Example: $\dfrac{3}{\sqrt{2}}$ has an irrational denominator.

If a fraction's denominator has a *monomial* containing a square root, we will multiply both the numerator and denominator by that square root. This will work because multiplying a square root by itself will eliminate the radical sign: $\sqrt{x} \cdot \sqrt{x} = x$.

Example: We can rationalize the denominator of $\dfrac{3}{\sqrt{2}}$ by multiplying by $\dfrac{\sqrt{2}}{\sqrt{2}}$, as in:

$$\frac{3}{\sqrt{2}} \cdot \frac{\sqrt{2}}{\sqrt{2}} = \frac{3 \cdot \sqrt{2}}{\sqrt{2} \cdot \sqrt{2}} = \frac{3\sqrt{2}}{2}$$

To rationalize a monomial denominator of a fraction:
1.   Find the radical in the denominator, and create a new fraction using this radical in the numerator and denominator (a form of 1). Multiply the two fractions.
2.   Simplify.

Example: To simplify $\dfrac{4}{3\sqrt{6}}$, multiply the fraction by $\dfrac{\sqrt{6}}{\sqrt{6}}$, which gives us

$$\frac{4}{3\sqrt{6}} \cdot \frac{\sqrt{6}}{\sqrt{6}} = \frac{4\sqrt{6}}{18} = \frac{2\sqrt{6}}{9}.$$

When adding or subtracting fractions, it is helpful to rationalize the denominators first.

MODEL PROBLEM 1:   *RATIONALIZING THE DENOMINATOR*

Rationalize the denominator of $\dfrac{10}{\sqrt{5}}$ and write the equivalent expression in simplest form.

Solution: **Explanation of steps:**

$$\begin{array}{ccc} \text{(A)} & \text{(B)} & \text{(C)} \end{array}$$

$$\dfrac{10}{\sqrt{5}} \cdot \left(\dfrac{\sqrt{5}}{\sqrt{5}}\right) = \dfrac{10\sqrt{5}}{5} = 2\sqrt{5}$$

(A) If the fraction has a single irrational square root term in the denominator [$\sqrt{5}$], create a new fraction with this radical as its numerator and denominator.

(B) Multiply the two fractions. The denominator of the product is now rational.

(C) Simplify.

PRACTICE PROBLEMS

1. Rationalize the denominator of $\dfrac{1}{\sqrt{7}}$.	2. Rationalize the denominator of $\dfrac{6}{\sqrt{2}}$ and simplify.
3. Rationalize the denominator of $\dfrac{5}{\sqrt{10}}$ and simplify.	4. Rationalize the denominator of $\dfrac{6}{\sqrt{21}}$ and simplify.

5. Rationalize the denominator of $\dfrac{8}{3\sqrt{6}}$ and simplify.

6. Rationalize the denominator of $\dfrac{10\sqrt{2}}{\sqrt{5}}$ and simplify.

7. Multiply $\dfrac{2}{\sqrt{3}} \times \dfrac{\sqrt{2}}{5}$ and express the product as a fraction with a rational denominator.

8. Simplify $\sqrt{\dfrac{16}{3}}$. Express as a fraction with a rational denominator.

MODEL PROBLEM 2:   *ADD FRACTIONS WITH IRRATIONAL DENOMINATORS*

Add $\dfrac{2}{\sqrt{3}} + \dfrac{1}{\sqrt{5}}$

Solution:

(A) $\dfrac{2}{\sqrt{3}} \cdot \left(\dfrac{\sqrt{3}}{\sqrt{3}}\right) = \dfrac{2\sqrt{3}}{3}$ $\dfrac{1}{\sqrt{5}} \cdot \left(\dfrac{\sqrt{5}}{\sqrt{5}}\right) = \dfrac{\sqrt{5}}{5}$

(B) $\dfrac{2\sqrt{3}}{3} + \dfrac{\sqrt{5}}{5} = \dfrac{2\sqrt{3}}{3} \cdot \left(\dfrac{5}{5}\right) + \dfrac{\sqrt{5}}{5} \cdot \left(\dfrac{3}{3}\right) = \dfrac{10\sqrt{3}}{15} + \dfrac{3\sqrt{5}}{15}$

(C) $= \dfrac{10\sqrt{3} + 3\sqrt{5}}{15}$

Explanation of steps:

(A)   When adding fractions, first rationalize the denominators of both fractions, and simplify each fraction if possible.

(B)   Now, add the fractions by finding the least common denominator *[the LCD is 15]* and converting the fractions into equivalent fractions with the same LCD.

(C)   Write the sum as a single fraction by adding the numerators and keeping the LCD as the denominator.

PRACTICE PROBLEMS

9. Add $\dfrac{1}{\sqrt{3}} + \dfrac{1}{\sqrt{2}}$.	10. Add $\dfrac{1}{\sqrt{2}} + \dfrac{3}{\sqrt{5}}$.

11. Add $\dfrac{3}{\sqrt{5}} + \dfrac{4}{\sqrt{6}}$.

12. What is $\dfrac{3 - \sqrt{8}}{\sqrt{3}}$ expressed in simplest form?

13. What is $\sqrt{\dfrac{4}{3}} - \sqrt{\dfrac{3}{4}}$ expressed in simplest form?

6.4   <u>Closure</u>

KEY TERMS AND CONCEPTS

The set of real numbers is made up of **rational numbers** and **irrational numbers**. (Using the language of sets, the set of reals is the union of the two disjoint sets: the set of rationals and the set of irrationals.)

A rational number is any number that can be expressed as a fraction $\frac{a}{b}$ where a is an integer and b is a non-zero integer. Expressed in decimal form, rational numbers are terminating or repeating decimals, such as –100, 1.75. or $2.\overline{6}$. So, an irrational number is any real number that *cannot* be expressed as a fraction of integers. Irrational numbers, such as π and $\sqrt{2}$, are non-terminating, non-repeating decimals.

In fact, the *square roots of all whole numbers that are not perfect squares are irrational*. Examples: $\sqrt{9}$ and $\sqrt{49}$ are rational, but $\sqrt{3}$ and $\sqrt{50}$ are irrational.

We have already seen (*in Section 1.1*) that that the set of *non-zero* rational numbers is *closed* under each of the four basic operations.

In contrast, the set of irrational numbers is **not closed** under any of the four basic operations.

Examples: We can add, subtract, multiply, or divide two irrational numbers and the result may be rational, as shown here.

$$\sqrt{2} + \left(-\sqrt{2}\right) = 0 \qquad \sqrt{2} - \sqrt{2} = 0 \qquad \sqrt{2} \cdot \sqrt{2} = 2 \qquad \frac{\sqrt{2}}{\sqrt{2}} = 1$$

When any of the four basic operations are performed on *non-zero* real numbers:
a) if both operands are **rational**, the result is **rational**;
b) if one of the operands is **rational** and the other operand is **irrational**, the result is *always* **irrational** (excluding zero as an operand for multiplication or division);
c) if both operands are **irrational**, the result may be **rational** (e.g., $\sqrt{2} \cdot \sqrt{8} = \sqrt{16} = 4$) or **irrational** (e.g., $\sqrt{2} \cdot \sqrt{3} = \sqrt{6}$).

How do we know that statement b) above is true?

Remember, an irrational number is a non-repeating, non-terminating decimal. If we were to, say, add such a number to a rational number (that is, a terminating or repeating decimal), the result would still be a non-repeating, non-terminating decimal.

Examples: (a) $2 + \sqrt{2} = 2 + 1.414213 \ldots = 3.414213 \ldots$

(b) $\frac{1}{3} + \pi = 0.33333 \ldots + 3.14159 \ldots = 3.47492 \ldots$

Another way to look at it is by using our knowledge of closure.

For example: Is it possible to have $a + b = c$ where a is rational, b is irrational, and c is rational? The answer is no, by the following proof:

1) If we solve the equation for b, we get $b = c - a$.
2) If both c and a are rational, and we know the set of rational numbers is closed under subtraction, then the difference $c - a$ would have to be rational.
3) This would mean that b would have to be rational, since $b = c - a$.
4) Since we originally said b is irrational, we've come to a contradiction.
5) So, it's not possible to have $a + b = c$ where a is rational, b is irrational, and c is rational. Therefore the sum c would have to be irrational.

This is known as a *proof by contradiction*. Similar explanations can be used to justify or prove this for the other basic operations.

MODEL PROBLEM

The famous "golden ratio" is defined as $\dfrac{1 + \sqrt{5}}{2}$. Is the golden ratio rational or irrational?

Solution:

$1 + \sqrt{5}$ is the sum of a rational and an irrational number, so it is irrational.

$\dfrac{1 + \sqrt{5}}{2}$ is the division of an irrational numerator and a rational denominator, so it is irrational.

Explanation of steps:

Look at each operation. If both operands are rational, then the result is rational. If one operand is rational and the other is irrational [as is the case with both operations performed here], then the result is irrational. An operation between two irrational numbers may have either a rational or irrational result.

169

PRACTICE PROBLEMS

1. Which of the following square roots is an irrational number? (1) $-\sqrt{16}$ (3) $\sqrt{64}$ (2) $\sqrt{8}$ (4) $\sqrt{\dfrac{1}{64}}$	2. State whether $2\sqrt{3}$ is rational or irrational.
3. State whether $\dfrac{\pi}{2}$ is rational or irrational. Justify your answer.	4. State whether $\dfrac{2-\sqrt{29}}{4}$ is rational or irrational. Justify your answer.
5. Name at least three possible values of x that would make $x\sqrt{3}$ a rational number.	6. $\dfrac{22}{7}$ and 3.14 are often used as a rational approximations of π. Which of these is closer to the actual value of π?

Chapter 7.   Univariate Data

7.1   Types of Data

KEY TERMS AND CONCEPTS

Statistics is the practice or science of collecting and analyzing data. A set of data may be qualitative or quantitative in nature:

Data is **qualitative** (from the word, "quality") if it is recorded as non-numeric characteristics. Qualitative data is also known as **categorical**.

Example: If a survey asks for a favorite soda, the responses are qualitative.

Data is **quantitative** (from the word, "quantity") if it is recorded as numeric values. Quantitative data allows for numerical analysis of the results, such as finding the average (mean) of the data. Quantitative data is also known as **numerical**.

Example: If a survey asks for test scores, the responses are quantitative.

Data is considered **univariate** if it can be recorded using a **single variable**. A frequency table, histogram, or dot plot uses univariate data. **Frequency** represents the number of times each result occurs in the data. Univariate data can also be represented by a box-and-whisker plot.

Example: A survey asks a sampling of people for their heights in inches.

Data is considered **bivariate** if it is recorded using **two variables**. Bivariate data can be represented by plotting points on a coordinate graph or scatter plot. For each result or response, an ordered pair represents the values of the two variables, usually x and y, for that point. Each variable may be qualitative or quantitative.

Example: A survey asks people for their heights in inches and their weights in pounds.

MODEL PROBLEM

For each of the following graphs, identify whether the data is (a) qualitative or quantitative, and (b) univariate or bivariate.

Types of Pitches in a Game

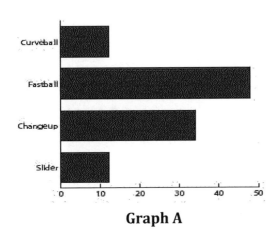

Graph A

Revenue for an Ice Cream Shop Dependent on Temperature

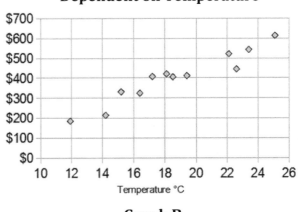

Graph B

Solution:

(A)   Graph A is qualitative and univariate.

(B)   Graph B is quantitative and bivariate.

Explanation:

(A)   Data is qualitative if their values are non-numerical *[curveball, fastball, etc.]* and univariate if it involves only one variable *[specifying which type of pitch].*
   [The numerical values on the x-axis of the bar graph represent the frequency of the data; for example, nearly 50 of the pitches were fastballs.]

(B)   Data is quantitative if their values are numerical *[a number of degrees and a number of dollars]* and bivariate if it involves two variables *[specifying the temperature in degrees Celsius and the revenue in dollars].*

PRACTICE PROBLEMS

1. Which is an example of bivariate data?
   (1) shoe sizes of the players on a high school basketball team
   (2) goals scored in hockey games over the course of a season
   (3) Calories consumed per day by a track athlete for one month
   (4) hours spent studying compared to test scores in a science course

2. An art studio posts information about each sculpture that is for sale. Which data would *not* be classified as quantitative?
   (1)   cost   (3)   artist
   (2)   height   (4)   weight

3. Specify whether the data used to create this chart is univariate or bivariate.

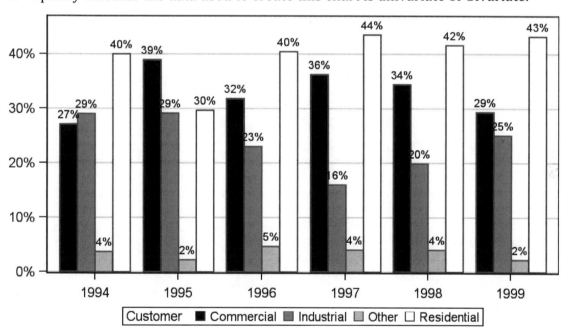

7.2   Frequency Tables and Histograms

KEY TERMS AND CONCEPTS

Frequency is the number of times that a particular result or value occurs in a list of data. Sometimes, data values are organized into **intervals** of equal sizes.

Examples: The **frequency table** on the left shows the scores of 30 students on a 5-point quiz. On the right, the **frequency table** shows the age intervals of 30 people.

Score	Frequency
0	4
1	3
2	5
3	5
4	6
5	7

Age Group	Frequency
20–29	9
30–39	7
40–49	10
50–59	4

A **frequency histogram** is a type of bar graph where the height of each bar represents the number of data items in that interval. To create a frequency histogram:

1. First create a **frequency table** by tallying each item of data in the Tally column, then counting the tallies for each interval and writing the count in the Frequency column. It is often helpful to count the frequencies using **tally** marks, with every 5 tally marks written as ⅢⅠ.

2. Create the frequency histogram by first labeling each interval along the horizontal axis and the range of frequencies along the vertical axis. The interval labels and the frequency labels must be equally spaced. If the lowest interval does not start at 0, the symbol ⌄ may be drawn on the horizontal axis to represent the gap.

3. For each interval, draw a shaded rectangular bar as high as its corresponding frequency. There should be no spaces between the bars.

Example: The data from the frequency table to the above right may be graphed using a frequency histogram, as shown to the right.

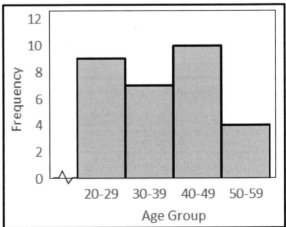

A **cumulative frequency histogram** is also a bar graph, but each bar represents the sum of all the frequencies from the *first* interval up to and including that interval. To create one:

1. Create a **cumulative frequency table** based on the frequency table. Each interval should be relabeled as spanning from the start of the *first* frequency table interval to the end of the current interval. The cumulative frequencies are the sums of the frequencies from the *first* interval up to and including that interval. *The last cumulative frequency should equal the number of data items.*

2. Create the cumulative frequency histogram by first labeling each interval along the horizontal axis and the range of cumulative frequencies along the vertical axis. The interval labels and the frequency labels must be equally spaced.

3. For each interval, draw a shaded rectangular bar as high as its corresponding cumulative frequency. There should be no spaces between the bars. *Each bar should be at least as tall as the bar to its left.*

Example: The same data used in the frequency histogram of the previous example may be displayed using a cumulative frequency histogram, as shown below.

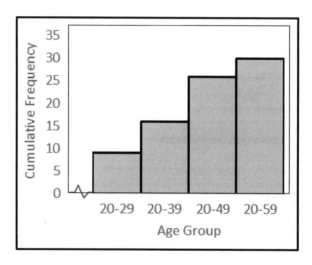

CALCULATOR TIP

To enter a set of data into the calculator:

1. Press [STAT][1] to select Edit.

2. If any values already appear in the L1 column (L stands for List), select the column heading and press [CLEAR][ENTER].

3. Enter the data values into the L1 column.

4. Press [2nd][QUIT] when you're done to return to the home screen.

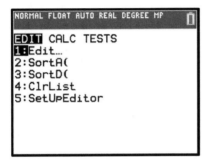 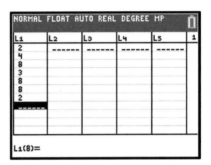

If any columns other than L1 appear in the table, you can either leave them there or delete them by selecting the column heading and pressing [DEL]. Also, if the L1 column is missing, you can add it by selecting an empty column heading and then pressing [2nd][L1][ENTER].

To sort and view your data as a horizontal list:

1. Press [STAT][2] to select SortA. [Or, press [STAT][3] select SortD for descending order.]

2. Press [2nd][L1][)][ENTER]. The word "Done" will appear.

3. View your data by pressing [2nd][L1][ENTER] and it will now be sorted.

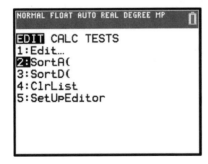 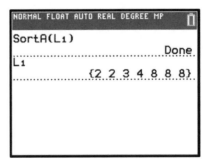

CALCULATOR TIP

To view a frequency histogram on the calculator for a set of data:

1. Press [2nd][STAT PLOT][1] to select Plot 1.

2. Select [On] and press [ENTER].

3. Select the third Type of graph (histogram) and press [ENTER].

4. For Xlist, if L1 isn't already selected, press [2nd][L1] to enter it.

5. For Freq, enter the value 1.

6. Press [GRAPH].

7. If you don't see the histogram, or prefer a larger view, press [ZOOM][9] for ZoomStat.

   You may also need to press [WINDOW] to adjust the dimension and scale values, as shown below.

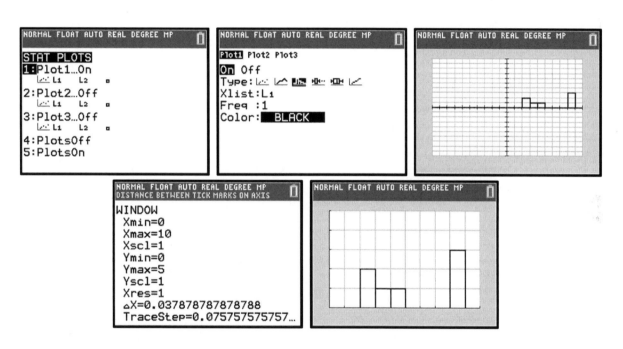

▓▓▒░ CALCULATOR TIP

To enter larger amounts of data into the calculator more efficiently, we can use a frequency table to enter each value and its frequency as L1 and L2, as shown below.

Example: For the data shown below, instead of entering 30 values into L1, we can enter each of the six possible values once into L1 but specify its frequency in L2.

Score	Frequency
0	4
1	3
2	5
3	5
4	6
5	7

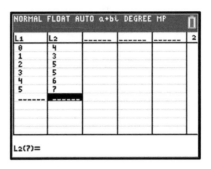

To enter a frequency table into the calculator:

1. Press [STAT][1] to select Edit.

2. If any values already appear in the L1 or L2 column, select the column heading and press [CLEAR][ENTER].

3. Enter each data value and its frequency into the L1 and L2 column, respectively.

4. Press [2nd][QUIT].

▒▒▒ CALCULATOR TIP

To view a frequency histogram on the calculator for a frequency table of data:

1. Press $\boxed{\text{2nd}}\boxed{\text{STAT PLOT}}\boxed{1}$ to select Plot 1.

2. Select $\boxed{\text{On}}$ and press $\boxed{\text{ENTER}}$.

3. Select the third Type of graph (histogram) and press $\boxed{\text{ENTER}}$.

4. For Xlist, enter L1 by pressing $\boxed{\text{2nd}}\boxed{\text{L1}}$.

5. For Freq, enter L2 by pressing $\boxed{\text{2nd}}\boxed{\text{L2}}$.

6. Press $\boxed{\text{GRAPH}}$.

7. If you don't see the histogram, or prefer a larger view, press $\boxed{\text{ZOOM}}\boxed{9}$ for ZoomStat.

   You may also need to press $\boxed{\text{WINDOW}}$ to adjust the dimension and scale values, as shown below.

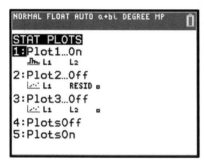  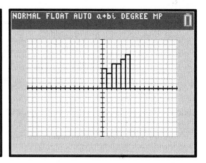

MODEL PROBLEM

Create a frequency histogram and cumulative frequency histogram for the following set of 36 test scores, using intervals of 10 points.

14, 17, 28, 28, 30, 36, 45, 52, 58, 58, 61, 64, 64, 68, 68, 77, 77,

81, 81, 81, 81, 87, 87, 94, 94, 95, 95, 95, 95, 95, 95, 97, 97, 97, 100, 100

Solution:

(A) Interval	(B) Tally	(C) Frequency
0-10		0
11-20	||	2
21-30	|||	3
31-40	|	1
41-50	|	1
51-60	|||	3
61-70	⊬⊬	5
71-80	||	2
81-90	⊬⊬ |	6
91-100	⊬⊬ ⊬⊬ |||	13

(D)

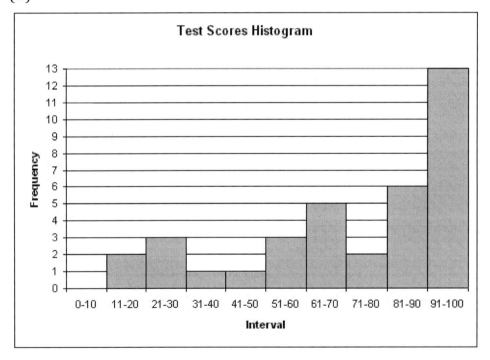

(Continued on next page...)

(Continued from previous page)

(E)   (F)   (G)

Interval	Cumulative Frequency
0-10	0
0-20	2
0-30	5
0-40	6
0-50	7
0-60	10
0-70	15
0-80	17
0-90	23
0-100	36

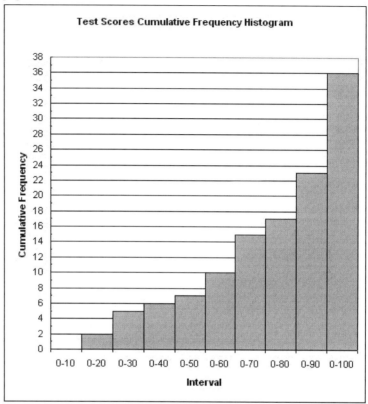

Explanation of steps:

(A)   Create the frequency table using equally wide intervals. *[Each is 10 points wide.]*

(B)   Tally each data item by writing a tally mark for the corresponding interval.

(C)   Count the tally marks and write each count as a number in the Frequency column.

(D)   Draw the frequency histogram.

(E)   Create the cumulative frequency table based on the frequency table. Re-label the intervals so that they all start with the *first* interval's minimum value *[0]*.

(F)   Enter the cumulative frequencies. The first interval's cumulative frequency is equal to the first interval's frequency. The cumulative frequency for each interval after the first is the sum of the preceding cumulative frequency plus the corresponding interval's frequency. *[For example, the cumulative frequency for 0-30 is the sum of the cumulative frequency for 0-20, which is 2, plus the frequency of the 21-30 interval, which is 3.]*

(G)   Draw the cumulative frequency histogram.

PRACTICE PROBLEMS

1. The accompanying histogram shows the heights of the students in Kyra's health class. What is the total number of students in the class?

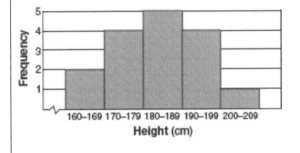

2. Casey talked to everyone in his apartment building to find out how many hours of television each person watched each day. The results are shown in the histogram below. Using the histogram, determine the total number of people in Casey's building.

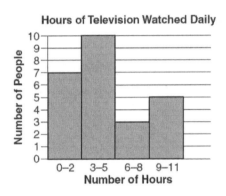

3. The table below shows a cumulative frequency distribution of runners' ages. According to the table, how many runners are in their forties?

Cumulative Frequency Distribution of Runners' Ages

Age Group	Total
20–29	8
20–39	18
20–49	25
20–59	31
20–69	35

4. Mr. Trapp recorded the height, in inches, of every student in his class. From the data collected, he created the cumulative frequency histogram shown below. Based on the histogram, how many students are in the class?

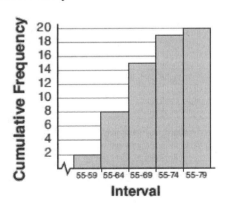

5. The cumulative frequency histogram below shows the distances swimmers completed in a swim team practice.

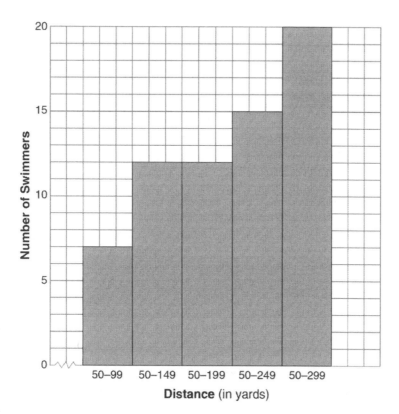

a) Based on the cumulative frequency histogram, determine the number of swimmers who swam between 200 and 249 yards.

b) Determine the number of swimmers who swam between 150 and 199 yards.

c) Determine the number of swimmers who participated in the swim team practice.

6. In the time trials for the 400-meter run at the state sectionals, the 15 runners recorded the times shown in the table below. Using the data from the frequency column, draw a frequency histogram on the grid below.

400-Meter Run	
Time (sec)	Frequency
50.0–50.9	
51.0–51.9	II
52.0–52.9	JHT I
53.0–53.9	III
54.0–54.9	IIII

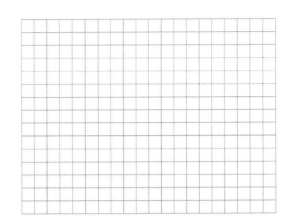

7. The following set of data represents the scores on a mathematics quiz:

58, 79, 81, 99, 68, 92, 76, 84, 53, 57,

81, 91, 77, 50, 65, 57, 51, 72, 84, 89

a) Complete the frequency table below.

b) On the grid below, draw and label a frequency histogram of these scores.

Mathematics Quiz Scores

Interval	Tally	Frequency
50–59		
60–69		
70–79		
80–89		
90–99		

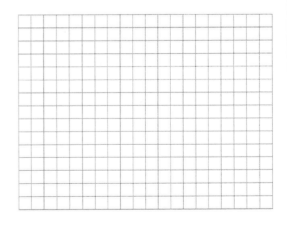

8.   Ms. Hopkins recorded her students' final exam scores in the frequency table below.

On the accompanying grid, construct a frequency histogram based on the table.

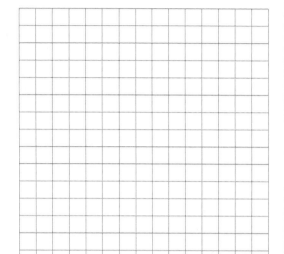

Interval	Tally	Frequency
61–70	﷽	5
71–80	IIII	4
81–90	IIII	9
91–100	I	6

9.   The test scores for 18 students in Ms. Rom's class are listed below.

86, 81, 79, 71, 58, 87, 52, 71, 87,

87, 93, 64, 94, 81, 76, 98, 94, 68

Complete the frequency table below. Then, draw and label a frequency histogram on the accompanying grid.

Interval	Tally	Frequency
51–60		
61–70		
71–80		
81–90		
91–100		

10. Twenty students were surveyed about the number of days they played outside in one week. The results of this survey are shown below.

6, 5, 4, 3, 0, 7, 1, 5, 4, 4, 3, 2, 2, 3, 2, 4, 3, 4, 0, 7

Complete the frequency table and cumulative frequency table below for these data.

Number of Days Outside

Interval	Tally	Frequency
0–1		
2–3		
4–5		
6–7		

Number of Days Outside

Interval	Cumulative Frequency
0–1	
0–3	
0–5	
0–7	

On the grid below, create a cumulative frequency histogram based on the table.

7.3   **Central Tendency**

KEY TERMS AND CONCEPTS

For the definitions below, we will refer to this sample set of quantitative data:

2, 4, 8, 3, 8, 8, 2

Each data value may be called an **observation**.

Example: For the sample data above, there are 7 observations.

The lowest value in the data set is called the **minimum**, the highest value is called the **maximum**, and the **range** is the *difference* between the *maximum* and *minimum* values. Range is a measure of **spread**, not central tendency, in that it measures how spread out the data set is.

Example: For the sample data, 2 is the minimum, 8 is the maximum, and the range is 6.

Three commonly used measures of **central tendency** are the mean, median and mode.

The **mean** (often written as $\bar{x}$) is calculated as a numerical average, by *adding* all the numbers in the data and *dividing* by how many data values (or *observations*) there are.

Example: The mean of the sample set of data is $\dfrac{2 + 4 + 8 + 3 + 8 + 8 + 2}{7} = \dfrac{35}{7} = 5.$

To find the **median** for a set of data, we must first arrange the data in ascending order. For an *odd* number of data values, the median is the *middle number*.

Example: The sample set of data is arranged as: 2, 2, 3, 4, 8, 8, 8.

There are 7 data values. The median, or middle number, is 4.

For an *even* number of values, the median is the *mean* (average) of the *two middle numbers*.

Example: Suppose we add another 2 to the data: 2, 2, 2, 3, 4, 8, 8, 8.

Now there are 8 values. The median is the average of 3 and 4, or 3.5.

The **mode** is the data value that appears *most often*. It is helpful to arrange the data in ascending order before determining the mode.

Example: The sample set of data is arranged as: 2, 2, 3, 4, 8, 8, 8.

Since the value 8 appears most often (three times), the mode is 8.

It is possible to have more than one mode. A set of data with two modes is called **bimodal**.

Example: Suppose we add another 2 to the sample data: 2, 2, 2, 3, 4, 8, 8, 8.

Now there are two modes, 2 and 8, since both numbers appear three times.

If each number appears with the same frequency, then there is **no mode**.

Example: This set of data has no mode: 2, 2, 3, 3, 4, 4.

Sometime, one of the measures of central tendency is a better indicator than another. In some cases there are one or a few data values, called **outliers**, which are much higher or lower than the rest of the data. Outliers can skew the mean.

Examples: Consider these two sets of data.

2, 3, 5, 5, 7, 8, 33   2, 3, 5, 5, 25, 25, 33

Mean = 9   Mean = 14

Median = 5   Median = 5

In the first set of data, an outlier (33) skews the mean so that the mean (9) is actually larger than 6 of the 7 data values. In this case, the median may be a better indicator of central tendency. In the second set of data, the mean (14) may be more appropriate, since nearly half the values are at least 25.

If we **add the same constant to each value** in a set of data, this will add that constant to the mean, median, and mode. The range will not change.

Example: Test scores in a class are originally 55, 60, 62, 70, 70.

The mean = 63.4, median = 62, and mode = 70.

The teacher decides to "curve" the test by adding 10 points to each score.

The data set becomes 65, 70, 72, 80, 80. Each new measure of central tendency is now 10 points higher: mean = 73.4, median = 72, and mode = 80.

The same is true if we **multiply each data value by the same constant** (other than zero). The mean, median and mode will also be multiplied by the same constant factor as a result. However, in this case the range will also multiplied by the same factor.

■■■□ CALCULATOR TIP

To find the measures of central tendency on the calculator:

1. First, press [STAT][1] and enter the data into the L1 column, or enter the data as a frequency table into L1 and L2.

2. Press [STAT], select [CALC] and press [1] for 1-Var Stats. Be sure that L1 is specified as the List, or press [2nd][L1] to enter it. If L2 contains frequencies, enter [2nd][L2] as FreqList; otherwise, leave it blank. Then, select Calculate.

   [On the TI-83, you need to enter L1 after the 1-Var Stats prompt by pressing [2nd][L1]. If L2 contains frequencies, press [,][2nd][L2]. Then, press [ENTER].]

3. The mean is the value of $\bar{x}$. Press the down arrow to Med for the median. Unfortunately, the calculator does not show the mode.

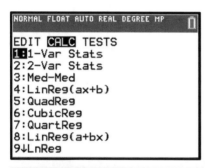

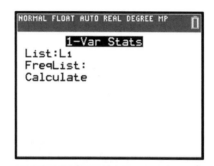

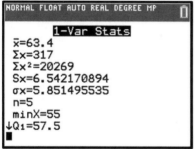

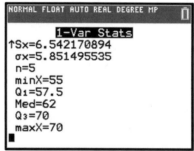

▓▓▓▒□ CALCULATOR TIP

You can also find the mean (or median) on the calculator by pressing ⟦2nd⟧⟦STAT⟧ and selecting ⟦MATH⟧. Then, press ⟦3⟧ for mean (or ⟦4⟧ for median), followed by ⟦2nd⟧⟦L1⟧⟦)⟧⟦ENTER⟧.

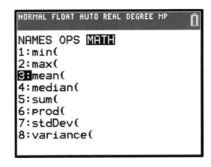 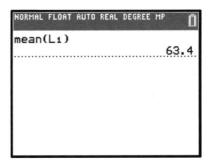

MODEL PROBLEM

For the given set of data, find the mean, median, and mode: 1, 3, 5, 7, 9, 13, 21, 25, 25, 31.

Solution:

(A) Mean: $\dfrac{1 + 3 + 5 + 7 + 9 + 13 + 21 + 25 + 25 + 31}{10} = \dfrac{140}{10} = 14$

(B) Median: $\dfrac{9 + 13}{2} = 11$

(C) Mode: 25

Explanation of steps:

(A) Find the mean by adding all the values and dividing this sum *[140]* by the number of data values *[10]*.

(B) For an even number of data values *[there are 10 values in this set]*, we need to take the mean (numerical average) of the middle two numbers *[9 and 13]*.

(C) The mode is the value that appears most often. *[Only 25 appears more than once.]*

PRACTICE PROBLEMS

1. For a school report, Luke contacted a car dealership to collect data on recent sales. He asked, "What color do buyers choose most often for their car?" White was the response. What statistical measure does the response "white" represent?

2. The weights of all the students in grade 9 are arranged from least to greatest. Which statistical measure separates the top half of this set of data from the bottom half?

3. Which of the following sets of data is bimodal?
   (1) 1, 1, 2, 5, 5, 6
   (2) 1, 1, 2, 2, 2, 3
   (3) 1, 2, 3, 4, 5, 6
   (4) 1, 1, 2, 2, 3, 3

4. Each value in a set of data is divided by two. How does this affect the mean, median and mode for this set of data?

5. Mr. Swift raised all his students' scores on a recent test by five points. How were the mean and the range of the scores affected?

6. The table below shows math quiz scores of seven students.

    5, 12, 7, 15, 20, 14, 7

    a) Determine the mean, median, and mode of the student scores, to the *nearest tenth*.

    b) Describe the effect on the mean, median, and mode if 5 bonus points are added to each of the students' scores.

7. The table shows the high and low temperatures for five cities. Which city had the greatest temperature range?

    TEMPERATURES ON OCTOBER 1ST
    FOR FIVE CITIES (in °F)

	High	Low
City A	72	50
City B	90	75
City C	83	72
City D	50	37
City E	92	72

8. Sara's test scores in mathematics were 64, 80, 88, 78, 60, 92, 84, 76, 86, 78, 72, and 90. Determine the mean, the median, and the mode of Sara's test scores.

9. Which statement is true about the data set 4, 5, 6, 6, 7, 9, 12?
   (1)   mean = mode
   (2)   mode = median
   (3)   mean < median
   (4)   mode > mean

10. What is the relationship between the measures of central tendency of these data?

   22, 14, 19, 22, 8, 17

   (1)   mode > median > mean
   (2)   median > mode > mean
   (3)   mean > median > mode
   (4)   mode > mean > median

11. Based on the frequency table of student test grades below, which statement is true for the data?
   (1)   mean > median > mode
   (2)   mean > mode > median
   (3)   mode > median > mean
   (4)   median > mean > mode

Score	Frequency
96	2
92	5
88	3
84	2
78	4
60	1

12. Two social studies classes took the same current events examination that was scored on the basis of 100 points.

   Mr. Wong's class had a median score of 78 and a range of 4 points, while Ms. Rizzo's class had a median score of 78 and a range of 22 points.

   Explain how these classes could have the same median score while having very different ranges.

13. The accompanying graph shows the high temperatures in Elmira, New York, for a 5-day period in January. Find the mean, median, and mode.

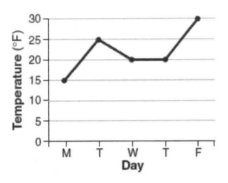

14. The table below shows the distribution of bowling scores. In which interval does the median lie?

Interval	Frequency
91–110	10
111–130	11
131–150	8
151–170	4
171–190	6
191–210	5

15. The values of 11 houses on West St. are shown in the table below.

Value per House	Number of Houses
$100,000	1
$175,000	5
$200,000	4
$700,000	1

Find the mean value and the median value of these houses in dollars.

State which measure of central tendency, the mean or the median, *best* represents the values of these 11 houses. Justify your answer.

16. The cumulative frequency table below shows the number of minutes students spent texting on a weekend.

Text-Use Interval (minutes)	Cumulative Frequency
41–50	2
41–60	5
41–70	10
41–80	19
41–90	31

Which 10-minute interval contains the median? Justify your choice.

7.4   <u>Distribution</u>

KEY TERMS AND CONCEPTS

A **dot plot** may be used to provide a graphic representation of a set of data. In a dot plot, each data value is represented by a dot, or by a similar symbol such as a plus sign (+) or asterisk (*). The dots are stacked on top of a number line. The height of a stacked column of dots represents the frequency for that data value, just like the height of a bar represents the frequency for a data value in a frequency histogram.

Example: 29 students were asked to time their trip to school one morning and to round their results to the nearest multiple of 5 minutes. Their responses were plotted below. From the dot plot, we can see that two students took about 5 minutes each, one student took about 10 minutes, and so on.

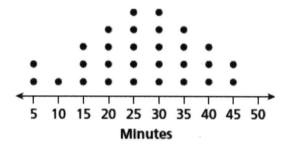

The **shape** of a dot plot can show the type of **distribution** of the data. If the data values are somewhat equally distributed, we call it a **uniform distribution**. In a **symmetrical distribution**, one could draw a vertical line on the dot plot that would divide it into two parts that are approximate mirror images of each other. A **skewed distribution** is neither uniform nor symmetric; the data is stacked mostly on the low end or on the high end of the dot plot.

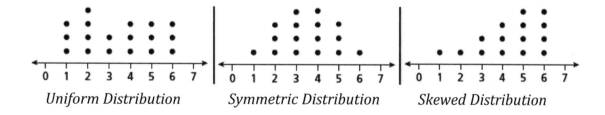

When the data tends to gather around a central value in a *symmetrical* dot plot, it is said to have a **normal distribution**, and the shape is often called a *bell curve*. The middle dot plot above is an example of a normal distribution of data; notice the bell-shaped curve as shown below:

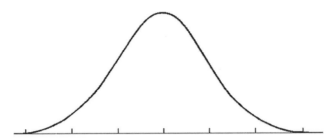

In a **skewed distribution**, if the graph appears to have a tail to the right (and more of the data to the left), it is **skewed to the right**, or *positively skewed*. If it appears to have its data stretched to the left like a tail, it is considered **skewed to the left**, or *negatively skewed*.

Example: The following dot plot is skewed to the left.

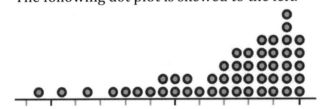

A *skewed distribution* can easily be seen in a frequency histogram. The histogram on the left shows a somewhat *symmetrical distribution*. We can draw a vertical line down the middle so that the left and right sides would have approximately the same shape. The histogram on the right is skewed to the right (*positively skewed*), in that it has a "tail" to the right and more of the data to the left.

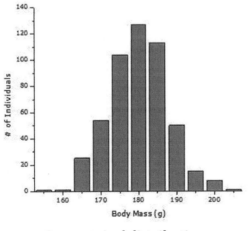
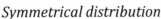
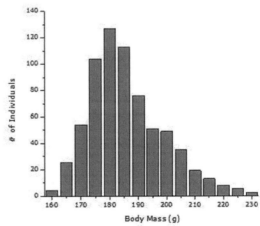

Symmetrical distribution   *Skewed distribution*

When the data has a symmetrical distribution, the mean and median tend to be approximately equal (at the center of the bell) and either can be used as measures of central tendancy. However, when the data is skewed, the median is usually a better indicator. The mean will be less than the median when the data is skewed left or greater than the median when the data is skewed right.

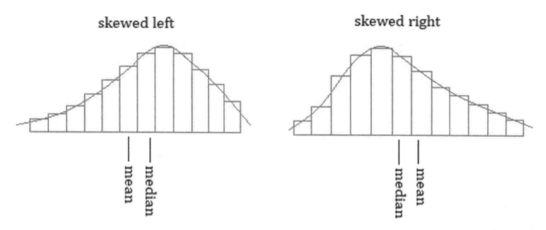

For a more informative analysis, the *standard deviation* can be calculated with the mean, or the *quartiles* may be calculated with the median; these will be presented in later sections.

MODEL PROBLEM 1:   *READING DOT PLOTS*

The following dot plot shows the fuel economy for a number of cars in miles per gallon (mpg). How many cars have a fuel economy between 30 and 40 mpg inclusive?

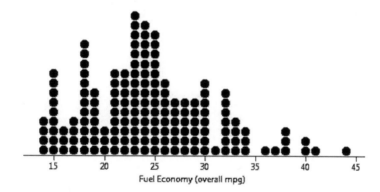

Solution:

> 30 cars

Explanation:

> Count the dots stacked vertically. *[There are 8 dots at the 30 mpg marker, 2 dots at the 40 mpg marker, and 20 more dots stacked between these two markers.]*

PRACTICE PROBLEMS

1. Given the dot plot below, what percent of the data values are less than 5?	2. Given the dot plot below, what are the mean, median, and mode of the data?
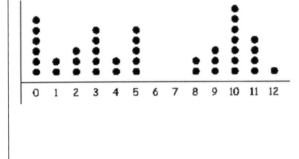	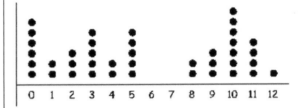

MODEL PROBLEM 2:   *DISTRIBUTION AND SHAPE*

The dotplot below shows the number of televisions owned by each family on a city block.

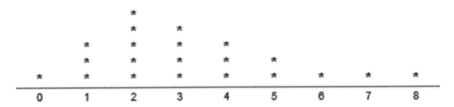

Which of the following statements are true?

    (1) The distribution is right-skewed with no outliers.

    (2) The distribution is right-skewed with one outlier.

    (3) The distribution is left-skewed with no outliers.

    (4) The distribution is left-skewed with one outlier.

    (5) The distribution is symmetric.

Solution:

The correct answer is (1).

Explanation:

Most of the observations are on the left side of the distribution, so the distribution is right-skewed. And none of the observations is extreme, so there are no outliers.

PRACTICE PROBLEMS

3. Identify the distribution of the data represented by the dot plot below. 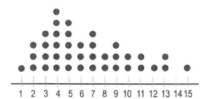	4. Describe the distribution. 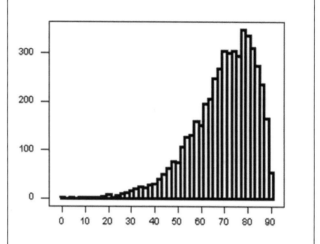
5. Describe the distribution. 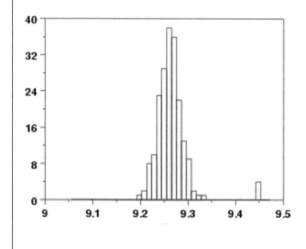	6. Draw a dot plot of data that has a symmetrical but *not* a normal distribution.

7.5 **Standard Deviation**

KEY TERMS AND CONCEPTS

The **standard deviation** is the most commonly used measure of the **spread** (also known as *variability* or *dispersion*) of a set of data. A *low* standard deviation means the data values tend to be *close to the mean*, while a *high* standard deviation means the values are *more spread out*. In other words, more **consistent** data values should result in a **lower** standard deviation.

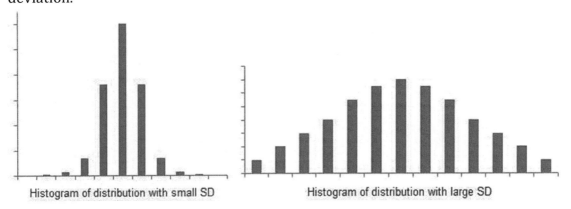

Histogram of distribution with small SD   Histogram of distribution with large SD

For the purposes of this course, we will calculate the **sample standard deviation**.

This can be expressed as a formula: $s = \sqrt{\dfrac{\sum(x-\overline{x})^2}{n-1}}$ (where $\sum$ means the *sum of each*).

To calculate the standard deviation of *n* data values:
1. Calculate the mean of the *n* values, often written as $\overline{x}$.
2. For each data value, find the square of the difference (*deviation*) from the mean.
3. Find the *variance*, which is the sum of these squares divided by $n - 1$.
4. Take the square root of the variance.

The *sample standard deviation* is preferred when we are attempting to generalize from a subset of the data. For example, suppose we want to find the average age among *all registered U.S. voters*. This group represents the **population**, estimated at over 150 million people (which is still only half of the estimated general population of the U.S.). To determine the average age, we might take a **sample** of, say, one million registered voters. Even if this sample is random and unbiased, the average age of the sample may be close to, but not necessarily equal to, the average age of the population. After all, even this very large sample is still less than 1% of the entire population of registered voters.

When the data is drawn from an entire population, statisticians will calculate the **population standard deviation**, in which case the *variance* is calculated as the sum of the squares of the deviations from the mean, *divided by N (the number of data in the population) rather than by n − 1*. The population standard deviation is often symbolized by the Greek letter σ (sigma).

A value computed from sample data is called a **statistic**. A statistic is often used to estimate the related population measure, called a **parameter**. Statisticians customarily use Roman letters for sample statistics and Greek letters for population parameters.

Examples: (a) The symbol $\bar{x}$ represents the mean of a sample and the Greek letter μ (mu) is used for the mean of the population.

(b) The letter *s* is used for the sample standard deviation and the Greek letter σ (sigma) is used for the population standard deviation.

 CALCULATOR TIP

To find the standard deviation on the calculator:

1. First, press [STAT][1] and enter the data into the L1 column, or enter the data as a frequency table into L1 and L2.

2. Press [STAT], select [CALC] and press [1] for 1-Var Stats. Be sure that L1 is specified as the List, or press [2nd][L1] to enter it. If L2 contains frequencies, enter [2nd][L2] as FreqList; otherwise, leave it blank. Then, select Calculate.

    [On the TI-83, you need to enter L1 after the 1-Var Stats prompt by pressing [2nd][L1]. If L2 contains frequencies, press [,][2nd][L2]. Then, press [ENTER].]

3. The sample standard deviation is the value of Sx.

    (If you need the population standard deviation, you would look at σx instead.)

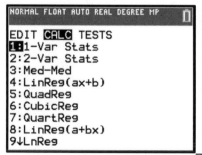
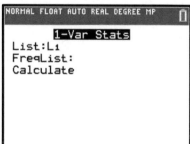
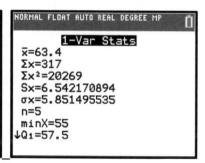

MODEL PROBLEM 1:   *POPULATION AND SAMPLE*

A survey of 1353 American households found that 18% of the households own a computer. Identify the population and sample.

Solution:

population = all American households

sample = the 1353 American houeholds that were surveyed

Explanation:

The population is the entire set we want to study. The sample is the subset that we actually survey.

PRACTICE PROBLEMS

1. Identify the population and the sample: A manufacturer received a large shipment of bolts. The bolts must meet certain specifications to be useful. Before accepting shipment, 100 bolts were selected, and it was determined whether or not each met specifications.	2. Identify the population and the sample: The average weight of every sixth person entering the mall within a 3 hour period was 146 lb.

MODEL PROBLEM 2:   *CONCEPTUALIZING STANDARD DEVIATION*

In the following chart, stock prices for companies UCX and SWC are recorded at the start of each month over a seven month period. Both stocks have the same mean price of $70 over that time. Which stock's monthly prices have a greater standard deviation, according to the graph?

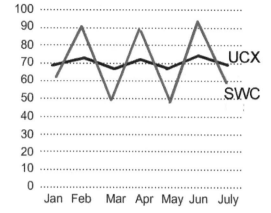

Solution:

SWC stock has a larger standard deviation.

Explanation:

The data set with the greater variability will have the higher standard deviation.

[The UCX prices are much more consistent, with prices closer to the mean, whereas the SWC prices fluctuate greatly, with monthly prices that are more distant from the mean.]

PRACTICE PROBLEMS

3. Jason and Eric discovered that the means of their grades for the first marking period in their math class were identical. They also noticed that the standard deviation of Jason's grades is 20.7, while the standard deviation of Eric's grades is 2.7. Which statement must be true?

(1) In general, Eric's grades were lower than Jason's grades.

(2) Eric's grades are more consistent than Jason's grades

(3) Eric had more failing grades during the marking period than Jason had.

(4) The median for Eric's grades is lower than the median for Jason's grades.

4. Billie's scores on five science tests were 98, 97, 99, 98, and 96. Her scores on five history tests were 78, 84, 95, 72, and 79. Which statement is true about the standard deviations for the scores?

(1) The standard deviation for the history scores is greater than the standard deviation for the science scores.

(2) The standard deviation for the science scores is greater than the standard deviation for the history scores.

(3) The standard deviations for both sets of scores are equal.

(4) More information is needed to determine the relationship between the standard deviations.

5. The mean for a set of data is 8.9 and the standard deviation is 1. The mean for a second set of data is 8.9 and the standard deviation is 2. In which data set do the values cluster closer to the mean?

6. On their college admission exams, Quincy College had a mean score of 875 and a standard deviation of 12. McCrane College had a mean score of 855 and a standard deviation of 20. In which school was there greater variability in the scores? Explain how you arrived at your answer.

MODEL PROBLEM 3:   *CALCULATING STANDARD DEVIATION*

Find the standard deviation of this set of data.

$$2, 4, 4, 4, 5, 5, 5, 7, 9$$

Solution:

(A) $\dfrac{2+4+4+4+5+5+5+7+9}{9} = \dfrac{45}{9} = 5$

(B)

value	(value – mean)^2	result
2	$(2-5)^2$	9
4	$(4-5)^2$	1
4	$(4-5)^2$	1
4	$(4-5)^2$	1
5	$(5-5)^2$	0
5	$(5-5)^2$	0
5	$(5-5)^2$	0
7	$(7-5)^2$	4
9	$(9-5)^2$	16

(C) $\dfrac{9+1+1+1+0+0+0+4+16}{9-1} = \dfrac{32}{8} = 4$

(D) The standard deviation $= \sqrt{4} = 2$.

Explanation of steps:

(A) Calculate the mean *[5]*.

(B) For each data value, find the square of the difference from the mean.

(C) Find the variance by dividing the sum of the squares by $n-1$ *[32 ÷ 8]*.

(D) Take the square root of the variance *[2]*.

PRACTICE PROBLEMS

7. Using the calculator, find the mean and standard deviation to the *nearest tenth*. 22, 99, 102, 33, 57, 75, 100, 81, 62, 29	8. Using the calculator, find the mean and standard deviation to the *nearest tenth*. 35, 50, 60, 60, 75, 65, 80
9. The scores on a mathematics test are: 42, 51, 58, 64, 70, 76, 76, 82, 84, 88, 88, 90, 94, 94, 94, 97 For this set of data, find the standard deviation to the *nearest tenth*.	10. The following Apgar scores were recorded on one day at a local hospital: 9, 8, 10, 9, 8, 10, 9, 10, 8, 10. Find the sample standard deviation of the scores, to the *nearest hundredth*.
11. A New York weather bureau recorded snowfalls of more than 6 inches over a four year period. The snowfall amounts, in inches, were as follows: 7.1, 9.2, 8.0, 6.1, 14.4, 8.5, 6.1, 6.8, 7.7, 21.5, 6.7, 9.0, 8.4, 7.0, 11.5, 14.1, 9.5, 8.6 Find the mean and sample standard deviation to the *nearest hundredth*.	12. Use the method shown in the model problem above to find the mean and standard deviation to the *nearest tenth*. 51, 48, 47, 46, 45, 43, 41, 40, 40, 39 Then verify your answer using the calculator.

13. This chart shows the weekly salary of five employees. Find the mean and standard deviation of this data.

Employee Number	Salary
3201	$612
2734	$588
2461	$604
3582	$625
3144	$621

14. This table shows the age at inauguration of ten presidents of the United States.

President	Age at Inauguration
Harry Truman	60
Dwight D. Eisenhower	62
John F. Kennedy	43
Lyndon B. Johnson	55
Richard M. Nixon	56
Gerald R. Ford	61
Jimmy Carter	52
Ronald Reagan	69
George Bush	64
Bill Clinton	46

Find, to the *nearest tenth*, the sample standard deviation of the age at inauguration of these ten presidents.

7.6   **Percentiles and Quartiles**

KEY TERMS AND CONCEPTS

A value's **percentile** is the percent of values in a set of data that lie below the given value. The percent is generally rounded to the nearest whole percent and the given data value is stated as being "at the pth percentile." A formula for calculating a percentile is $p = \frac{b}{n}$, where b is the number of values that are below the given value, and n is the number of data values in the set.

Examples: (1) Jake is the third tallest in a group of ten students. Since 7 out of the 10 students are shorter than Jake, his height is at the 70th percentile.

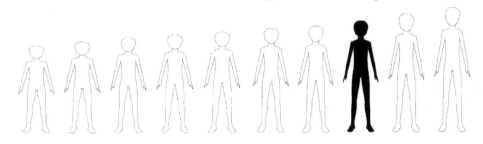

(2) Andy scores an 85 on an exam, which is better than 300 of the 325 exam scores. Andy's score is at the 92nd percentile. $(300 \div 325 \approx 92.3\%.)$

For a set of data, the value at the 25th percentile is called the **first quartile** or **lower quartile** (and is often denoted as Q_1). The value at the 50th percentile is called the **second quartile** or **median** (or Q_2), and the value at the 75th percentile is called the **third quartile** or **upper quartile** (or Q_3).

The difference between the upper and lower quartiles is called the **interquartile range** (or IQR). The interquartile range is another measure of spread, along with range and standard deviation.

The IQR can be used to identify *outliers*, which are extremely high or low values in the data. A data value should be considered an outlier if it is more than $1.5 \times$ IQR below the lower quartile or above the upper quartile.

Example: For a set of data, $Q_1 = 20$, $Q_2 = 50$, and $Q_3 = 100$. The IQR is $100 - 20 = 80$. Since $1.5 \times 80 = 120$, a value that is above $100 + 120 = 220$, such as 240, would be considered an outlier.

To identify the quartiles for a set of data:

1. Arrange the data in ascending order.

2. First find the *median (or second quartile)*, and label it Q_2. It is the middle value (for an odd number of data values), or the average of the two middle values (for an even number of data values).

   > **Use this tip:** For an *odd number* of data values, *circle* the middle value, but for an *even number* of data values, *draw a vertical line* between the two middle values. When we find the quartiles in the next steps, we will ignore a circled value but include values to the left or right of a line.

3. Find the *lower (first) quartile* by looking only at the subgroup of values that are to the *left* of the middle (that is, to the left of a circled value or line). The median of this subgroup is the lower quartile.

4. Find the *upper (third) quartile* by looking only at the subgroup of values that are to the *right* of the middle (to the right of a circled value or line). The median of this subgroup is the upper quartile.

 CALCULATOR TIP

To find the quartiles on the calculator:

1. First, press [STAT][1] and enter the data into the L1 column, or enter the data as a frequency table into L1 and L2.

2. Press [STAT], select |CALC| and press [1] for 1-Var Stats. Be sure that L1 is specified as the List, or press [2nd][L1] to enter it. If L2 contains frequencies, enter [2nd][L2] as FreqList; otherwise, leave it blank. Then, select Calculate.

   [On the TI-83, you need to enter L1 after the 1-Var Stats prompt by pressing [2nd][L1]. If L2 contains frequencies, press [,][2nd][L2]. Then, press [ENTER].]

3. Scroll down to find the number of data values, n; the minimum, minX; the first quartile, Q1; the median, Med; the third quartile, Q3; and the maximum, maxX.

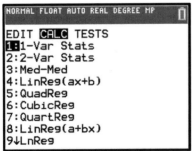
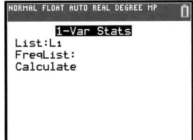
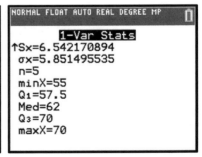

MODEL PROBLEM

Identify the first, second and third quartiles and calculate the interquartile range for the following set of ten data values:

86, 72, 85, 89, 86, 92, 73, 71, 91, 82

Solution:

(A)

71, 72, ⑦③ 82, 85, | 86, 86, ⑧⑨ 91, 92

(B) Q_2 (median) = 85.5
(C) Q_1 = 73 and Q_3 = 89
(D) IQR = 89 – 73 = 16

Explanation of steps:

(A) Arrange the data in ascending order.
(B) Find the median. *[Since there is an even number of values, we draw a line between the two middle values, 85 and 86, and calculate the median (or second quartile) as the average of these two middle values.]*
(C) Find the lower and upper quartiles. *[For the subgroup of 5 values to the left of the line, the middle number (73) is the lower quartile. For the subgroup of 5 values to the right of the line, the middle number (89) is the upper quartile.]*
(D) Calculate the interquartile range (IQR) as the difference between Q_3 and Q_1.

PRACTICE PROBLEMS

1. The weights of 40 students were recorded. If the 75th percentile of their weights was 150 pounds, what is the total number of students who weighed *more than* 150 pounds?	2. Brian's score on a college entrance exam exceeded the scores of 95,000 of the 125,000 students who took the exam. What was his score's percentile?

3. Dawn scored higher than 22 out of the 30 students in her class. What was her score's percentile?

4. For the given set of data, what percentile is the value 70?

   25, 90, 87, 58, 42, 95, 64, 75, 39, 70

5. The students at Adams High School held a canned food drive for 12 weeks. The results are summarized in the table below.

   Canned Food Drive Results

Week	1	2	3	4	5	6	7	8	9	10	11	12
Number of Cans	20	35	32	45	58	46	28	23	31	79	65	62

   Find the second quartile of the number of cans of food collected.

6. Find the first, second and third quartiles for the following set of data:

   5, 6, 7, 8, 12, 14, 17, 17, 18, 19, 19

7. Find the first, second and third quartiles for the following set of data:

   3, 6, 7, 7, 8, 9, 9, 9, 10, 12, 13, 15

8. Find the first, second and third quartiles, and the interquartile range, for the following set of data:

   33, 28, 45, 21, 32, 53, 41, 28, 50

9. The heights, in inches, of 10 high school varsity basketball players are given below. Find the interquartile range of this data set.

   78, 79, 79, 72, 75, 71, 74, 74, 83, 71

10. For the set of test scores shown by the frequency table below, find the first, second and third quartiles.

Score	Frequency
60	1
70	9
80	8
90	2
100	5

11. The cumulative frequency table below shows the length of time that 30 students spent texting on a weekend.

Minutes Used	Cumulative Frequency
31–40	2
31–50	5
31–60	10
31–70	19
31–80	30

    Which 10-minute interval contains the first quartile?

7.7   **Box Plots**

KEY TERMS AND CONCEPTS

A **box-and-whisker plot** (or **box plot**) is a used to represent a set of data graphically. The "box" marks the values of the *first, second,* and *third quartiles* of the data set. The "whiskers" show the *minimum* (lowest) and *maximum* (highest) values of the data set.

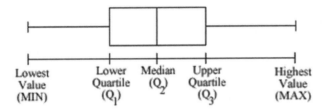

The lowest value in the data set is called the **minimum**, the highest value is called the **maximum**, and the **range** is the *difference* between the *maximum* and *minimum* values.

By the definition of quartiles, each section of a box plot represents 25% (one quarter) of the data values. 25% of the data is at or below the lower quartile, 50% is at or below the median, and 75% is at or below the upper quartile.

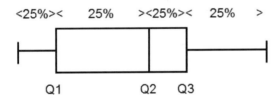

If the data has **symmetrical** (*normal*) **distribution**, the whiskers will be about the same length and the median will be at about the center of the data. For a **skewed distribution**, the whisker on the side of the "tail" will be longer and the median will be closer to the shorter whisker.

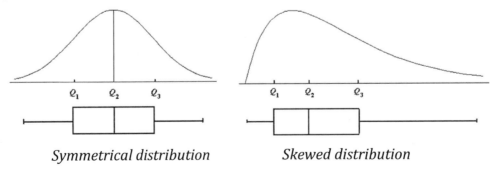

Symmetrical distribution   *Skewed distribution*

To create a box plot:

1. Arrange the data from smallest to largest.
2. Draw a number line from the minimum (or below) to the maximum (or above).
3. Find the median and plot it as a line.
4. Find the lower and upper quartiles, plot them as lines, and connect the box.
5. Plot the minimum and maximum as smaller lines and connect the whiskers.

 CALCULATOR TIP

The calculator can be used to display a box plot.

1. First, press [STAT][1] and enter the data into the L1 column, or enter the data as a frequency table into L1 and L2.

2. Press [2nd][STAT PLOT][1] to select Plot1. Select [On] [ENTER]. For the Type, select the fifth chart type, ⊞⊢. For Xlist, if L1 isn't already selected, press [2nd][L1] to enter it. For Freq, enter 1 if all of your data is in L1, or enter [2nd][L2] if your data is entered as a frequency table with the frequencies stored in L2.

3. Press [ZOOM][1] for ZBox. You may need to adjust the [WINDOW] settings, as shown below, to see the entire box plot clearly, depending on the range of values.

4. Press [TRACE] and then the [◄][►] keys to see the five summary numbers: minX, Q1, Med, Q2, and maxX.

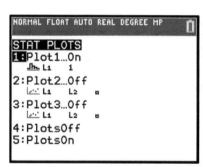

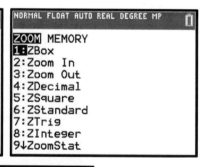

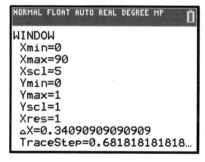
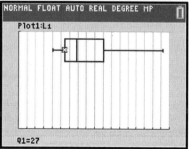

Box plots with outliers: Sometimes, outliers are drawn separately as dots (or similar symbols such as asterisks) on a box plot and excluded from the lengths of the whiskers. Remember, an outlier is considered to be any data value that is more than $1.5 \times IQR$ above the upper quartile or more than $1.5 \times IQR$ below the lower quartile. IQR is the interquartile range.

Example: Consider the data set, {20, 25, 25, 27, 28, 31, 33, 34, 36, 37, 44, 50, 59, 85, 86}. The quartiles are 27, 34, and 50, so the box plot would look like this:

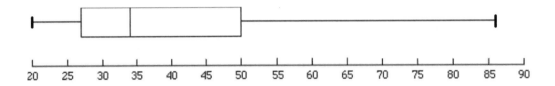

Notice the long right whisker due to the fact that two outliers, 85 and 86, are included. We know these are outliers because they are more than $1.5 \times IQR$ above the upper quartile.

$$IQR = Q_3 - Q_1 = 50 - 27 = 23$$
$$Q_3 + (1.5 \times IQR) = 50 + (1.5 \times 23) = 84.5$$

So, any values above 84.5 are outliers. Therefore, 85 and 86 are outliers.

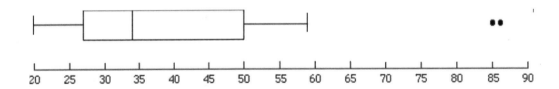

If we show these outliers as dots, the box plot would appear as above. The right whisker is shortened in length to the next largest (*adjacent*) value below the outliers, which happens to be 59. This now shows a big gap below the outliers.

MODEL PROBLEM

Create a box plot for the following data:

2, 4, 8, 10, 14, 18, 20, 22, 30, 32, 38

Solution:

(B)

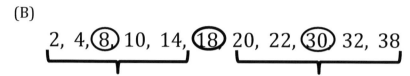

(C)

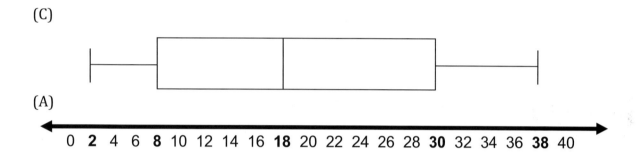

(A)

Explanation of steps:

(A) Once the data is arranged in ascending order *[as this data already is]*, draw a number line from below the minimum *[2]* to above the maximum *[38]*, and label the intervals. *[Our number line can go from 0 to 40 in 2-unit intervals.]*

(B) Find the median *[18]* and the lower and upper quartiles *[8 and 30]*.

(C) Plot the median as a line *[over 18]* and the lower and upper quartiles as lines *[over 8 and 30]* and connect the box. Add whiskers (shorter lines) over the minimum *[2]* and maximum *[38]* and connect them to the box as whiskers.

PRACTICE PROBLEMS

1. The accompanying diagram shows a box plot of student test scores. What is the median score? 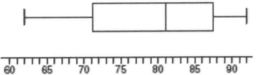	2. The accompanying box plot represents the scores earned on a science test. What is the median score? 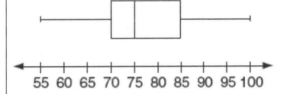
3. What is the value of the third quartile shown on the box-and-whisker plot below? 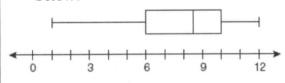	4. The box-and-whisker plot below represents students' scores on a recent test. What is the value of the upper quartile? 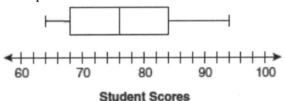 **Student Scores**
5. In the box-and-whisker plot below, what is the 2nd quartile? 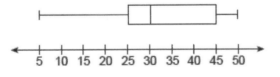	6. In the box-and-whisker plot below, what is the 1st quartile? 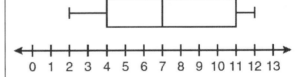

7. What is the range of the data represented in the box-and-whisker plot shown below?

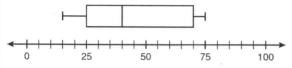

8. The box-and-whisker plot below represents the math test scores of 20 students.

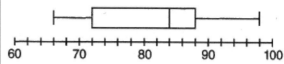

    What percentage of the test scores are *less than 72?*

9. The box-and-whisker plot below represents a set of grades in an algebra class.

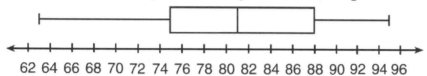

    62 64 66 68 70 72 74 76 78 80 82 84 86 88 90 92 94 96

    Which interval contains exactly 50% of the grades?

    (1)   63-88   (3)   75-81

    (2)   63-95   (4)   75-88

10. Create a box plot for the following data:
        89, 73, 84, 91, 87, 77, 94

11. Create a box plot for the following data:

    65, 75, 92, 84, 62, 96, 88, 79, 82

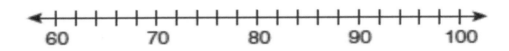

12. Create a box plot for the following data:

    72, 73, 66, 71, 82, 85, 95, 85, 86, 89, 91, 92

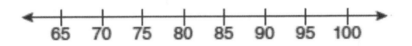

13. Using the line provided, construct a box-and-whisker plot for the 12 scores below.

    26, 32, 19, 65, 57, 16, 28, 42, 40, 21, 38, 10

Chapter 8.   Bivariate Data

8.1   <u>Two-Way Frequency Tables</u>

KEY TERMS AND CONCEPTS

A **two-way table** (or *pivot table*) shows frequencies for bivariate data.

Example: A bakery holds a taste test in which participants select their favorite cup cake icing flavor. The two-way table below shows the results for 50 adults - 20 women and 30 men. In this survey, only 2 out of 20 women preferred vanilla, but 16 out of the 30 men chose vanilla.

	Vanilla	Chocolate	Strawberry	Total
Women	2	10	8	20
Men	16	6	8	30
Total	18	16	16	50

Entries in the body of the table are called **joint frequencies**. Entries in the "Total" row and "Total" column are called **marginal frequencies**. The marginal frequencies are the sums of the joint frequencies on that row or column of the table. The **grand total** in the lower right hand cell is the total number of data points. It should equal the sum of each set of marginal frequencies.

Sometimes we may prefer to show ratios (in *percent, decimal,* or *fraction* format). In this case, each entry, called a **relative frequency**, is a ratio of the frequency for that cell to the total number of data points. The total percentage written in the lower right hand cell is always 100%.

Example: We could have represented the above table using relative frequencies, below.

	Vanilla	Chocolate	Strawberry	Total
Women	4%	20%	16%	40%
Men	32%	12%	16%	60%
Total	36%	32%	32%	100%

Two-way tables help us to find conditional relative frequencies. A **conditional relative frequency** is one that is calculated given that a certain condition (row or column) is true.

Example: Using the relative frequency table above, we could say that among *women*, 10% prefer vanilla (4% divided by the 40% who are women). The given condition, "among women," restricts us to the top row. Or, we could say that among those who prefer *strawberry*, half are women (16% divided by 32%). In this case, the given condition restricts us to the column labelled "Strawberry."

MODEL PROBLEM

A public opinion survey explored the relationship between age and support for increasing the minimum wage. The results are summarized in the two-way table below.

	For	Against	No opinion	Total
21 – 40	25	20	5	50
41 – 60	20	35	20	75
Over 60	55	15	5	75
Total	100	70	30	200

In the 21 to 40 age group, what percent supports increasing the minimum wage?

Solution: 50%

Explanation:

A total of 50 people in the 21 to 40 age group were surveyed. Of those, 25 were "for" increasing the minimum wage. Therefore, 50% (25 ÷ 50) of the respondents in this age group supported the increase.

PRACTICE PROBLEMS

1. In a survey of eighth and ninth grade students, participants were asked what grade they were in and whether they planned to watch the Super Bowl. Results are shown in the table below. Round your answers to the *nearest tenth of a percent.*

	Watching	Not Watching	Undecided	Total
8th Grade	25	20	8	53
9th Grade	31	22	7	60
Total	56	42	15	113

a) What percent of the students are undecided?

b) What percent of the ninth graders are watching?

2. The first table shows the number of books sold at a library sale. Complete this *joint frequency table* by writing the *marginal frequencies* in the blank cells. Then, using the same data, create an equivalent two-way *relative frequency table* in the second table below.

	Fiction	Nonfiction	Total
Hardcover	28	52	
Paperback	94	36	
Total			

	Fiction	Nonfiction	Total
Hardcover			
Paperback			
Total			

3. You go to a dance and help clean up afterwards. To help, you collect the soda cans, Coca-Cola and Sprite, and organize them. Some cans were on the table and some were in the garbage. 72 total cans were found. 42 total cans were found in the garbage and 50 total cans were Coca-Cola. 14 Sprite cans were found on the table. From the given information, complete the two-way joint frequency table below.

	Coca-Cola	Sprite	Total
Table			
Garbage			
Total			

8.2   **Scatter Plots**

KEY TERMS AND CONCEPTS

A **scatter plot** is a graph used to plot pairs of bivariate data values in a coordinate plane. They are often used for gathering experimental data to determine whether a correlation exists between the two variables. The **independent** variable is represented by *x*-**values** in a horizontal axis and the **dependent** variable is represented by *y*-**values** in a vertical axis. Only points are plotted; the points are not connected by lines.

The bivariate data can be written using a table. The *x*-**values** are always written first (the top row in a horizontal table or the left column in a vertical table), followed by the corresponding *y*-**values**. Each pair of values in the table can be plotted as a single point.

Example: Park administrators use a table to keep track of daily temperatures and the number of daily visitors to the beach. The points are then plotted on a scatter plot, using the temperatures as *x*-values and visitors as *y*-values. The first data column is plotted as the point (84, 225) on the scatter plot.

Temp (*x*)	84	86	82	87	86	92	88	89	94	96	94
Visitors (*y*)	225	350	100	125	300	450	455	525	600	565	510

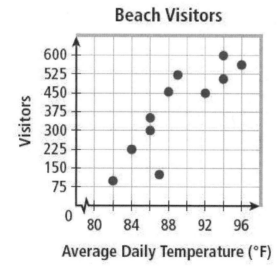

223

Each axis must include **labels** in equal intervals to cover the range of *x* or *y* values in the data, and should include an axis **title** describing what the axis labels represent.

Example: In the scatter plot above, the *x*-axis is labeled from 80 to 96 in intervals of 4, where each grid square is 2 units wide. To save room, you may omit labels between 0 and the first tick by using a $\sqrt{\ }$ symbol, as shown between 0 and 80 on the *x*-axis. To cover values as high as 600 visitors, intervals of 75 visitors are used on the *y*-axis.

 CALCULATOR TIP

To enter bivariate data into the calculator:

1. Press $\boxed{\text{STAT}}\boxed{1}$ to select Edit.
2. If any values already appear in the L1 or L2 columns, select the column heading and press $\boxed{\text{CLEAR}}\boxed{\text{ENTER}}$.
3. Enter the *x* values into the L1 column and the corresponding *y* values into the L2 column.

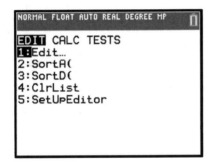
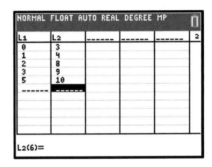

If any columns other than L1 or L2 appear in the table, you can either leave them there or delete them by selecting the column heading and pressing $\boxed{\text{DEL}}$. Also, if either the L1 or L2 column is missing, you can add it by selecting an empty column heading and then pressing $\boxed{\text{2nd}}\boxed{\text{L1}}\boxed{\text{ENTER}}$ or $\boxed{\text{2nd}}\boxed{\text{L2}}\boxed{\text{ENTER}}$.

CALCULATOR TIP

To view a scatter plot on the graphing calculator:

1. Enter the x and y values into L1 and L2 as described above.

2. Press [2nd][STAT PLOT][1] for Plot1. Select [On] [ENTER]. Be sure the Type is set at the first option [image], Xlist is L1, and Ylist is L2.

3. Press [ZOOM][9] for ZoomStat. You may need to adjust the dimensions and scale of the scatter plot by pressing [WINDOW], as shown below.

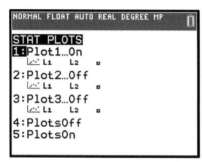

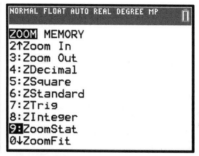

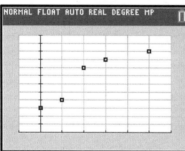

MODEL PROBLEM

A teacher records how many hours her students studied during the week leading up to their state exam and the scores they received. The data is shown in the following table. Create a scatter plot for the data.

Hours	3	5	2	6	7	1	2	7	1	7
Score	80	90	75	80	90	50	65	85	40	100

Solution:

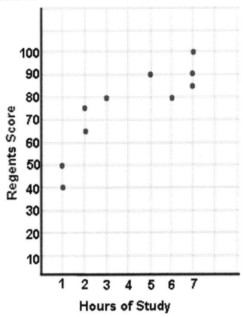

Explanation of steps:

(A) Draw a grid. Label the *x*-axis using equal intervals covering the range of x values in the table *[1 through 7, with intervals of 1]*.

Label the *y*-axis similarly to cover the range of y values *[10 through 100, with intervals of 10]*.

Add appropriate axis titles.

(B) Plot each pair of data values as a point on the grid *[the first point in the table is (3, 80)]*.

Enter the table into the calculator and create a scatter plot according to the instructions at the top of this page.

PRACTICE PROBLEMS

1. For 10 days, a real estate agent kept a record of the number of hours she spent showing homes to potential buyers. The information is shown in the table below.

Day	1	2	3	4	5	6	7	8	9	10
Hours	9	3	2	6	8	6	10	4	5	2

Which scatter plot shows the agent's data graphically?

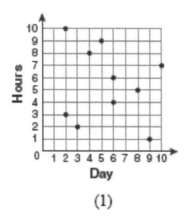

(1)

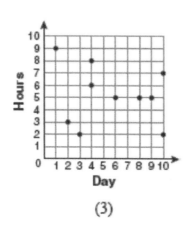

(3)

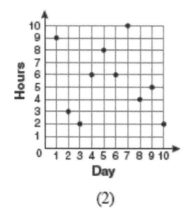

(2)

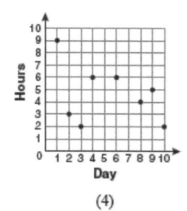

(4)

2.   The table shows the height (in inches) and the weight (in pounds) of five starters on a high school basketball team. Create the corresponding scatter plot.

Height (x)	67	72	77	74	69
Weight (y)	155	220	240	195	175

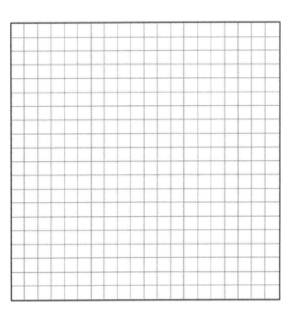

3. The following table lists weights (in hundreds of pounds) and highway fuel usage
    rates (in mpg) for a sample of domestic cars. Create the corresponding scatter plot.

Weight (x)	29	35	28	44	25	34	30	33	28	24
Fuel (y)	31	27	29	25	31	29	28	28	28	33

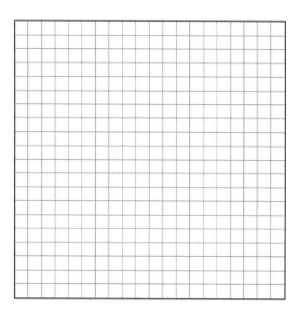

8.3 **Correlation and Causality**

KEY TERMS AND CONCEPTS

In a set of bivariate data, **correlation** (or *association*) is a statistical relationship between the two variables.

If the two variables are *x* and *y*, the data is said to have a **positive correlation** if, as *x* increases, *y* also increases, and as *x* decreases, *y* also decreases.

Example: As the temperature *increases*, *more* ice cream cones are sold. As the temperature *decreases*, *less* ice cream cones are sold. This shows a positive correlation.

There is a **negative correlation** when, as *x* increases, *y* decreases, and as *x* decreases, *y* increases.

Example: As the temperature *increases*, *less* cups of hot chocolate are sold. As the temperature *decreases*, *more* cups of hot chocolate are sold. This shows a negative correlation.

In some cases, a change in one variable is directly responsible for the change in the second variable. These are called **causal** relationships.

Example: When boiling a pot of water, the relationship between the time spent on the stove and the temperature of the water is causal.

However, the existence of a correlation does not necessarily mean that the relationship is causal. For example, a study of middle school students found a positive correlation between shoe sizes and reading comprehension scores. Clearly, a larger shoe size does not cause an increase in reading comprehension, or vice-versa, so this is *not a causal relationship*. In fact, a missing factor in this research is the age of the students: older children tend to have larger feet, and also tend to have higher reading scores.

Almost all real life relationships would have some hidden factors, but for our purposes we will define a "cause" as a primary factor responsible.

Example: In the above example about boiling water, a number of other factors could be partially responsible for the rise in water temperature. But certainly, placing a pot of water on a hot stove for a period of time will directly cause the temperature of the water to increase.

MODEL PROBLEM

A number of children between the ages of 5 and 15 are measured for height. How would you describe the relationship between the ages and heights? Is there a correlation, and if so, is it positive or negative? Is it a causal relationship?

Solution:

Children grow as they get older, so there is a positive correlation and a causal relationship.

Explanation of steps:

If an increase or decrease in the first variable *causes* a change in the second variable, there is a causal relationship. *[Yes, there are other hidden factors, such as nutrition, genetics, etc., but it safe to say that aging is a primary cause of growth within this age group.]* If an increase in one variable results in an increase in the other, it is a positive correlation, but if an increase in one variable results in a decrease in the other, it is a negative correlation.

PRACTICE PROBLEMS

1. Which of the following best describes the relationship between the distance driven and the amount of gasoline used?
 	
    (1)   causal, but not correlated
 	
    (2)   correlated, but not causal
 	
    (3)   both correlated and causal
 	
    (4)   neither correlated nor causal
	2. A study showed that a decrease in the cost of a quart of milk led to an increase in the number of quarts of milk sold. Which statement best describes this relationship?
	
	    (1) positive correlation and causal
	
	    (2) negative correlation and causal
	
	    (3) positive correlation and not causal
	
	    (4) negative correlation and not causal

3. Identify the correlation you would expect to see (*positive*, *negative*, or *none*) between each pair of data sets. Explain.

a) children's ages and their weights

b) the volume of water poured into a container and the amount of empty space left in the container

c) a woman's shoe size and the length of her hair

d) the outside temperature and the number of people at the beach

4. For each research finding below, (a) determine whether there is a *positive, negative, or no correlation*; (b) decide if there is a *causal relationship*; and (c) if a correlation is *not* causal, state what missing factors, if any, may be the cause of the results.

a) As the volume of air in a balloon increases, its diameter increases as well.

b) As the number of workers increases, the number of days required to complete a job decreases.

c) The more firefighters sent to a fire, the longer it takes to put out the fire.

d) Over the past few centuries, the number of pirates worldwide has decreased while the level of CO_2 in the atmosphere has increased.

8.4   **Identify Correlation in Scatter Plots**

KEY TERMS AND CONCEPTS

Although the points in a scatter plot may not be collinear (i.e., they may not lie in a straight line), one can visually determine if the **correlation** between the variables is positive or negative, or if no discernible correlation exists.

As with slope, the variables have a **positive correlation** if, as the *x*-values (*independent variable*) increase, so do the *y*-values (*dependent variable*) tend to increase. The variables have a **negative correlation** if the general tendency is that, as the *x*-values increase, the *y*-values decrease. It's also possible that the points show no such tendencies, in which case there is **no correlation**.

Example: The following diagrams show that (a) there is *no correlation* between a person's arm length and his or her results on an exam; (b) there is a *positive correlation* between the time a person spends revising the exam essay and the results on the exam; and (c) there is a *negative correlation* between the number of absences from school and the exam results.

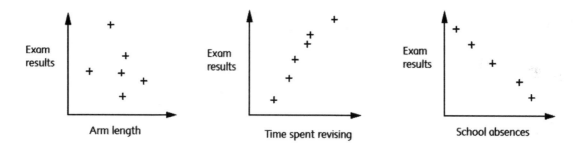

A linear correlation is considered **strong** if the points closely approximate a straight line.

Example: The first graph below shows a stronger positive correlation than the second.

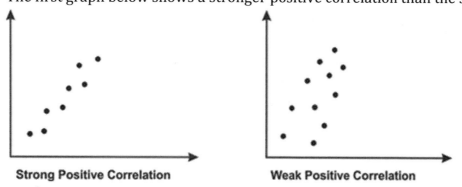

MODEL PROBLEM

Which diagram shows a negative correlation?

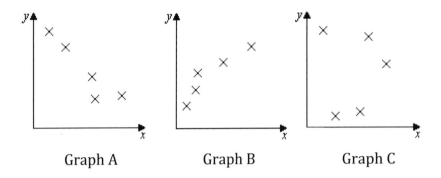

Graph A   Graph B   Graph C

Solution: Graph A

Explanation of steps:

A graph has a negative correlation if, as the *x*-values increase, the *y*-values tend to decrease. *[Graph B shows a positive correlation and Graph C shows no correlation.]*

PRACTICE PROBLEMS

1. Which diagram shows the strongest positive correlation?

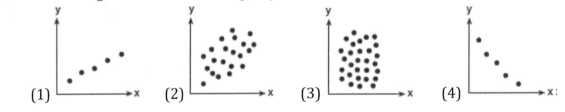

2. State whether the diagram below shows a positive, negative, or no correlation.

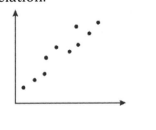

3. State whether the diagram below shows a positive, negative, or no correlation.

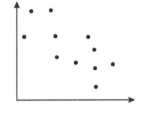

234

4. State whether the scatter plot below shows a positive, negative, or no correlation.

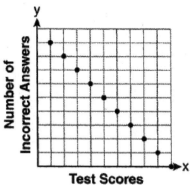

5. State whether the scatter plot below shows a positive, negative, or no correlation.

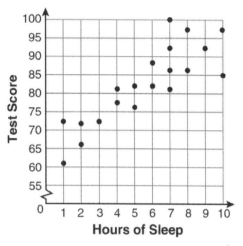

6. State whether the scatter plot below shows a positive, negative, or no correlation.

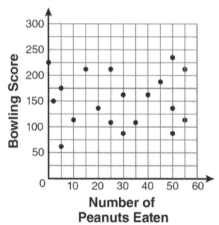

7. State whether the scatter plot below shows a positive, negative, or no correlation.

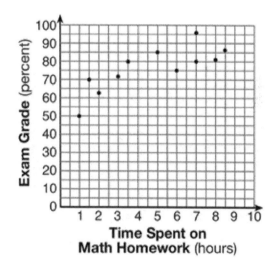

8.5   Lines of Fit

KEY TERMS AND CONCEPTS

When a scatter plot shows a linear correlation, a line which approximates this relationship is called a **line of fit** (or *trend line*).

Example: For the following scatter plot, a line of fit may be drawn as shown. Because the graph shows a positive correlation, the line will have a positive slope.

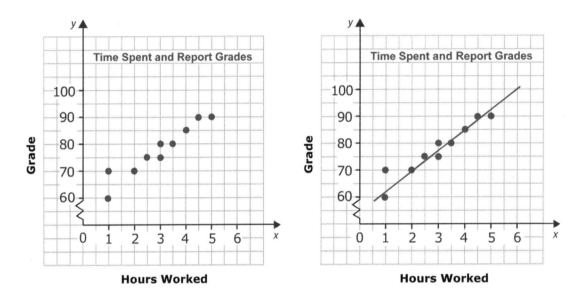

We can create a **line of fit** and find its equation by one of two methods: either by *drawing* an appropriate line by hand (using a straight edge) or by using the *calculator*. The calculator finds the **linear regression** (also known as the **least-squares line**), which passes through the mean point $(\overline{x}, \overline{y})$, where $\overline{x}$ is the mean of the x's and $\overline{y}$ is the mean of the y's. This line minimizes the combined distances of the points from the line, and so it is usually called a **line of best fit**.

Drawing a Line of Fit:

When drawing a straight line, we try to have the points lie as close to the line as possible, and preferably with as many points above the line as below it.

We can then determine its equation by finding two points which appear to lie directly on the line. Try not to pick points that are too close to each other. From these two points, we can determine a slope and y-intercept.

Example: The line above appears to run through points $(2, 70)$ and $(4, 85)$.

$$\text{Using these points, the slope } m = \frac{85 - 70}{4 - 2} = \frac{15}{2} = 7.5.$$

Substituting point $(2, 70)$ for x and y and the slope 7.5 for m in the general equation $y = mx + b$, we can find b:

$$70 = 7.5(2) + b$$
$$70 = 15 + b$$
$$b = 55$$

Therefore, the equation for this line of fit is $y = 7.5x + 55$.

▓▓▓ CALCULATOR TIP

Using the calculator to find a line of best fit:

1. Press [STAT][1] and enter the *x* and *y* coordinates of the points as L1 and L2.

2. Press [STAT] [CALC] [4] to select LinReg(ax+b).

3. On the next screen, select L1 for Xlist, L2 for Ylist, and Y1 (by pressing [ALPHA][F4][1]) for Store RegEQ in order to store the equation in Y1.
    [On the TI-83, this screen is skipped; instead, after the LinReg(ax+b) *prompt, press* [VARS] [Y-VARS] [1][1] *to select* Y1, *and press* [ENTER].*]*

4. The screen will show the equation y = ax + b along with the values of *a* (the slope) and *b* (the *y*-intercept).

5. To view the resulting line of best fit, press [ZOOM][9] for ZoomStat.

6. To see the equation of the line, press [Y=].

Example: If we enter the points as they appear in the graph on the previous page, the calculator will create the equation Y1 = 6.651718984X + 57.877429. Rounding to the *nearest tenth*, the equation would be $y = 6.7x + 57.9$.

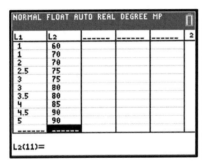

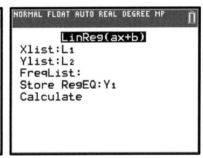

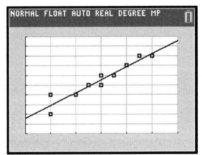

The line of fit helps us to **predict** values not included in the original data. We can **extrapolate** about data that is outside (but near) the range of given *x*-values, or **interpolate** about data that is within the range of *x*-values but not already included in the data.

Example: Using the graph above, if a student submits a project on which he has worked 1.5 hours, we can predict his grade by looking at a line of fit or by using its equation. This would be *interpolation*, since 1.5 is within the range of *x* values. Either of the following predictions would be acceptable:

a) Substituting 1.5 for *x* in the equation of the drawn line, we get
$$y = 7.5(1.5) + 55 = 66.25 \approx 66.$$

b) Using the equation of the calculator's linear regression, we get
$$y = 6.7(1.5) + 57.9 = 67.95 \approx 68.$$

CALCULATOR TIP

For part b) above, since we have already stored the line of best fit into Y1, we could also have the calculator find this value by entering ALPHA F4 1 (1 . 5) ENTER *[or on the TI-83,* VARS Y-VARS 1 1 (1 . 5) ENTER*].*

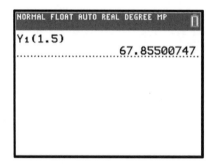

MODEL PROBLEM

Given the data table below, create a scatter plot. Draw a reasonable line of fit and state its equation. Use the equation to extrapolate the next y value for an x value of 7.

x	0	1	2	3	4	5	6
y	2	4.5	9	11	13	18	19.5

Solution:

(A)

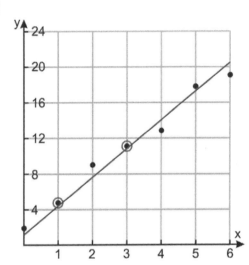

(B) From points $(1, 4.5)$ and $(3, 11)$,
$$m = \frac{11 - 4.5}{3 - 1} = \frac{6.5}{2} = 3.25.$$

(C) Using $(3, 11)$ and $m = 3.25$:
$$y = mx + b$$
$$11 = 3.25(3) + b$$
$$b = 1.25$$

(D) Equation for the line of fit is
$$y = 3.25x + 1.25$$

(E) For an x value of 7,
$$y = 3.25(7) + 1.25 = 24$$

Explanation of steps:

(A) Draw the scatter plot and a reasonable line of fit, where about as many points are above the line as below it. For our purposes, any reasonable line will be acceptable.

(B) Find two points that appear to lie on the line or are closest to it. Calculate the slope of the line between these two points using the slope formula.

(C) Use one of the points and the slope to substitute for x, y, and m in the general equation $y = mx + b$, and solve for b.

(D) Write the equation of the line.

(E) To extrapolate (or interpolate), use the new given value and substitute it into the equation to find the value of the other variable. *[Substitute 7 for x, and find y = 24.]*

The equation of the calculator's regression line for this data would round to $y = 3x + 2$. It would start near the point $(0,2)$ and have a slightly smaller slope than the drawn line. Using this line of best fit, we would extrapolate $y = 3(7) + 2 = 23$. Either answer is acceptable.

PRACTICE PROBLEMS

1. The following chart shows students' typing speeds in words per minute (wpm) after a certain number of weeks of practice.

   a) Based on the line of fit shown, approximately how fast would you expect a student to type after 8 weeks of practice?

   b) By how many words per minute, approximately, can an employee expect to increase her or his speed for each additional week of practice?

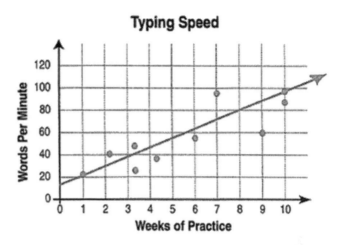

2. The scatter plots below display the same data about the ages of eight health club members and their heart rates during exercises. Which line is a better fit for the data? Explain your reasoning.

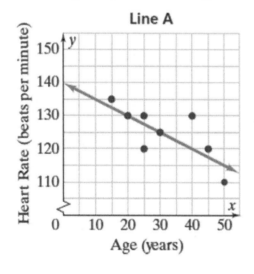

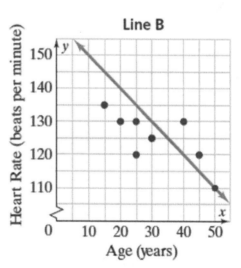

3. The local ice cream shop keeps track of daily sales (in dollars) and the temperature (in Celsius) on that day. On the scatter plot below, draw a line of fit.

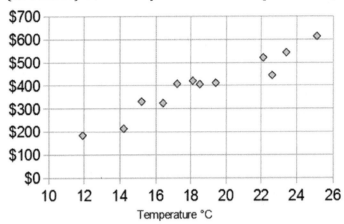

4. Write an equation for the line of fit shown in the scatter plot below.

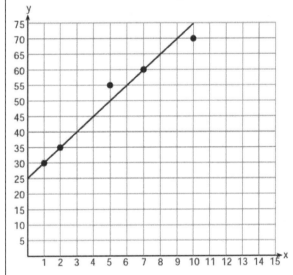

5. Write an equation for the line of fit shown in the scatter plot below.

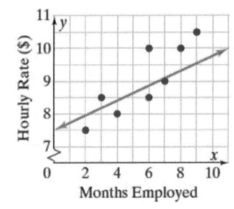

6. The data below shows hours spent researching the stock market per week and the percent gain for an investor.

Hours	6	8	10	12	14	16	18
% Gain	17	20.5	26.5	29	32.5	37.5	41

   Find an equation of the line of best fit for gain with respect to hours of study.

7. A random sample of graduates from a particular college program reported their ages and incomes in response to a survey. Each point on the scatter plot below represents the age and income of a different graduate. Of the following equations, which best fits the data?

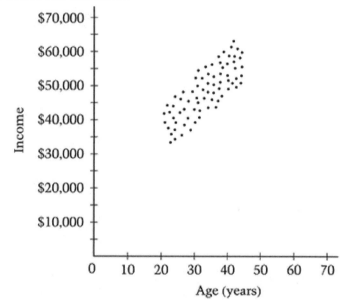

(1) $y = -1,000x + 15,000$ (3) $y = 1,000x + 15,000$

(2) $y = 1,000x$ (4) $y = 10,000x + 15,000$

8. Based on the data in the scatter plot of the previous question, predictions can be made about the income of a 35 year old and the income of a 65 year old. For which age is the prediction more likely to be accurate? Justify your answer.

9. Which equation most closely represents the line of best fit for the scatter plot below?

Money Earned from Babysitting

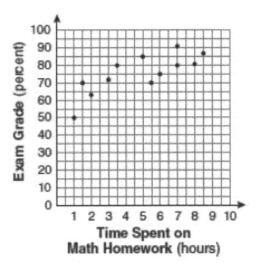

Babysitting Time (hours)

(1) $y = x$

(2) $y = \frac{2}{3}x + 1$

(3) $y = \frac{3}{2}x + 4$

(4) $y = \frac{3}{2}x + 1$

10. Based on a line of best fit for the scatter plot below, which exam grade is the best prediction for a student who spends 4 hours on math homework?

Time Spent on Math Homework (hours)

(1)   62   (3)   82

(2)   72   (4)   92

11. Based on the line of best fit drawn below, which value could be expected for the data in June 2015?

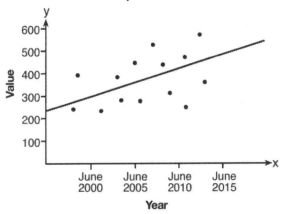

Year

(1) 230   (3) 480

(2) 310   (4) 540

12. Based on the line of best fit drawn below, what is the best estimate for profit in the 18th month?

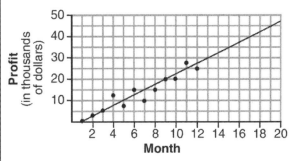

Month

(1) $35,000   (3) $42,500

(2) $37,750   (4) $45,000

13. A new business' goal is to reach a profit of $20,000 in its 18th month of business. The table and scatter plot below represent the profit, *P*, in thousands of dollars, that the business made during the first 12 months.

t (months)	P (profit, in thousands of dollars)
1	3.0
2	2.5
3	4.0
4	5.0
5	6.5
6	5.5
7	7.0
8	6.0
9	7.5
10	7.0
11	9.0
12	9.5

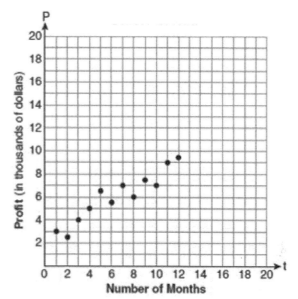

Draw a reasonable line of best fit. Using the line of best fit, predict whether the business will reach its goal in the 18th month. Justify your answer.

14. The table shows the temperature, *t* degrees Fahrenheit, displayed on an oven while it was heating as a function of the amount of time, *s* seconds, since it was turned on. Create a scatter plot for this data. Find the equation for its line of best fit.

s	t
31	175
61	200
104	225
158	250
202	275
250	300
285	325
327	350
380	375
428	400

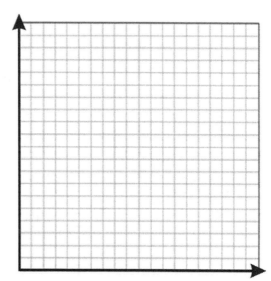

15. The table below shows ocean temperatures at various depths.

Water Depth (x) (meters)	Temperature (y) (°C)
50	18
75	15
100	12
150	7
200	1

a) Write the linear regression equation for this set of data, rounding all values to the *nearest thousandth*.

b) Using this equation, predict the temperature, to the *nearest integer*, at a water depth of 255 meters.

16. The table below shows the number of new crime cases reported in a city over a period of four years.

Year (x)	New Cases (y)
1999	440
2000	457
2001	369
2002	351

a) Write the linear regression equation for this set of data.
(Let $x = 0$ represent 1999.)

b) Using this equation, find the projected number of new cases for 2009, rounded to the *nearest whole number*.

8.6   **Correlation Coefficients**

KEY TERMS AND CONCEPTS

The **correlation coefficient** tells us the degree of correlation; in other words, how close the entire set of points is from the line. It is a value between –1 and 1, with *negative* values used for best-fit lines with *negative* slopes and *positive* values used for lines with *positive* slopes. A correlation coefficient of 0 means no correlation; a value close to 0 ($|r| < 0.3$) represents a weak correlation. A value of –1 or 1 would represent data points that are collinear (all points are on the regression line); a value close to –1 or 1 ($|r| \geq 0.7$) represents a strong correlation.

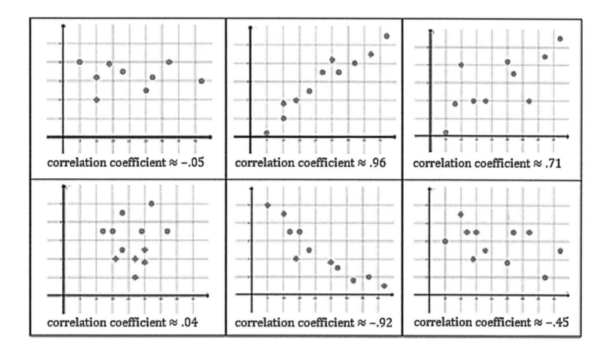

◧▥◨ CALCULATOR TIP

We can find the correlation coefficient on the calculator:

If you turn Diagnostics on, then any time you calculate a linear regression, you will be told the correlation coefficient *r* along with the values of *a* and *b*.

- On the TI-84, you can turn Diagnostics on by pressing MODE, scrolling down to Stat Diagnostics and selecting On.

- On the TI-83, you can turn Diagnostics on by pressing 2nd[CATALOG], scrolling down to DiagnosticOn and then pressing ENTER twice.

Now, when you find a linear regression using LinReg, instead of showing the screen to the left below, the calculator will display a screen like the one to the right, including *r*.

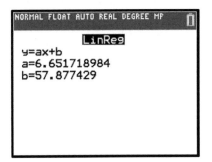 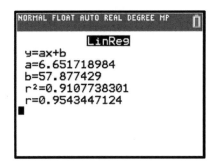

MODEL PROBLEM

Use the calculator to find the correlation coefficient for the data below, rounded to the *nearest thousandth.*

x	3	4	5	6	7	8	9	10
y	6.25	8.0	10.5	13.75	15.5	17.75	19.0	20.75

Solution:

(A)
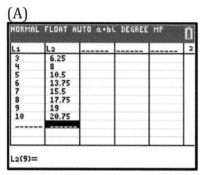

(B)

(C)
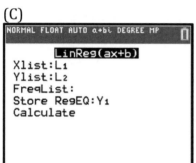

(D)
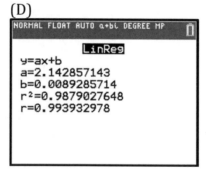

$r \approx 0.994$

Explanation of steps:

(A) Press the Mode key and turn Stat Diagnostics on. Enter the data into L1 and L2.

(B) Press the Stat key and select CALC for the linear regression (LinReg) function.

(C) Select L1 and L2 for the Xlist and Ylist, and store the equation in Y1.

(D) The correlation coefficient is calculated as *r [the equation is $y = 2.143x + 0.009$].*

PRACTICE PROBLEMS

1. Which value of *r* represents data with a strong positive linear correlation between two variables?

   (1) 0.89   (3) 1.04

   (2) 0.34   (4) 0.01

2. What could be the approximate value of the correlation coefficient for the accompanying scatter plot?

   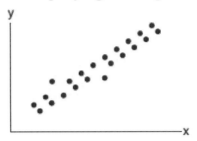

   (1) −0.85   (3) 0.21

   (2) −0.16   (4) 0.90

3. Which graph would have a linear correlation coefficient closest to −1?

   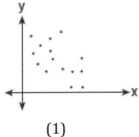

   (1)

   (3)

   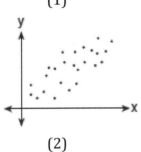

   (2)

   (4)

4. What could be the approximate value of the correlation coefficient for the accompanying scatter plot?

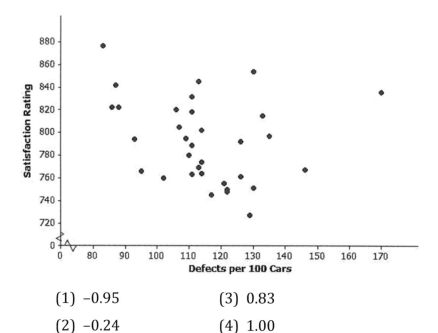

(1) –0.95   (3) 0.83

(2) –0.24   (4) 1.00

5. The correlation coefficients for the six scatter plots shown below are
        -0.85, -0.40, 0, 0.50, 0.90, 0.99

    Match each scatter plot with the correct correlation coefficient.

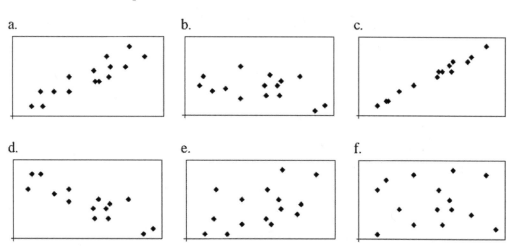

6. Find the correlation coefficient for the data below.

Woman's Shoe Size	5	6	7	8
Foot Length (in)	9.00	9.25	9.50	9.75

7. Use the calculator to find the correlation coefficient for the data below, rounded to the *nearest thousandth*.

Exit #	2	39	48	57	67	75	91	110
Toll	1.50	2.50	3.00	3.50	4.25	4.50	5.50	6.50

8. Use the calculator to find the correlation coefficient for the data below, rounded to the *nearest thousandth*.

Age (years)	Target Heart Rate (beats per minute)
20	135
25	132
30	129
35	125
40	122
45	119
50	115

8.7   **Residuals [CC]**

KEY TERMS AND CONCEPTS

The **residual** of a data point is a measure of how far the y-value of the point is from the line of best fit (i.e., the predicted value). It is calculated as **actual y-value — predicted y-value**. Points *above* the line will have *positive* residuals; points *below* will have *negative* residuals.

Example: The point with the largest residual on the graph below, meaning the farthest point from the line of best fit, is (9,60).

Suppose the equation for the line of best fit for this graph is $y = 8.7x + 12.3$.

To find the residual for point (9,60), substitute 9 for x in the equation, giving us $y = 8.7(9) + 12.3 = 90.6$, so the residual of (9,60) is $60 - 90.6 = -30.6$.

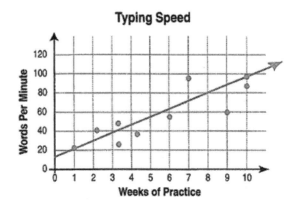

A **residual plot** is made by plotting the *x-values* on the *horizontal axis* and the corresponding *residuals* on the *vertical axis*.

A scatter plot with a line of best fit is shown below. Line segments are added to show the residual of each point. The length of each segment represents the point's residual. When plotted on a residual plot, the line of best fit is drawn as a horizontal line at 0, and the points are plotted using the same *x*-values along the horizontal axis but with the *labels on the vertical axis representing their residuals.*

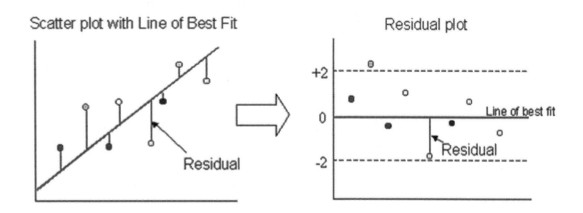

When creating a residual plot from a scatter plot, we can imagine residual line segments as strings tying the points to the regression line, and visualize rotating the regression line so that it becomes horizontal, while keeping the residual line segments (strings) vertical. Example:

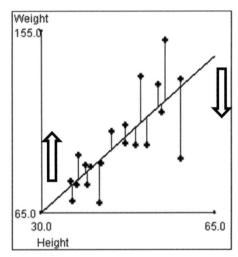 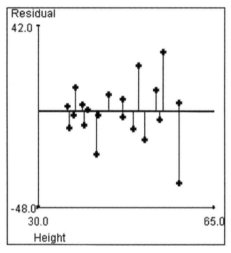

![Calculator icon] **CALCULATOR TIP**

To create a residual plot on the calculator:

1. First, create a scatter plot for the data and store the equation of the linear regression in Y1. The regression equation must be stored in Y1 for this to work.

2. Turn off Plot1 by pressing [2nd][STAT PLOT][1] [Off] [ENTER].

3. Select [Plot2] at the top of the screen and press [ENTER] [On] [ENTER]. Select the first option [⌐·] for Type and L1 for Xlist. For Ylist, press [2nd][LIST][7] for RESID.

4. Press [ZOOM][9] for ZoomStat. Adjust the [WINDOW] dimensions and scales as needed.

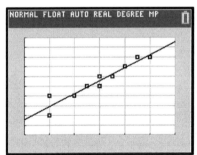  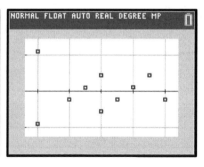

In a residual plot, the points should not show any pattern or curve. If they do, then the *linear* regression may not have been appropriate for the data.

Example: The first residual plot is shown on data for which a linear regression is appropriate. The residuals are more or less evenly distributed above and below the axis and show no particular pattern. The second residual plot does show a pattern, so a linear regression should not have been used. In other words, a *line* was not a best fit for this set of data.

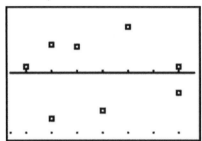   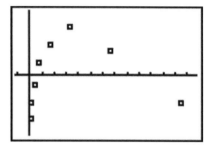

MODEL PROBLEM

Which residual plot below shows that an inappropriate regression may have been used?

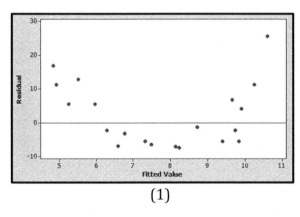   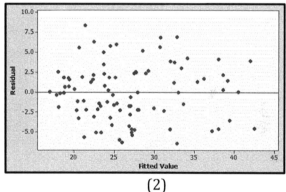

(1)   (2)

Solution: (1)

Explanation:

A residual plot is problematic if a pattern can be seen in the residuals that would allow someone to predict a residual based on a value. *[In plot (1), a clear pattern is seen in the residual plot. This pattern allows us to predict, for example, that a value of 8 would have a negative residual but a value of 5 or 11 would have a positive residual. For an appropriate regression, the residuals should not be predictable, as shown in the patternless plot (2).]*

PRACTICE PROBLEMS

1. Based on a regression line, it is predicted that a 10 year old Toyota Corolla should cost $14,050. Its actual cost is $12,550. What is the residual?

2. The table below shows study time, in hours, and test scores based on a linear model for which $y = 8.8x + 58.4$ is the equation of a line of fit. Complete the table to show the predicted test score and residual for each point.

Study Time in Hours (x)	Test Score (y)	Predicted Test Score	Residual
0.5	63		
1	67		
1.5	72		
2	76		
2.5	80		
3	85		
3.5	89		

3. A linear regression equation to predict the number of points scored by an NFL team in one game, y, based on the team's time of possession (in minutes) in that game, x, is $y = 0.75x - 0.25$.

a) How many points would you predict a team to score if their time of possession was 22 minutes?

b) Say a team had 34 minutes of possession and scored 32 points. What is their residual?

c) A team had 28 minutes of possession and a residual of -0.75. How many points did they score?

4. Complete the following table using the equation $y = 0.5x$ as the line of fit to determine the predicted values. Round to the *nearest tenths*.

x	y	Predicted Value	Residual
5	3		
10	4		
15	9		
20	7		
25	13		
30	15		

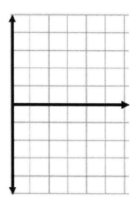

Then plot the residuals on the grid to the right.

Does the residual plot suggest a linear relationship? Explain.

5. Complete the following table using the equation $y = -0.4x + 16.3$ as the line of fit to determine the predicted values. Round to the *nearest tenths*.

x	y	Predicted Value	Residual
2	5		
4	15		
6	26		
8	23		
10	11		
12	3		

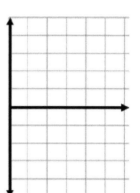

Then plot the residuals on the grid to the right.

Does the residual plot suggest a linear relationship? Explain.

6. Airlines charge different prices based on the distance of the flight being purchased. The table below shows the distances and prices of different flights for a given airline at an airport.

Destination	Distance (miles)	Airfare ($)	Predicted Price ($)	Residual
Atlanta	576	178		
Boston	370	138		
Chicago	612	94		
Dallas/Fort Worth	1,216	278		
Detroit	409	158		
Denver	1,502	258		
Miami	946	198		
New Orleans	998	188		
New York	189	98		
Orlando	787	179		
Pittsburgh	210	138		
St. Louis	737	98		

a) Find the equation for the line of best fit using the calculator.

b) Using this equation, calculate the predicted price for each flight and enter the predicted prices in the table above.

c) Calculate the residuals and enter them into the table above.

d) Using the grid below, graph the residual plot. Use your calculator to verify that your residual plot is correct.

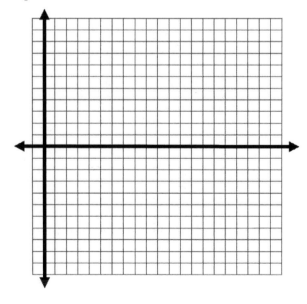

Chapter 9.   Introduction to Functions

9.1   <u>Recognize Functions</u>

KEY TERMS AND CONCEPTS

An **ordered pair** is a pair of two values (*entries*) written in a certain order. The coordinates of a point on a graph are usually represented by an ordered pair in parentheses, with the *x*-coordinate (*abscissa*) written first and the *y*-coordinate (*ordinate*) written second, as in $(3, -2)$.

A **relation** is a set of ordered pairs. It may be graphed as a set of points.

A **function** is a type of relation in which every first entry is mapped to exactly one second entry. In a function, no two ordered pairs can have the same first entries but different second entries. Represented as a graph, a relation is a function only if no points have the same *x*-coordinates but different *y*-coordinates.

Given its graph, we can test whether a relation is a function by using the **vertical line test**. If we can draw a vertical line that intersects the graph at two or more points, then these points have the same *x*-values but different *y*-values, and therefore the relation is not a function. It is a function only if it is *impossible* to draw a vertical line that would intersect the graph at multiple points.

function   not a function

MODEL PROBLEM 1:   *DETERMINING IF A RELATION IS A FUNCTION*

Determine whether the relation, $\{(1, -1), (0,0), (1,1), (4,2)\}$, is a function or is *not* a function.

Solution:

It is *not* a function.

Explanation of steps:

Look for any two ordered pairs that have the same *x*-coordinate but different *y*-coordinates *[(1, -1) and (1,1)]*. A relation is a function only if no such cases can be found.

PRACTICE PROBLEMS

1. Which relation is *not* a function? (1) $\{(1,2), (3,4), (4,5), (5,6)\}$ (2) $\{(3,1), (2,1), (1,2), (3,2)\}$ (3) $\{(4,1), (5,1), (6,1), (7,1)\}$ (4) $\{(0,0), (1,1), (2,2), (3,3)\}$	2. Which relation is *not* a function? (1) $\{(3,-2), (4,-3), (5,-4), (6,-5)\}$ (2) $\{(3,-2), (3,-4), (4,-1), (4,-3)\}$ (3) $\{(3,-2), (5,-2), (4,-2), (-1,-2)\}$ (4) $\{(3,-2), (-2,3), (4,-1), (-1,4)\}$
3. Which relation is a function? (1) $\{(2,1), (3,1), (4,1), (5,1)\}$ (2) $\{(1,2), (1,3), (1,4), (1,5)\}$ (3) $\{(2,3), (3,2), (4,2), (2,4)\}$ (4) $\{(1,6), (2,8), (3,9), (3,12)\}$	4. Which relation is a function? (1) $\{(3,4), (3,5), (3,6), (3,7)\}$ (2) $\{(1,2), (3,4), (4,3), (2,1)\}$ (3) $\{(6,7), (7,8), (8,9), (6,5)\}$ (4) $\{(0,2), (3,4), (0,8), (5,6)\}$

5. The table to the right shows all the ordered pairs (x, y) that define a relation between the variables x and y.

Is y a function of x? Justify your answer.

x	y
-2	3
-1	0
0	-1
1	0
2	3
3	8

MODEL PROBLEM 2:   *DETERMINING IF A GRAPH REPRESENTS A FUNCTION*

Determine whether the graph below represents a function.

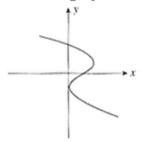

Solution:

The graph is *not* a function.

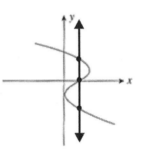

Explanation of steps:

A graph is not a function if we are able to draw any vertical line that intersects the graph at two or more points. *[We can draw the vertical line shown to the right, for just one example. Since it crosses the graph in three points, this cannot be a function.]*

PRACTICE PROBLEMS

6. Which graph represents a function?

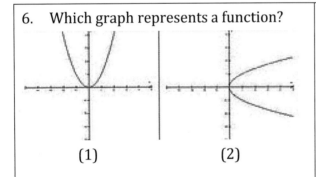

(1)   (2)

7. Which graph represents a function?

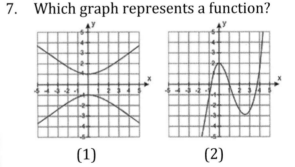

(1)   (2)

8. Which graph does *not* represent a function?

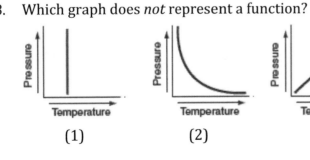

(1)   (2)   (3)   (4)

9.   Which graph represents a function?

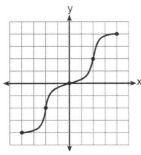

(1)

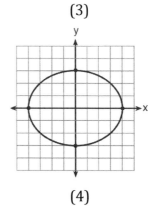

(3)

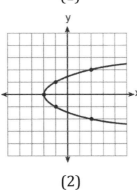

(2)

(4)

10. Which graph represents a function?

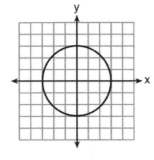

(1)

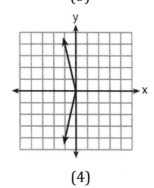

(3)

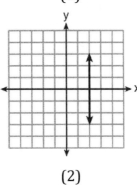

(2)

(4)

9.2   <u>**Function Graphs**</u>

KEY TERMS AND CONCEPTS

As we have seen, a function may be represented as a set of ordered pairs (x, y) such that each x is paired with a unique y. Often, the relationship between each x and its corresponding y can be represented by an algebraic expression.

Example: Considering the function represented by the expression $3x + 5$, for each x-value, the corresponding y-value is 5 more than 3 times the x-value. Note that for each x-value, there is only one possible y-value.

A function is named using a letter (often f) followed by the expression's independent variable (often x) in parentheses, as in $f(x)$. This is read as "f of x". We could **define** the function by writing that it is equal to an expression in terms of the independent variable.

Examples: $f(x) = 3x + 5$ $A(n) = n^2 - 2n + 1$

When a function $f(x)$ is graphed on a coordinate graph, the y-values are the values produced by the function. For this reason, the y-axis is often labelled $f(x)$.

Example: $f(x) = 3x + 5$ is graphed as the line $y = 3x + 5$. So, $f(x) = y$.

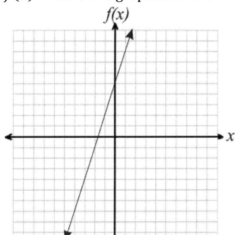

$$\boxed{\begin{array}{c} \text{Linear Function} \\ y = mx + b \\ f(x) = mx + b \end{array}}$$

A function's value, $f(x)$, for a given value of x can be determined by finding the y-value of a point (x, y) for the given x on a graph of the function.

Example: For the function $f(x) = 3x + 5$ shown above, $f(-1) = 2$, because $(-1, 2)$ is a point on the line.

As we have seen, you can **determine whether a point is in the solution set of an equation** by substituting the x and y coordinates for the variables x and y in the equation and then checking if these values make the equation true. When the equation is written as a function definition, we can simply replace $f(x)$ with y to give us an equation in x and y.

Example: $(-3,1)$ is a point that lies on the graph of the function $f(x) = x^2 + 3x + 1$.

We can check this by substituting -3 for x and 1 for y in the equation $y = x^2 + 3x + 1$, giving us $1 = (-3)^2 + 3(-3) + 1$, which is true.

MODEL PROBLEM

Below is a graph of $f(x)$. _[Assume the points graphed with closed circles have integer coordinates and the lines between them are straight.]_

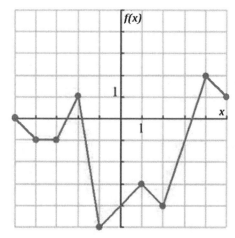

(A)   What is $f(2)$?

(B)   What is $f(0)$?

(C)   For what value of x does $f(x) = -5$?

(D)   Which of the following does _not_ equal -1?

     (1) $f(-4)$ (2) $f(-3)$ (3) $f(3)$ (4) $f(4)$

Solution:

(A) -4

(B) -4

(C) $x = -1$

(D) (4)

Explanation of steps:

(A) $f(2) = -4$ because $(2, -4)$ is a point on the graph of $f(x)$.

(B) $f(0) = -4$ because the graph of $f(x)$ crosses the y-axis at the point $(0, -4)$.

(C) $f(-1) = -5$ because $(-1, -5)$ is a point on the graph of $f(x)$.

(D) $f(4) = 2$ because $(4,2)$ is a point on the graph of $f(x)$.

PRACTICE PROBLEMS

1. Complete the table based on the graph of the function $f(x)$ below.

x	f(x)
0	
1	
2	
3	
4	
5	

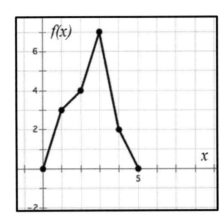

2. The function $f(x)$ is graphed below.

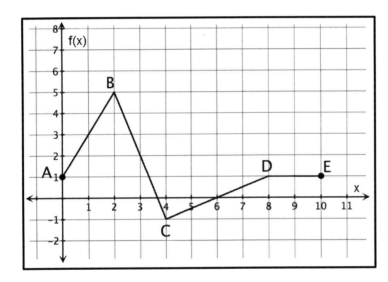

a) What is $f(9)$?

b) For what values of x does $f(x) = 2$?

9.3   **Evaluate Functions**

KEY TERMS AND CONCEPTS

We saw in the previous section that we can find the value of $f(x)$ for a given x by looking at a graph of the function. More frequently, however, we will use the function's definition. We can find $f(x)$ for a given value of x by **substituting and evaluating** the expression.

Example: For the function $f(x) = 3x + 5$ shown below, $f(-1) = 2$,

(a) because $(-1,2)$ is a point on the line, and also

(b) because $f(x) = 3x + 5 = 3(-1) + 5 = 2$.

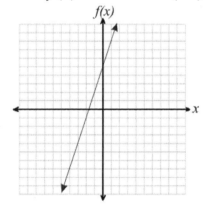

⬛▦⬛ CALCULATOR TIP

We can also evaluate a function on the calculator:

1.   Press [Y=] and type the equation of the function as Y1. Then, press [2nd][QUIT].

2.   On the TI-84 models, press [ALPHA][F4][1] to select Y1. On the TI-83 models, press [VARS] Y-VARS [1][1] instead.

3.   Enter the given value and press [)] [ENTER].

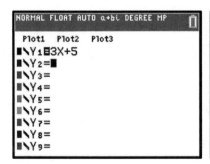
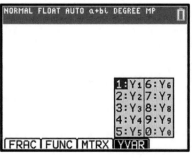
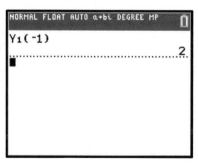

The **y-intercept** of a function $f(x)$ is the value of $f(0)$.

Example: For the function $f(x) = 3x + 5$ shown above, $f(0) = 3(0) + 5 = 5$,
so the y-intercept is 5.

We can also **evaluate a function at a given expression** by replacing the variable in the original function with the expression, using parentheses to avoid errors.

Example: If $f(x) = 3x + 5$, find $f(n + 1)$.

$$f(n + 1) = 3(n + 1) + 5$$
$$= 3n + 3 + 5$$
$$= 3n + 8$$

Model Problem

Given $f(x) = 3x^2 - 2x + 5$, find $f(1) + f(2)$.

Solution:

$f(1) = 3(1)^2 - 2(1) + 5 = 6$ and $f(2) = 3(2)^2 - 2(2) + 5 = 13$,
so $f(1) + f(2) = 6 + 13 = 19$

Explanation of steps:

To evaluate a function of x for a given value, substitute the value for x in the expression. *[Find $f(1)$ by substituting 1 for x in $3x^2 - 2x + 5$ and find $f(2)$ by substituting 2 for x in $3x^2 - 2x + 5$.]*

PRACTICE PROBLEMS

1. Find $f(3)$ given $f(x) = -2x^2 - 3x - 6$.	2. If $f(a) = a^2 - 2a + 1$, find $f(-3)$.
3. If $f(x) = (x - 3)^2$, find $f(0)$.	4. $f(m) = 0.5^m$. Evaluate the function for $m = 2$.
5. If $f(x) = 3x - 4$ and $g(x) = x^2$, find the value of $f(3) - g(2)$.	6. If $h(x) = 2x - 1$, find the product $h(0) \cdot h(-2)$.

7. For what integer value of x is $f(x) = -10$ if $f(x) = -4x + 2$?	8. If $f(x) = kx^2$, and $f(2) = 12$, then what is the value of k?
9. If $g(x) = 2x^2 + 6x - 3$, find $g(4a)$ in terms of a.	10. Find $f(a + 2)$ in terms of a, given $f(x) = x^2 + 2x - 1$.

11. $P(t) = 0.0089t^2 + 1.1149t + 78.4491$ models the U. S. population, P, in millions since 1900. If t represents the number of years after 1900, then what is the estimated population in 2025 to the *nearest tenth of a million*?

9.4   **Features of Function Graphs**

KEY TERMS AND CONCEPTS

When looking at the behavior of a function on a graph, it is helpful to identify key features of the graph. We should recognize where the function is positive or negative, increasing or decreasing, and its end behavior. We should also recognize its extrema.

Example: For the discussion to follow, we will refer to the graph below.

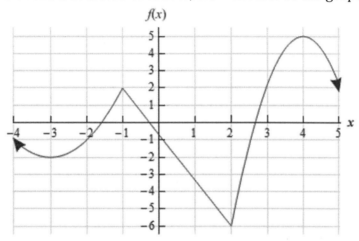

A function is **positive** where its graph lies above the *x*-axis, and **negative** where its graph lies below the *x*-axis. It is **increasing** where the graph goes up, when moving from left to right, and **decreasing** where it goes down. Its **end behavior** describes the function at the arrowheads; that is, at the leftmost or rightmost extremes of the graph.

Example:

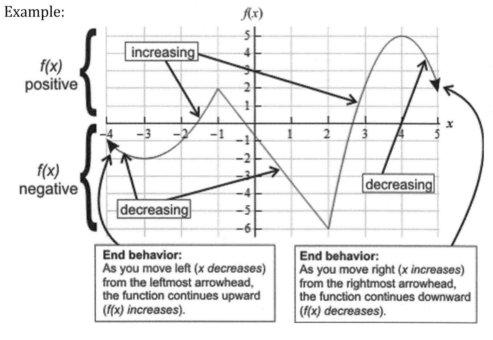

Some points on the graph of a function can be described as a relative maximum (plural, *maxima*) or a relative minimum (plural, *minima*). A **relative maximum** is a point where no other nearby points have a greater function value (*y*-coordinate), and a **relative minimum** is a point where no other nearby points have a lesser function value. These points are also called **extrema**. The function is *neither increasing nor decreasing* at the extrema.

Example:

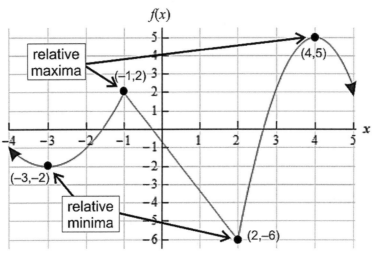

MODEL PROBLEM

Describe the features of the function graph below.

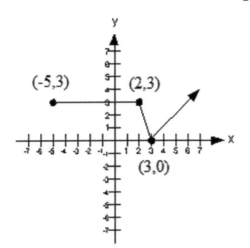

Solution:

The function is constant in the interval $-5 < x < 2$, decreasing where $2 < x < 3$, and increasing at $x > 3$. There is a relative minimum at $(3,0)$. There are no relative maxima.

PRACTICE PROBLEMS

1. The function $f(x)$ is graphed below.

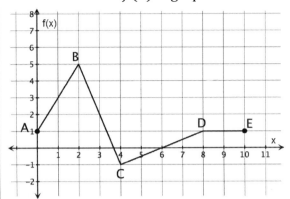

a) Over which interval(s) is $f(x)$ increasing?

b) Over which interval(s) is $f(x)$ decreasing?

c) Over which interval(s) is $f(x)$ constant?

2. For the graph of the function below,

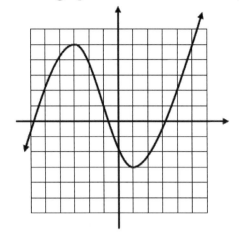

a) which point is a relative maximum?

b) which point is a relative minimum?

Note: you may assume integer coordinates.

3. For the graph of the function below,
a) state all the intervals where the function is positive or negative
b) state all the intervals where the function is increasing, decreasing, or constant
c) state the coordinates of any relative maxima or minima

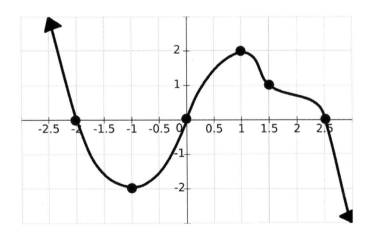

9.5   <u>**Domain and Range**</u>

KEY TERMS AND CONCEPTS

For a function, the set of possible *x*-values is called the **domain**, and the set of *y*-values that are produced by the function is called the **range**.

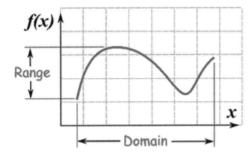

The function is like a machine in that for any given **input** value from the *domain*, the function produces a unique **output** value in the *range*.

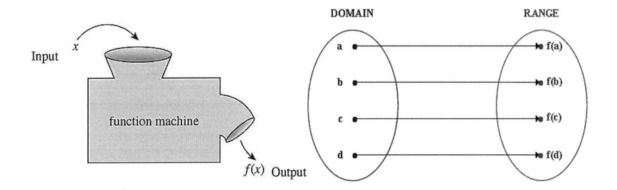

A **discrete domain** is a set of input values that consist of only certain numbers in an interval, whereas a **continuous domain** consists of all numbers in an interval. Likewise, the range of a function may be either discrete or continuous.

Example: A domain of *counting* numbers from 1 to 5 would be *discrete*.

A domain of *real* numbers from 1 to 5 would be *continuous*.

We can express a continuous domain or range as a **compound inequality**, or by using **interval notation** or **set-builder notation**.

Example: A domain of real numbers from 3 to 7, including 3 but excluding 7, could be written as $3 \leq x < 7$, or as $[3, 7)$, or as $\{x \mid x \geq 3 \text{ and } x < 7\}$.

If the domain or range extends _infinitely_ in the negative or positive direction, we may use the symbols $-\infty$ or ∞, respectively.

Example: If $f(x) = x$ is defined for the domain of all real numbers $-\infty < x < \infty$, then the range would also include all real numbers, $-\infty < y < \infty$.

Restrictions on the domain:

If the domain is not specified, it is assumed to be the set of real numbers. However, the domain may be restricted to only certain intervals of the real numbers such as $0 \leq x < \infty$ or $-2 \leq x \leq 2$, or to _discrete_ sets such as the set of integers, or even to _finite_ sets such as $\{-2, -1, 0, 1, 2\}$. Or the domain may simply exclude certain values of x; for example, the domain for the function $f(x) = \frac{1}{x}$ for $x \neq 0$ excludes 0 from the domain because $\frac{1}{0}$ is undefined.

Restrictions on the domain may derive from the situation that the function models.

Examples: (a) If x represents the length of a side of a triangle, then $0 < x < \infty$ would be an appropriate domain for $f(x)$.

(b) If x represents a number of people, then _the set of whole numbers_ would be an appropriate domain for $f(x)$.

(c) If x is the result of rolling a six-sided die, then the domain $\{1, 2, 3, 4, 5, 6\}$ would be appropriate for $f(x)$.

The properties of the set of real numbers may also dictate restrictions on the domain.

Example: If $f(x) = \frac{\sqrt{x-2}}{x-10}$, then we need to restrict the domain in two ways.

To avoid a square root of a negative number in the numerator, we need $x - 2 \geq 0$, or $x \geq 2$. Also, to avoid division by zero, we need $x - 10 \neq 0$, or $x \neq 10$. So, our domain for f can be written as $\{x \mid x \geq 2, x \neq 10\}$.

On a graph, and **open circle** can be used to show an endpoint that is not included. Just as we saw when graphing inequalities, an **open circle** means the point is *excluded*, but a **closed circle** means the point is *included*.

Example: The linear graph below shows the function $f(x) = 2x - 1$ restricted to the domain $-2 \leq x < 4$. Note the open circle shows that the graph does not include $f(4)$.

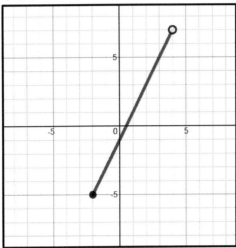

Determining the range:

Not all functions map to all real values of y.

Example: Suppose $f(x) = |x|$ (the absolute value of x) for the domain of all real numbers. The range cannot include negative numbers, so the range is $y \geq 0$.

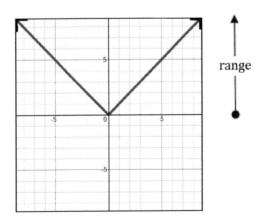

For a simple linear function with a restricted domain, we can find the range by finding the _y_-values (ie, evaluating the function) at the _endpoints_ of the line segment.

Example: If $f(x) = 2x - 1$ is defined on the domain $-2 \leq x < 4$, we can find the range by finding $f(-2) = 2(-2) - 1 = -5$ and $f(4) = 2(4) - 1 = 7$. The range will include all _y_-values between –5 and 7, but _excluding_ 7, which is written as $-5 \leq y < 7$.

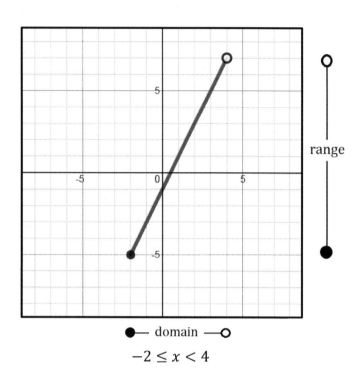

$$-2 \leq x < 4$$

This method for determining the range works for linear functions, but *other types of functions* may require more work.

Example: Here's the graph of the quadratic function $f(x) = x^2 - 5$ defined on the domain $-2 \leq x \leq 3$. We cannot assume the range includes only those values between $f(-2) = -1$ and $f(3) = 4$, or $-1 \leq y \leq 4$. As we can see by the graph, the range includes *y*-values as low as -5, so the actual range is $-5 \leq y \leq 4$.

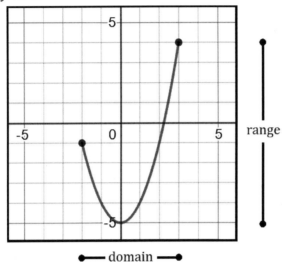

Note: In an upcoming unit on quadratic functions, you'll learn how to find the minimum or maximum value in the range, without having to graph, by finding the *y*-value of the vertex.

MODEL PROBLEM

The graph below represents the function $f(x)$ on the domain, $-5 \leq x < 5$. Based on the graph, describe the range.

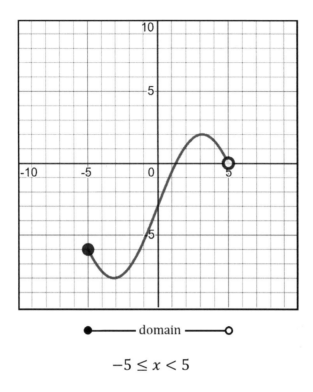

$\bullet\!\!-\!\!-\!\!-$ domain $-\!\!-\!\!-\!\!\circ$

$$-5 \leq x < 5$$

Solution:

The range is approximately $-8 \leq y \leq 2$.

Explanation of steps:

The range of this continuous function extends from the lowest point (minimum, or least value of y) to the highest point (maximum, or greatest value of y). Without knowing the equation of the function, we can only approximate these values from the graph.

[The graph appears to go as low as –8 at $(-3, -8)$ and as high as 2 at $(3, 2)$.]

PRACTICE PROBLEMS

1. State the range of the following function. $\{(-1,2), (1,3), (2,51), (8,22), (9,51)\}$	2. What is an appropriate domain of the function $f(x) = \dfrac{1}{x}$?
3. State the domain and range of the function shown in the graph. 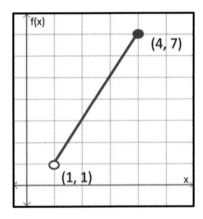	4. State the domain and range of the function shown in the graph. 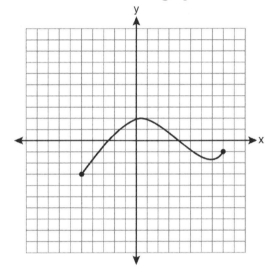

5. The graph below shows the effect of pH on the action of a certain enzyme.

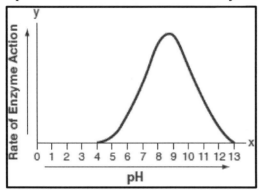

What is the approximate domain of this function?

6. Data collected from an experiment are shown in the graph below.

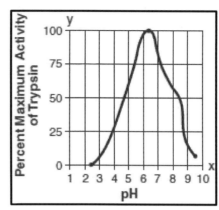

What is the approximate range of this function?

7. The graph shows the elevation of a region along a 12-mile hiker's trail.

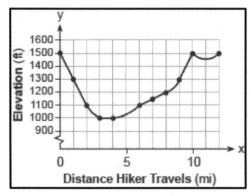

What is the approximate domain of this function?

8. The graph below shows the relative humidity during a 24-hour period.

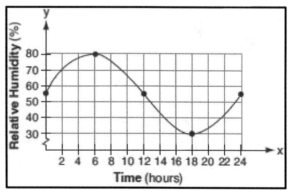

What is the approximate range of this function?

9. Suppose $g(n) = n + 1$ for the domain of whole numbers, n. Describe the range of this function.

10. Find the range of $f(x) = 3x + 10$ where $f(x)$ is defined on the domain $5 \leq x < 10$.

11. Given $f(x) = x^2$ for all real numbers, x.

a) What is the range of this function?

b) Suppose we restrict the domain of this function to $-3 \leq x \leq 3$. How does this affect the range?

12. Suppose n represents the number of multiple-choice questions answered correctly on a 20-question test. The function $f(n)$ represents the points earned on the test, where each question is worth 5 points with no partial credit.

a) Define the function $f(n)$.

b) What is an appropriate domain?

c) What is the range?

9.6   **Absolute Value Functions**

KEY TERMS AND CONCEPTS

An **absolute value function** can be graphed using a table or a calculator.

Example: We can graph $y = |x|$ as follows.

x	$\lvert x \rvert$	y	(x, y)
-2	$\lvert -2 \rvert$	2	$(-2, 2)$
-1	$\lvert -1 \rvert$	1	$(-1, 1)$
0	$\lvert 0 \rvert$	0	$(0, 0)$
1	$\lvert 1 \rvert$	1	$(1, 1)$
2	$\lvert 2 \rvert$	2	$(2, 2)$

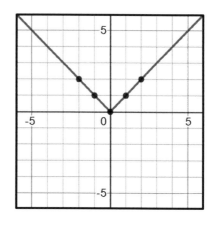

▦▦ CALCULATOR TIP

To graph $y = |x|$ on the calculator:

On the TI-84, enter: [Y=][ALPHA][F2][1][X,T,Θ,*n*][▸][GRAPH].

On the TI-83, enter: [Y=][MATH] NUM [1][X,T,Θ,*n*][ )][GRAPH].

An absolute value function will have a **V shape** (or an upside down V shape).

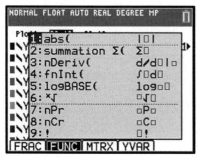 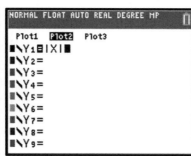 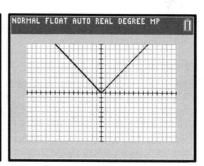

MODEL PROBLEM

Use a table to graph the function $y = 2|x + 1|$.

Solution:

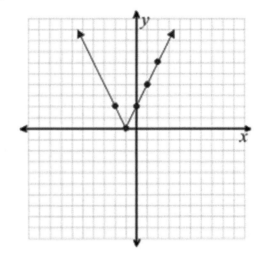

(A)	(B)	(C)	(D)
x	$2\|x + 1\|$	y	(x, y)
-2	$2\|-2 + 1\|$	2	$(-2,2)$
-1	$2\|-1 + 1\|$	0	$(-1,0)$
0	$2\|0 + 1\|$	2	$(0,2)$
1	$2\|1 + 1\|$	4	$(1,4)$
2	$2\|2 + 1\|$	6	$(2,6)$

Explanation of steps:

(A)   Pick values of x that will evaluate to both positive and negative expressions inside the absolute value sign, allowing you to see both sides of the V shape in the graph.

(B)   Substitute the values of x into the expression on the right side of the equation.

(C)   Evaluate for y.

(D)   Plot the resulting points on the graph and extend the rays infinitely with arrow heads.

PRACTICE PROBLEMS

1. Which graph represents the equation $y = |x - 2|$?

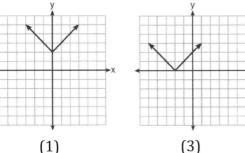

(1)   (3)

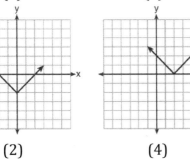

(2)   (4)

2. The graph below represents $f(x)$.

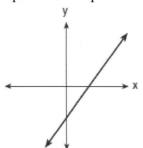

Which graph best represents $|f(x)|$?

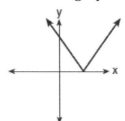

(1)   (3)

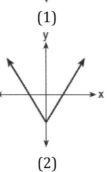

(2)   (4)

3. Graph $y = |x| - 3$.

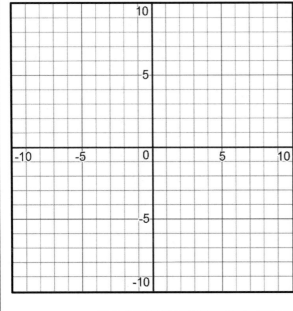

4. Graph $y = -|x|$.

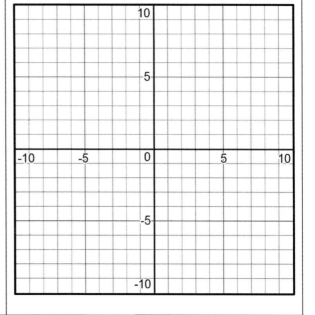

5.   Graph $y = 3|x|$.

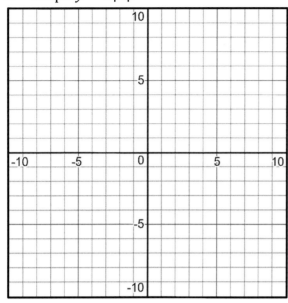

6.   Graph $y = \frac{1}{2}|x - 1|$.

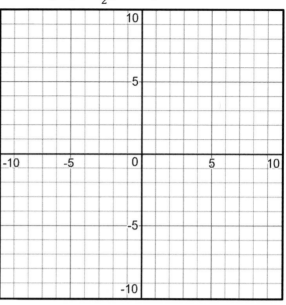

7.   Graph $y = 2|x + 3|$ over the interval $-7 \le x \le 1$.

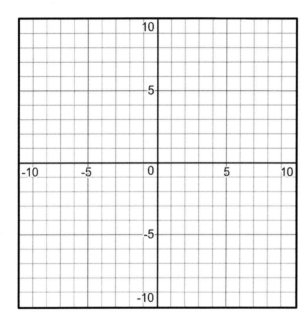

Chapter 10. Functions as Models

10.1 <u>**Write a Function from a Table**</u>

KEY TERMS AND CONCEPTS

We have seen that a linear equation may be written in slope-intercept form as $y = mx + b$ or in point-slope form as $y - y_1 = m(x - x_1)$.

We can convert the general slope-intercept form into function notation by changing y to $f(x)$ and changing the y-intercept, b, to $f(0)$, which gives us $f(x) = mx + f(0)$.

We can also write the general point-slope form in function notation. Instead of (x_1, y_1), we'll express the given point as $(n, f(n))$, where n is any value in the domain. So, $y - y_1 = m(x - x_1)$ is converted to function notation as follows:

    1) $y - f(n) = m(x - n)$ Substitute n for x_1 and $f(n)$ for y_1

    2) $y = m(x - n) + f(n)$ Isolate y by adding $f(n)$ to both sides

    3) $f(x) = m(x - n) + f(n)$ Change y to $f(x)$

We can use these forms to write linear functions for tables of coordinates with x-values given at equal intervals. If a table includes $x = 0$, we can use the simpler slope-intercept form, $f(x) = mx + f(0)$. If a table doesn't include $x = 0$, we'll use the form derived from the point-slope form, $f(x) = m(x - n) + f(n)$.

Note: When $n = 0$, the form, $f(x) = m(x - n) + f(n)$ becomes $f(x) = mx + f(0)$.

To write an equation for a linear function given a table including $x = 0$:

1. Find the slope m using the first two given points.
2. The value of b would be the y-intercept, $f(0)$.
3. Write the function in the form, $f(x) = mx + f(0)$.

Example: In the table below,

x	0	5	10	15
$f(x)$	10	12	14	16

the slope $m = \dfrac{12 - 10}{5 - 0} = \dfrac{2}{5}$ and the y-intercept, $f(0)$, is 10, so the linear

equation is $f(x) = \dfrac{2}{5}x + 10$.

To write an equation for a linear function given a table that *does not* include $x = 0$:

1. Find the slope m using the first two given points.
2. The first given point gives us n and $f(n)$.
3. Write the function in the form, $f(x) = m(x - n) + f(n)$.

Example: In the table below,

x	1	3	5	7
$f(x)$	8	14	20	26

the slope $m = \dfrac{14 - 8}{3 - 1} = \dfrac{6}{2} = 3$ and the first point $(1,8)$ gives us n and $f(n)$, so

the linear equation is $f(x) = 3(x - 1) + 8$, which simplifies to $f(x) = 3x + 5$.

MODEL PROBLEM

Write an equation of the linear function represented by the table below.

x	2	4	6	8
$f(x)$	13	21	29	37

Solution:

(A) $m = \frac{8}{2} = 4$

(B) $f(x) = 4(x - 2) + 13$

(C) $f(x) = 4x - 8 + 13$

   $f(x) = 4x + 5$

Explanation of steps:

(A) Find the slope.

   [Use the points, (2,13) and (4,21).]

(B) Write the function in the form,

   $f(x) = m(x - n) + f(n).$

   [Using the first point, (2,13), substitute 2 for n and 13 for f(n).]

(C) Simplify.

PRACTICE PROBLEMS

1. Write the linear function represented by the table below.	2. Write the linear function represented by the table below.
<table><tr><td>x</td><td>0</td><td>1</td><td>2</td><td>3</td><td>4</td></tr><tr><td>$f(x)$</td><td>9</td><td>13</td><td>17</td><td>21</td><td>25</td></tr></table>	<table><tr><td>x</td><td>0</td><td>3</td><td>6</td><td>9</td><td>12</td></tr><tr><td>$f(x)$</td><td>10</td><td>15</td><td>20</td><td>25</td><td>30</td></tr></table>

3. Write the linear function represented by the table below.

x	1	2	3	4	5
$f(x)$	7	10	13	16	19

4. Write the linear function represented by the table below.

x	1	5	9	13	17
$f(x)$	−5	−3	−1	1	3

5. Write the linear function represented by the table below.

x	2	4	6	8	10
$f(x)$	9	5	1	−3	−7

6. Write the linear function represented by the table below.

x	11	12	13	14	15
$f(x)$	0	5	10	15	20

10.2   **Graph Linear Functions**

KEY TERMS AND CONCEPTS

Graphs of functions are often used to model real world situations. The **independent** variable is represented by **x-values** in a horizontal axis and the **dependent** variable is represented by **y-values** in a vertical axis. Very often in a real event, time is the independent variable.

An important first step in creating graphs of functions to model a situation is to determine what **units of measure** are used for the horizontal and vertical axes.

Example: To graph a function representing the gasoline in a car's tank during a trip, we could use distance (miles) for one axis and gasoline (gallons) for the other.

The real world situation may also require certain **contraints**, such as minimum or maximum values of the variables. A linear graph, therefore, may be a line segment rather than a line.

Example: The most commonly used units for the independent variables are units of time, which are generally constrained to non-negative real numbers.

Also, there may be **restrictions on the domain**.

Example: If an axis represents a number of people, or a number of items produced, we would restrict its values to counting numbers only.

Since the measurements or values in real world problems are not always small integers, we may need to **scale** our coordinate axes to fit the situation. It is very possible that a grid square in our graph may not represent a one unit by one unit square. No matter what scale we choose to use for an axis, we must use consistent intervals on that axis.

Example: The graph below uses a grid square of 1 hour by 25 pages.

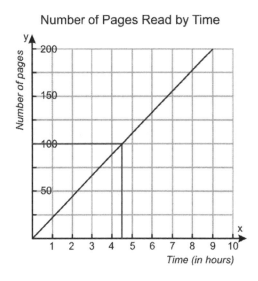

MODEL PROBLEM

A swimming pool with a maximum capacity of 450 gallons contains 100 gallons of water before a hose begins to fill the pool by depositing 50 gallons of water each minute. Write and graph an equation that relates x, the number of minutes, to $g(x)$, the number of gallons, for the interval $100 \leq g(x) \leq 450$ only.

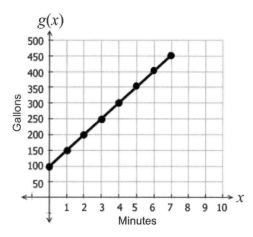

Solution:

(A) $g(x) = 50x + 100$

(B)   (C)

Explanation of steps:

(A)   Write an equation.

(B)   Create a grid with appropriately scaled axes.

(C)   Graph the line. *[Due to the given constraints, the line segment should start at (0, 100) and stop when g(x) reaches 450 at (7, 450).]*

PRACTICE PROBLEMS

1. A cell phone company charges a monthly rate of $25 for a data plan plus $5 per gigabyte of data used. Write an equation for $c(g)$, the cost of the plan with g gigabytes of data usage. Graph $c(g)$ below.

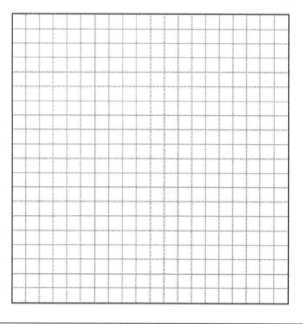

2. A handyman charges $1.00 per square foot plus an additional fee of $25.00 to paint a deck floor. Write an equation for $c(x)$, the cost, in dollars, for painting a deck floor that is x square feet in area. Graph $c(x)$ below.

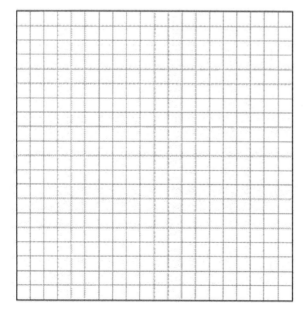

3. An elementary school is sponsoring a dance. The cost of a disk jockey is $40, and tickets sell for $2 each. Write a linear equation and, on the grid below, graph the equation to represent the relationship between the number of tickets sold and the profit from the dance.

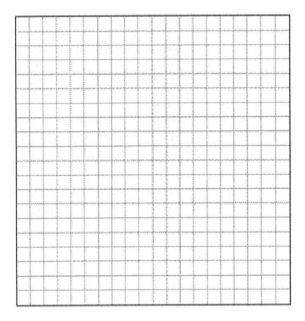

4. The rate at which crickets chirp is a linear function of temperature. At 59° F they make 76 chirps per minute, and at 65° F they make 100 chirps per minute. Write an equation for $c(t)$, the chirping rate at temperature t. Then, graph $c(t)$ over the domain $50 \leq t \leq 75$ on the grid below.

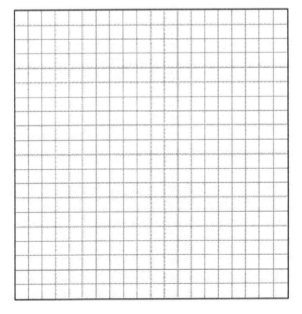

10.3 **Rate of Change for Linear Functions**

KEY TERMS AND CONCEPTS

A **rate of change** is a rate that describes how one quantity changes in relation to another quantity. If a graph of a function forms a straight line, it is called a **linear** function, and the rate of change can be calculated as the **slope of the line**. Like we saw with *correlation*, if the line has a **positive slope**, there is a **positive rate of change**. If the line has a **negative slope**, there is a **negative rate of change**. If the line is horizontal, the slope is zero and therefore the rate of change is zero.

Example: Every two hours, a driver records the total time and distance traveled. The bivariate table and graph below show the results. A positive slope indicates a *positive rate of change*. Since the slope is 40, the rate is 40 miles per hour.

Time Driving (h)	Distance Traveled (mi)
x	*y*
2	80
4	160
6	240

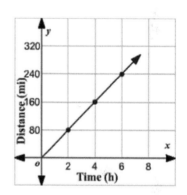

The **absolute value of the slope** will determine how **steep** it is. A graph with a slope of 5 will be steeper than a graph with a slope of 2, while a graph with a -5 slope will be steeper than a graph with a -2 slope.

If the line *passes through the origin*, then $y = mx$ and the variables are in **direct variation**. The slope *m* represents the **constant of variation** when comparing *y* to *x*. The above graph is an example of direct variation. The slope, 40, is the constant of variation of *miles* to *hours*.

If the line does not pass through the origin, then the constant term *b* (the *y*-intercept) in the equation $y = mx + b$ often represents the **starting value** in the model, especially where the *x* axis represents time passed.

MODEL PROBLEM

A candle has a starting length of 10 inches. Thirty minutes after lighting it, the length is 7 inches. The candle continues to get shorter at the same rate over time, as shown by the graph below. Is there a positive or negative rate of change in the length of the candle over time?

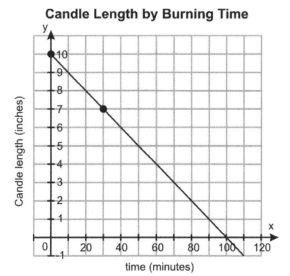

Candle Length by Burning Time

Solution:

Negative

Explanation of steps:

If the graph shows a line with a positive slope, the rate of change is positive. But if the slope of the line is negative, the rate of change is negative.

[Note that the y-intercept of 10 in the graph represents the starting length of the candle.]

PRACTICE PROBLEMS

1. In a linear equation, the independent variable *increases* at a constant rate while the dependent variable *decreases* at a constant rate.	2. In a linear equation, the independent variable *increases* at a constant rate while the dependent variable *increases* at a constant rate.
The slope of this line is	The slope of this line is
(1) zero (3) positive	(1) zero (3) positive
(2) negative (4) undefined	(2) negative (4) undefined

3. Identify the rate of change in the following graph as positive or negative.

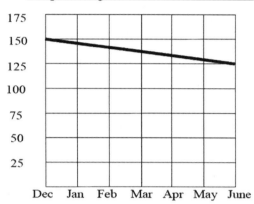

Weight Changes over the Last Six Months

4. Identify the rate of change in the following table as positive or negative.

x	y
0.5	9.0
1	8.75
1.5	8.5
2	8.25
2.5	8.0

5. The following table shows a constant rate of change in distance over time. Is the rate of change positive or negative? Calculate the rate.

Time (hours)	Distance (miles)
4	232
6	348
8	464
10	580

6. In a linear equation, *x* represents the distance that a car travels, in miles, and *y* represents the amount of gas in the car's gas tank, in gallons. As the car travels, is the constant rate of change positive or negative?

10.4 __Average Rate of Change__

KEY TERMS AND CONCEPTS

When we calculated the rate of change for linear functions, we simply calculated the slope of the line. For a linear function, the rate of change is constant because the slope is constant. But not all functions are linear. Nevertheless, we can still find an **average rate of change** between any two points on a curve by calculating the slope of the line through those two points, which is called the **secant line**.

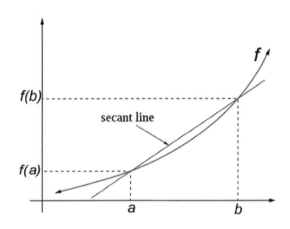

As we know, the formula for the slope of a line through points (x_1, y_1) and (x_2, y_2) is $m = \dfrac{y_2 - y_1}{x_2 - x_1}$. So, using function notation, we could say the average rate of change R over the interval $a \leq x \leq b$ is the slope of the secant line through points $(a, f(a))$ and $(b, f(b))$, which is $R = \dfrac{f(b) - f(a)}{b - a}$. We will use this formula to calculate average rate of change.

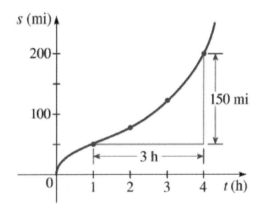

For example, suppose you take a car trip and record the distance that you travel every hour. The graph to the right shows the distance s (in miles) as a function of time t (in hours). If we want to calculate the average rate of change over the interval $1 \leq t \leq 4$, we simply find the slope between the points $(1,50)$ and $(4,200)$. So, the average rate of change (or average speed in this case) is $\dfrac{s(b) - s(a)}{b - a} = \dfrac{200 - 50}{4 - 1} = \dfrac{150}{3} = 50$ mph.

For non-linear functions, the **average rate of change may vary** for different intervals.

Example:　　In the example above, the average rate of change (ie, average speed) over the

interval $2 \leq t \leq 4$ is $\dfrac{200 - 75}{4 - 2} = \dfrac{125}{2} = 62.5$ mph.

MODEL PROBLEM 1:   *FROM A GRAPH OR SET OF POINTS*

A ball is shot straight up in the air from ground level and its height is recorded every 0.5 seconds until it lands 4 seconds later. A graph of the height of the ball over time (in the shape of a parabola) is shown to the right. Find the average rate of change in the ball's height between seconds 2 and 3.

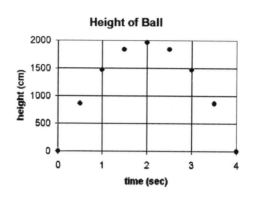

Solution:

(A)   (2,2000) and (3,1500)

(B) $\dfrac{1500 - 2000}{3 - 2} = \dfrac{-500}{1} = -500$ cm/sec

Explanation of steps:

(A)   Find the points at the start and end of the given interval *[at 2 seconds, the height is at its maximum of 2000cm; at 3 seconds, the height is 1500cm].*

(B)   Find the slope of the line between the two points *[a negative slope as it is falling].*

PRACTICE PROBLEMS

1.   From the graph below,

a)   find the average rate of change in the interval $1 \leq x \leq 3$

b)   find the average rate of change in the interval $-1 \leq x \leq 2$

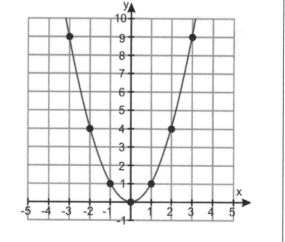

2. The following table shows the average prices of movie tickets over a period of years.

Year	1987	1991	1995	1999	2003	2007	2009
Price ($)	3.91	4.21	4.35	5.06	6.03	6.88	7.50

Determine which interval has the higher average rate of change:

(1) 1987 – 1999   (2) 1999 – 2009

MODEL PROBLEM 2:   *FROM A FUNCTION DEFINITION*

If an object is dropped from a tall building, then the distance it has fallen after t seconds is given by the function $d(t) = 16t^2$. Find its average speed (average rate of change) over the interval between 1 second and 5 seconds.

Solution:

(A) At 1 second, $d(1) = 16(1)^2 = 16$. At 5 seconds, $d(5) = 16(5)^2 = 16 \cdot 25 = 400$.

(B) Slope of the line through points (1,16) and (5,400) is $\dfrac{400 - 16}{5 - 1} = \dfrac{384}{4} = 96$ ft/sec.

Explanation of steps:

(A) Find the points at the start and end of the given interval.

   [Think of each point as the ordered pair of t and d(t). At t = 1, d(t) = 16,
   and at t = 5, d(t) = 400, so the points are (1,16) and (5,400)]

(B) Find the slope of the line between the two points.

PRACTICE PROBLEMS

3. Calculate the average rate of change of a function, $f(x) = x^2 + 2$ as x changes from 5 to 15?	4. Find the average rate of change for the function $f(x) = x^2 + 10x + 16$ over the interval $-3 \leq x \leq 3$.

10.5   **Functions of Time**

KEY TERMS AND CONCEPTS

Distance-Time functions: One of the most common types of graphs shows distance over time. Before being able to create such graphs, one needs to know how to interpret them.

If an object moves at a constant speed (*constant rate of change*) away from a starting base, the graph will show a straight line with a positive slope (*the distance steadily increases as time increases*). If it returns to base at a constant speed, the graph will show a straight line with a negative slope (*the distance is steadily decreasing over time*). If the object is stationary, we would see a horizontal line with a zero slope (*the distance remains the same as time passes*).

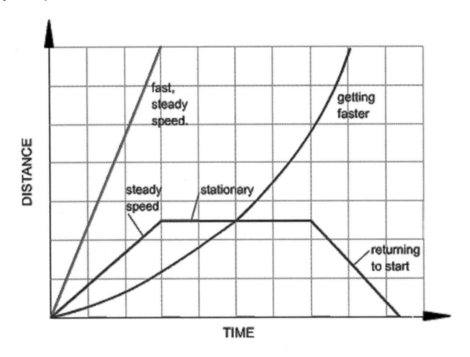

Generally, the horizontal (*x*, or often *t*) axis represents the amount of time passed. A negative value of time would be impossible, so the *domain* of the function is restricted to non-negative values. The vertical (*y*, or often *d*) axis represents the distance from a starting location. A measure of distance, and thus the *range* of the function, is also limited to non-negative values.

Speed-Time functions: Another type of graph shows an object's speed (or *velocity*) over time. In these graphs, the *y* axis represents the object's velocity, not its distance.

Example: The graph below shows the speed of a sprinter in a race. From a standstill (*zero velocity*) at the start of the race, the runner increases his speed (*accelerates*) until he reaches his maximum speed of 12.5 m/s about 4 seconds into the race. He continues to run at this same speed for more than four seconds before he slows down (*decelerates*) near the finish line.

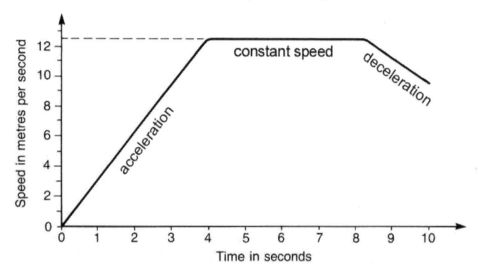

The slopes in this type of graph need to be interpreted differently than in a distance-time graph:

Feature of Graph	Distance-Time Graph	Speed-Time Graph
line with positive slope	constant speed (away from base)	steadily increasing speed
horizontal line (0 slope)	standing still	constant speed
line with negative slope	constant speed (back to base)	steadily decreasing speed

A **piecewise linear function** is one whose graph is made up of multiple line segments, like the one shown above. Some of the examples in this section will involve these types of graphs.

303

MODEL PROBLEM

A car travels away from its starting location at a constant rate of 2 km every 5 minutes for 15 minutes. The car stops and remains idle for the next 20 minutes. It then continues in the same direction at a constant rate of 1 km every 5 minutes for the next 10 minutes. Graph this event on a distance-time graph.

Solution:

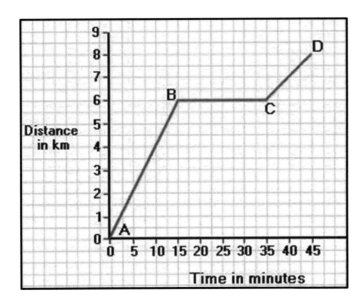

Explanation of steps:

(A)   The *y*-intercept of the graph is the distance at the start time *[we can consider the starting location as a distance of zero].*

(B)   An object moving at a constant rate will show as a straight line. The slope can be determined by moving up (the rise) by a certain distance *[2 km]* and to the right (the run) by a certain amount of time *[5 minutes].*

(C)   A stationary object will not change its distance (*y* stays the same), but time will pass (*x* increases), resulting in a horizontal line
      [15 + 20 mins = 35 mins].

(D)   If the distance increases at a slower rate, the line will have a smaller slope *[rise of 1 km and run of 5 minutes].*

PRACTICE PROBLEMS

1. A caterpillar travels up a tree, from the ground, over a 3-minute interval. It travels fast at first and then slows down. It stops for a minute, then proceeds slowly, speeding up as it goes. Which sketch best illustrates the caterpillar's distance (*d*) from the ground over the 3-minute interval (*t*)?

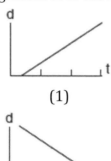

(1)

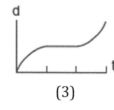

(3)

(2)

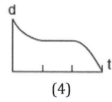

(4)

2. John walked 3 blocks from home to his school, as shown in the graph below.

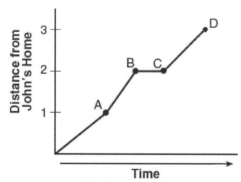

Which of the following may have happened between points B and C of the graph?

(1) John arrived at school and stayed throughout the day.

(2) John waited before crossing a busy street.

(3) John returned home to get his mathematics homework.

(4) John reached the top of a hill and began walking on level ground.

3. Rover's electronic water dish measures and records the amount of water in his dish over a period of time, as shown by the graph below.

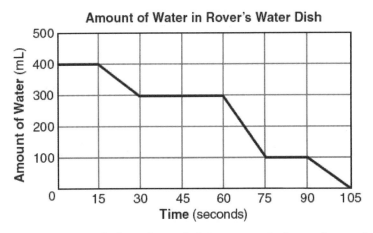

According to the graph, how long did Rover wait from the end of his first drink to the start of his second drink of water?

4. Tom went to the grocery store. The graph below shows Tom's distance from home during his trip. Tom stopped twice to rest on his trip to the store. What is the total amount of time, in minutes, that he spent resting?

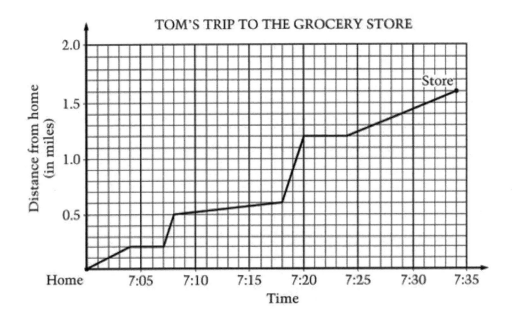

5. Marie works as a doctor at a suburban hospital that is 20 miles from her home. The graph below depicts one of her morning commutes from home to work.

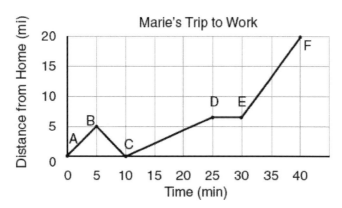

a) Marie left some patients' files at home and had to return home to get them. Which point represents when she turned back around to go home?

b) Marie also had to wait at railroad tracks for a train to pass. How long did she wait?

6. Spencer and McKenna are on a long-distance bicycle ride. Spencer leaves one hour before McKenna. The graph below shows each rider's distance in miles from his or her house as a function of time since McKenna left to catch up with Spencer.

a) Which function represents Spencer's distance? Which function represents McKenna's distance?

b) One rider is speeding up as time passes and the other one is slowing down. Which one is which, and how can you tell from the graphs?

c) Estimate when McKenna catches up to Spencer. How far have they traveled at that point in time?

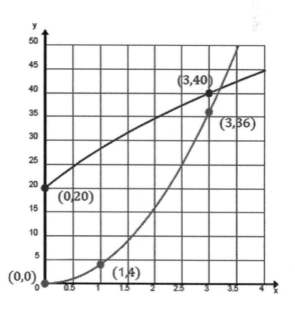

7. The graph below shows distance versus time for a race between runners *A* and *B*. The race is already in progress, and the graph shows only the portion of the race that occurred after 11 A.M. The table below lists several characteristics of the graph. Interpret these characteristics in terms of what happened during this portion of the race. Include times and distances to support your interpretation. (*A sample response is given in the table.*)

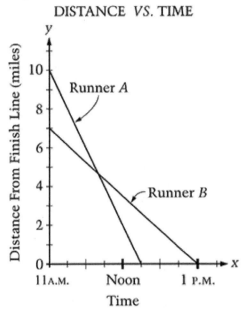

DISTANCE *VS.* TIME

Characteristic of Graph	Interpretation in Terms of the Race
y-intercepts	At 11 A.M. Runner *A* is 10 miles from the finish line and Runner *B* is 7 miles from the finish line.
Slopes	
Point of intersection	
x-intercepts	

10.6 Systems of Functions

KEY TERMS AND CONCEPTS

We can solve a system of functions graphically, by graphing both functions and finding their point of intersection. Or, we can solve the system algebraically, as follows.

We have seen that, if given two equations, such as $y = 3x - 5$ and $y = -x + 11$, we can solve the system of equations by *substitution*. We start by writing the new equation $3x - 5 = -x + 11$. We can then solve for x, and substitute this value of x into either of the original equations to find the corresponding value for y.

Note that in the example above, since y is already the isolated variable on the left sides of both equations, we can set the two expressions of x equal to each other, since they are both equal to y. This is known as the **transitive property of equality:** if $a = b$ and $b = c$, then $a = c$.

Similarly, if we have two functions of x, we can also determine when their values are the same by setting their expressions equal to each other and solving for the variable x.

Example: If $f(x) = 3x - 5$ and $g(x) = -x + 11$, then to determine when $f(x) = g(x)$, we set $3x - 5 = -x + 11$ and solve for x. Solving gives us $x = 4$.

Note that when we set two functions of x equal to each other, as in $f(x) = g(x)$, there are no y variables in the resulting equation. Therefore, the solutions to $f(x) = g(x)$ are the x-values at the points of intersection.

MODEL PROBLEM

Congress is considering two possible income tax plans for citizens. In the *flat* tax plan, citizens pay 30% of their entire income. In the *graduated* tax plan, citizens pay no taxes on the first $15,000 income but pay 35% of any income above $15,000. In function notation. write $f(x)$ to represent the taxes paid in the flat tax plan for an income of x, and write $g(x)$ to represent the taxes paid in the graduated tax plan for an income of x. Determine the amount of income x for which a citizen would pay the same amount in taxes under both plans.

Solution:

(A) $f(x) = 0.30x$

　　　$g(x) = 0.35(x - 15000)$

　　　　　$= 0.35x - 5250$

(B) $0.30x = 0.35x - 5250$

　　　$-0.05x = -5250$

　　　　　　$x = 105{,}000$

　　　Income of $105,000

Explanation of steps:

(A) Write the functions using the given information, simplifying if possible.

(B) Set the function expressions equal to each other and solve for the variable.

PRACTICE PROBLEMS

1. Two health clubs, Club *A* and Club *B*, offer different membership plans. The cost for each plan includes a membership fee plus a monthly charge. The graph below represents the total membership costs of the two plans for one year.

a) What is the membership fee for Club *A*?

b) What is the number of the month when the total cost is the same for both clubs, and what is the total cost for each club at that time?

c) What is the monthly charge for Club *B*?

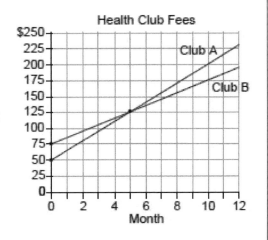

2. Both Tasha and her brother Tyson get an allowance of $5 each week. Tasha currently has $60 and decides to save her entire allowance each week. Tyson currently has $135 but spends all of his allowance plus an additional $10 each week. After how many weeks will they have the same amount of money?

3. A company produces and sells widgets. The company earns $25 for each widget sold, but it costs $20 per widget plus an annual fixed cost of $50,000 to produce them.

a) In function notation, write $R(x)$ for the revenue earned by selling x widgets.

b) In function notation, write $C(x)$ for the annual cost of producing x widgets.

c) How many widgets need to be sold in a year to "break even" (that is, to have the cost equal to the revenue)?

4. Michael is trying to decide between two plumbing companies to fix his sink. The first company, Flow-Rite, charges $50 for a service call, plus an additional $36 per hour of labor. The second company, Gunk-Gone, charges $35 for a service call, plus an additional $39 per hour of labor. Let h represent the number of hours of labor.

a) Write a rule for the function $f(h)$, which gives the cost of using Flow-Rite.

b) Write a rule for the function $g(h)$, which gives the cost of using Gunk-Gone.

c) At how many hours will the two companies charge the same amount of money?

10.7 **Combine Functions**

KEY TERMS AND CONCEPTS

We can perform **operations on functions**. For examples, we can define a function to be the sum, difference, product, or quotient of other functions.

Example: If $f(x) = x + 1$ and $g(x) = x - 2$, then we can find $h(x) = f(x) + g(x)$ by adding $(x + 1) + (x - 2) = 2x - 1$, so $h(x) = 2x - 1$.

We can check for any value of x. If $x = 5$, then $f(5) = 5 + 1 = 6$ and $g(5) = 5 - 2 = 3$, so $f(5) + g(5) = 6 + 3 = 9$. Also, $h(5) = 2(5) - 1 = 9$.

It is also common to use the following notation for combining functions:

$$(f + g)(x) = f(x) + g(x) \qquad\qquad (f - g)(x) = f(x) - g(x)$$

$$(fg)(x) = f(x)g(x) \qquad\qquad \left(\frac{f}{g}\right)(x) = \frac{f(x)}{g(x)} \text{ where } g(x) \neq 0$$

MODEL PROBLEM

If $f(x) = x^2 + 5$ and $g(x) = 2x - 1$, find $h(x) = f(x) - g(x)$. Find $h(-3)$.

Solution:

$$h(x) = f(x) - g(x)$$
(A) $= (x^2 + 5) - (2x - 1)$
(B) $= x^2 + 5 - 2x + 1$
$$h(x) = x^2 - 2x + 6$$
(C) $h(-3) = (-3)^2 - 2(-3) + 6$
$$= 9 + 6 + 6 = 21$$

Explanation of steps:

(A)   Substitute the rule for each function, using parentheses around each expression.

(B)   Simplify and express the resulting function rule in standard form.

(C)   To evaluate a function for a given value, substitute the value for the variable.
[To check, $h(-3)$ should equal
$f(-3) - g(-3) =$
$[(-3)^2 + 5] - [2(-3) - 1] =$
$14 - (-7) = 21.]$

PRACTICE PROBLEMS

1. If $f(x) = x^2 + x + 1$ and $g(x) = x - 5$, find $h(x) = f(x) + g(x)$.	2. If $f(x) = 2x + 1$ and $g(x) = x - 2$, find $h(x) = f(x) \cdot g(x)$.

3. To raise funds, a club is publishing and selling a calendar. The club has sold $500 in advertising and will sell copies of the calendar for $20 each. The cost of printing each calendar is $6. Let c be the number of calendars to be printed and sold.

a) Write a rule for the function $R(c)$, which gives the revenue generated.

b) Write a rule for the function $E(c)$, which gives the printing expenses.

c) Describe how the function $P(c)$, which gives the club's profit, is related to $R(c)$ and $E(c)$, and write a rule for $P(c)$.

Chapter 11. Exponential Functions

11.1 Exponential Growth and Decay

KEY TERMS AND CONCEPTS

When an amount is **increased** by a certain percent, r (for *rate*), we can calculate the new value by multiplying the original amount by $1 + r$, since $1 = 100\%$.

Example: A $50 investment increases by 4%. To calculate the new value,

$$50(1 + 0.04) = 50(1.04) = \$52.$$

Similarly, if an amount is **decreased** by a rate of r, we can multiply the amount by $1 - r$ to find the new value, since $1 = 100\%$.

Example: A $50 investment loses 6% of its value. It is now worth

$$50(1 - 0.06) = 50(0.94) = \$47.$$

A 6% loss results in a new amount that is 94% of the original amount.

Often, an increase or decrease is calculated in regular intervals of time. This represents **exponential growth** (increase) or **exponential decay** (decrease).

An example of exponential growth is **compound interest**.

Example: Suppose a $2,000 investment (principal) is invested in an account which earns 5% interest compounded annually over 4 years. This is represented by

$$2000(1.05)(1.05)(1.05)(1.05) = 2000(1.05)^4.$$

Exponential decay can be used to calculate **depreciation**, which is a decrease in an asset's value over time.

Example: Suppose an industrial machine originally purchased for $50,000 loses 10% of its value every year for 5 years. This is represented by

$$50000(0.90)(0.90)(0.90)(0.90)(0.90) = 50000(0.90)^5.$$

The opposite of depreciation is **appreciation**, or the increase in an asset's value over time.

The **formula for exponential growth** is $y = a(1 + r)^x$, where a is the original amount, r is the constant rate of *increase*, x is the number of times the rate is applied, and y is the final amount. The **formula for exponential decay** is $y = a(1 - r)^x$ where r is the constant rate of *decrease*.

If we set b to the growth $(1 + r)$ or decay $(1 - r)$ factor, we can build a **general formula for exponential growth or decay**: $y = ab^x$ where $a > 0, b > 0, b \neq 1$. The formula represents *growth* when $b > 1$ or *decay* when $0 < b < 1$. The variable x is usually given in units of time.

This can also be written in *function notation*; for example, $f(x) = ab^x$.

MODEL PROBLEM

The principal of a school predicts that enrollment at her school will increase by 15% each year for the next 4 years. If the current enrollment is 400 students, what would the enrollment be after the fourth year, *to the nearest whole number*, if the principal's predictions are true?

Solution:

    (A)   (B)

$$y = 400(1.15)^4 = 699.6025 \approx 700$$

Explanation of steps:

(A)   Use the formula $y = ab^x$, where a is the original amount *[400]*, b is the growth factor *[115% or 1.15]*, and x is the number of times the rate is applied *[4, once each year]*.

(B)   Use your calculator to find the result, rounding as directed.

PRACTICE PROBLEMS

1. If x is the starting value before an exponential growth of 10% per day, write an expression for the value after 20 days.	2. If x is the starting value before an exponential decay of 2% per day, write an expression for the value after n days.
3. $2,500 is invested in a savings account that earns 3% interest compounded annually. Write an expression for the number of dollars in this account at the end of 4 years.	4. The current population of a town is 10,000. If the population increases by 20% each year, write an expression for population after t years?
5. If you invest $1500 in an account that pays 5% interest compounded annually, and you make no deposits or withdrawals on the account in 6 years, how much money do you have, to the *nearest cent*, at the end of 6 years?	6. If you invest $1000 in an account that pays 3% interest compounded annually, and you make no deposits or withdrawals on the account, how much money do you have, to the *nearest cent*, at the end of 5 years?

7. $2000 is invested in an account at a 3.5% interest rate compounded annually. No deposits or withdrawals are made on the account for 4 years. Determine, to the *nearest dollar*, the balance in the account after the 4 years.

8. A school raised $30,000 for an athletics fund. Each year the fund will decrease by 5%. Determine the amount of money, to the *nearest cent*, that will be left in the fund after 4 years.

9. A mouse population is 25,000 and is decreasing at a rate of 20% per year. What is the population after 3 years?

10. The population of Jacksonville is 3,810 and is growing at an annual rate of 3.5%. If this growth rate continues, what will be the approximate population in five years?

11. The value of a car purchased for $20,000 decreases at a rate of 12% per year. What will be the value of the car after 3 years?

12. A used car is purchased in July 2019 for $11,900. If the car depreciates (loses) 13% of its value each year, what is the value of the car, to the nearest hundred dollars, in July 2022?

13. On January 1, 2000, the price of gasoline was $1.39 per gallon. If the price increased by 0.5% per month, what was the cost of one gallon of gasoline, to the nearest cent, on January 1, 2001?

14. In a certain game tournament, 75% of the players are eliminated each round. If the tournament starts with 256 players, how many remain after three rounds?

11.2   **Graphs of Exponential Functions**

KEY TERMS AND CONCEPTS

An **exponential function** is a function in which x appears as an exponent in the equation.
For this course, equations are limited to $f(x) = ab^x$ where $a \neq 0$, $b > 0$, and $b \neq 1$.
Examples: $f(x) = 5^x$ or $g(x) = -3(0.5)^x$

An exponential function can be graphed using a table or a graphing calculator.
Example: We can graph $f(x) = 2^x$ as follows, using $y = f(x)$.

x	2^x	$y = f(x)$	(x, y)
-1	2^{-1}	$\frac{1}{2}$	$\left(-1, \frac{1}{2}\right)$
0	2^0	1	$(0,1)$
1	2^1	2	$(1,2)$
2	2^2	4	$(2,4)$
3	2^3	8	$(3,8)$

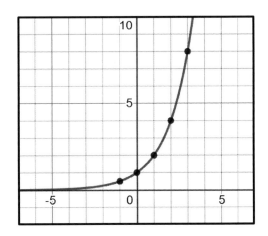

▦◨   **CALCULATOR TIP**

To graph $y = 2^x$ on the calculator:

Press $\boxed{\text{Y=}}\boxed{2}\boxed{\wedge}\boxed{\text{X,T,Θ,}n}\boxed{\text{GRAPH}}$

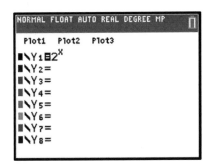

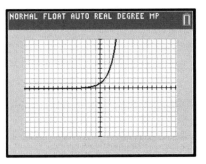

320

The behavior of the graph of an exponential function $f(x) = ab^x$ will depend on the values of a and b:

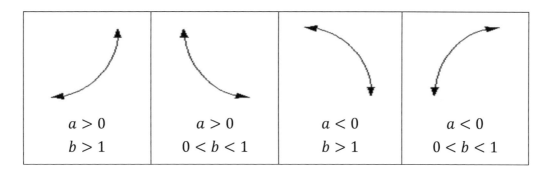

$a > 0$	$a > 0$	$a < 0$	$a < 0$
$b > 1$	$0 < b < 1$	$b > 1$	$0 < b < 1$

Example: The graph of the function $y = \left(\frac{1}{2}\right)^x$ looks like this.

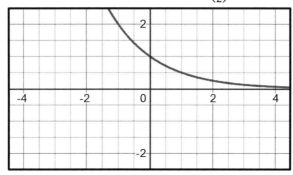

In general, $y = b^x$ will **increase** over the entire domain when $b > 1$ or **decrease** over the entire domain when $0 < b < 1$.

In the function $y = ab^x$, the **constant a** will tell us where the curve crosses the y-axis. Therefore, a is the y-intercept. (To find the y-intercept, substitute 0 for x; $b^0 = 1$.)

Example: For the function $y = 100 \left(\frac{1}{2}\right)^x$, where $a = 100$ and $b = \frac{1}{2}$, the graph would intersect the y-axis at $(0,100)$, as shown below.

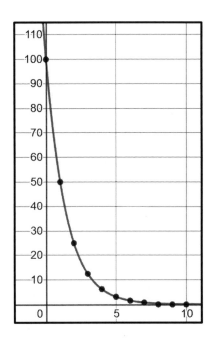

An exponential function $y = ab^x$ will **never actually touch** (intersect) the x-axis. Neither a nor b is equal to zero, so ab^x (and therefore y) will never equal zero.

When **a is negative**, the graph of $y = ab^x$ is negative over the entire domain.

Example: The graph of $y = -3^x$ will look like the graph of $y = 3^x$ but **reflected** (flipped) over the x-axis.

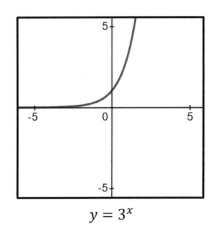

$y = 3^x$

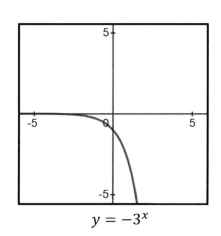

$y = -3^x$

Exponential functions may be used to represent **exponential growth** and **exponential decay**. In these special cases, the equation $y = ab^x$ is limited to $a > 0$.

- When $b > 1$, the function shows **exponential growth**.
- When $0 < b < 1$, the function shows **exponential decay**.

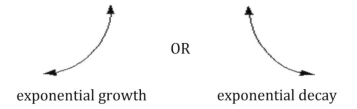

exponential growth   exponential decay

In these cases, the y-intercept, a, represents the starting value at time $x = 0$. The value of b equals 1 plus or minus the percent of change at each of the x intervals of time.

Example: The function $y = 1000(1.05)^x$ represents the value of a bank account that is compounded annually for x years. The y-intercept (or starting value, a) is $1000, while $b = 1.05$ shows an exponential growth (interest) of 5% per year.

Finding the equation from a set of points:

If given a table or graph of a exponential function, you can use the calculator to find the equation. After entering the coordinates of the points, calculate the **exponential regression**. The exponential regression is just like a linear regression, except that it finds the *exponential* equation that best fits the set of points. The calculator instructions are given below.

Note that the exponential regression can only be calculated for a function that is always *positive* (that is, when $a > 0$). However, for a function with all negative y values, you can enter their additive inverses (positive values of y that produce a reflection of the function over the x-axis) and then negate the a that is found by the regression.

CALCULATOR TIP

Using the calculator to find the equation for an exponential function:

1. Enter the x and y coordinates of the points as L1 and L2.

2. Press [STAT] [CALC] [0] for ExpReg.

3. On the next screen prompt, make sure L1 and L2 are selected for Xlist and Ylist.

   Next to Store RegEQ, enter [ALPHA][F4][1] to store the equation in Y1.

   [On the TI-83, you'll see an ExpReg prompt instead. Enter [VARS] Y-VARS [1][1].]

4. The screen will show the equation y=a*b^x along with the values of a and b.

5. To view the graph, press [GRAPH].

6. To see the equation, press [Y=].

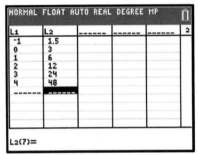
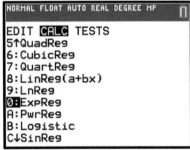
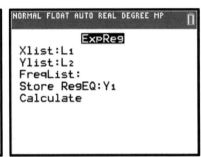

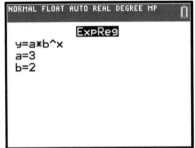
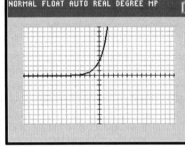
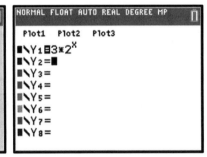

MODEL PROBLEM 1:   *GRAPH AN EXPONENTIAL FUNCTION*

Graph the function $y = \frac{3}{2} \cdot 2^x$.

Solution:

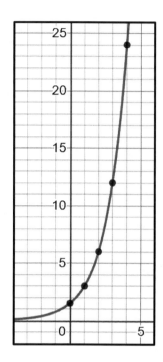

(A) x	(B) $\frac{3}{2} \cdot 2^x$	(C) y	(D) (x, y)
0	$\frac{3}{2} \cdot 2^0 = \frac{3}{2} \cdot 1$	1.5	(0,1.5)
1	$\frac{3}{2} \cdot 2^1 = \frac{3}{2} \cdot 2$	3	(1,3)
2	$\frac{3}{2} \cdot 2^2 = \frac{3}{2} \cdot 4$	6	(2,6)
3	$\frac{3}{2} \cdot 2^3 = \frac{3}{2} \cdot 8$	12	(3,12)
4	$\frac{3}{2} \cdot 2^4 = \frac{3}{2} \cdot 16$	24	(4,24)

Explanation of steps:

(A)   Pick values of x.

(B)   Substitute the values of x into the expression.

(C)   Evaluate for y.

(D)   Plot the resulting points on the graph.

PRACTICE PROBLEMS

1. Which graph may represent the exponential decay of a radioactive element?

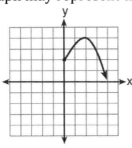

(1)

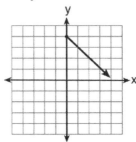

(3)

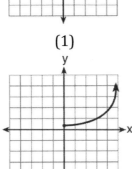

(2)

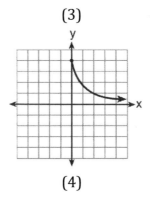

(4)

2. On the grid below, graph $y = 2^x$ over the interval $-1 \leq x \leq 3$.

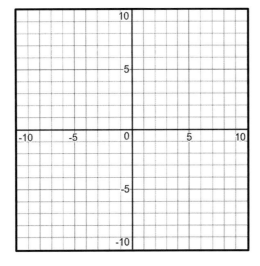

3. On the grid below, graph $y = 3^x$ over the interval $-1 \leq x \leq 2$.

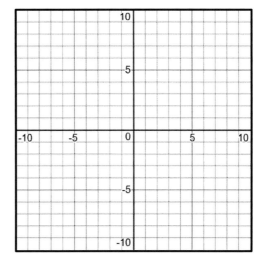

4. On the calculator, graph $y = \frac{1}{3} \cdot 2^x$.
   Sketch the graph below.

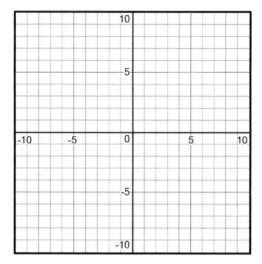

5. On the calculator, graph $y = 3 \cdot \left(\frac{1}{2}\right)^x$.
   Sketch the graph below.

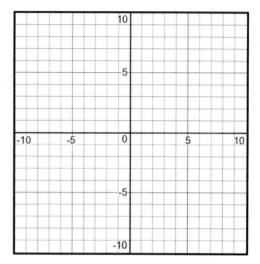

6. On the calculator, graph $y = 12(1.5)^x$.
   Sketch the graph below.

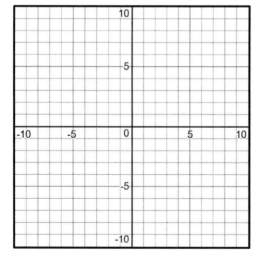

7. On the calculator, graph $y = 12(0.5)^x$.
   Sketch the graph below.

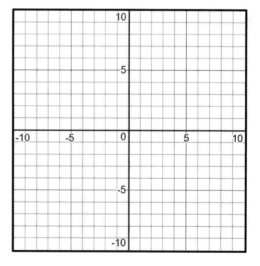

8.   On the grid below, graph $y = -2^x$.

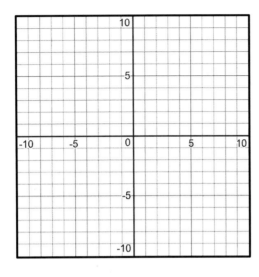

9.   On the grid below, graph $y = 2^x - 5$ and explain how this graph differs from the exponential function $y = 2^x$.

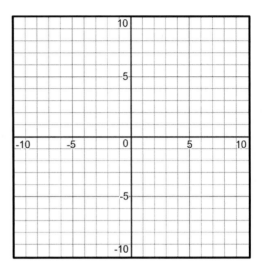

MODEL PROBLEM 2:   *DETERMINE THE EQUATION*

Write an equation for the exponential function using the values given in the table below.

x	1	2	3	4	5
y	0.75	2.25	6.75	20.25	60.75

Solution:

$$y = 0.25(3)^x$$

Explanation of steps:

On the calculator, press $\boxed{\text{STAT}}\boxed{1}$ to enter the values as L1 and L2, then use $\boxed{\text{STAT}}\boxed{\text{CALC}}\boxed{0}$ for ExpReg to determine the equation. *[a = 0.25 and b = 3]*

PRACTICE PROBLEMS

10. Write an equation for the exponential function using values given in the table below.

x	0	1	2	3	4
y	0.1	0.4	1.6	6.4	25.6

11. Write an equation for the exponential function graphed below.

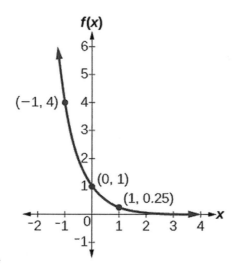

12. A spectrophotometer measures the concentration of ozone in the atmosphere at different altitudes, as shown by the table below. Write the exponential regression equation that models these data, rounding all values to the *nearest thousandth*.

Concentration of Ozone

Altitude (x)	Ozone Units (y)
0	0.7
5	0.6
10	1.1
15	3.0
20	4.9

13. The amount of radioactive substance decreases over times as a result of radioactive decay. The table below shows the amount of a certain radiactive substance remaining for selected years after 1990.

Years After 1990 (x)	0	2	5	9	14	17	19
Amount (y)	750	451	219	84	25	12	8

a) Write an exponential regression equation for this set of data, rounding all values to the *nearest thousandth*.

b) Using this equation, determine the amount of the substance that remained in 2002, to the *nearest integer*.

14. When a piece of paper is folded in half, the total thickness doubles. An unfolded piece of paper is 0.1 millimeter thick.

a) Write an equation for the total thickness, t, as an exponential function of the number of folds, n.

b) Graph the function for a discrete domain of whole numbers, $0 \leq n \leq 8$.

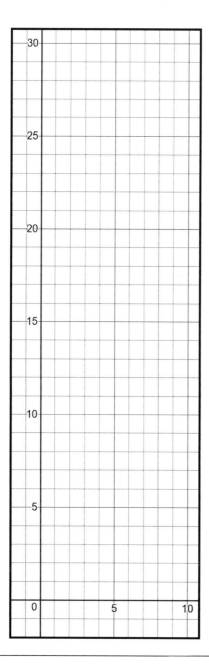

15. A ball is dropped from an initial height of 30 inches. On its first bounce, the ball reaches a height of 15 inches. On the second bounce, the ball reaches a height of 7.5 inches.

a) Write an equation for the height of the ball, h, as an exponential function of the number of bounces, n.

b) Graph the function for a discrete domain of whole numbers, $0 \leq n \leq 6$.

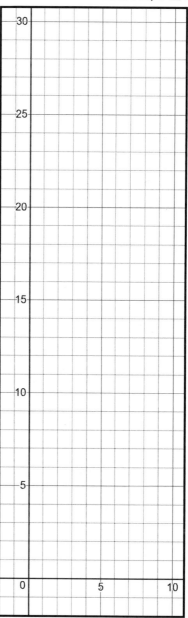

16. The average salary of baseball players in 1984 was $290,000. The table below shows the players' average salary over the following nine years.

Baseball Players' Salaries

Numbers of Years Since 1984	Average Salary (thousands of dollars)
0	290
1	320
2	400
3	495
4	600
5	700
6	820
7	1,000
8	1,250
9	1,580

a) Using this data, create a scatter plot on the grid below.

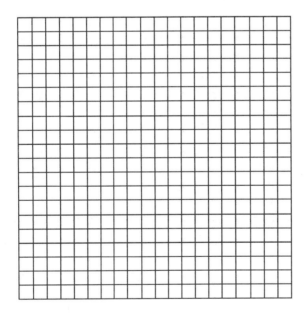

b) State the exponential regression equation with all values rounded to the *nearest hundredth*.

c) Using this equation, estimate the salary of a baseball player in the year 2005, to the *nearest thousand dollars*.

11.3 **Rewrite Exponential Expressions**

KEY TERMS AND CONCEPTS

It may help to use the properties of exponents to rewrite expressions for exponential functions.

Examples: $f(x) = 2^{3x}$ can be rewritten as $f(x) = 8^x$ since $2^{3x} = (2^3)^x$.

$g(x) = 3^{x+2}$ can be rewritten as $g(x) = 9(3)^x$ since $3^{x+2} = (3^x)(3^2)$.

CALCULATOR TIP

We can use the calculator to check whether two expressions appear to be equivalent by using an arbitrary value of the variable and testing the equality of the two expressions. Although this method doesn't confirm that the expressions are equivalent for *all* values, it can help us recognize a likely error if they are not equal for the arbitrary value.

1. Store an arbitrary, preferably non-integer, value into x. For example, we can store 12.3 into x by pressing 1 2 . 3 STO▶ X,T,Θ,n.

2. Now, test whether the two expressions are equal using 2nd [TEST] 1 for the equal sign. A result of 1 means they are equal, or a result of 0 means they are not.

Example: The screenshots below show how to test whether $3^{x+2} = 9(3^x)$.

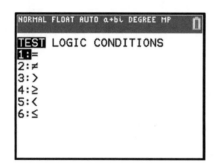
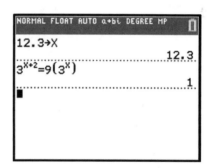

MODEL PROBLEM

If $f(x) = 2(0.5)^{3x}$, which of the following is an equivalent function?

     (1) $g(x) = 8(0.125)^x$ (3) $g(x) = 2(0.125)^x$

     (2) $g(x) = 6(1.5)^x$ (4) $g(x) = 2(1.5)^x$

Solution: (3)

Explanation of steps:

Only the quantity in parentheses *[(0.5)]* is being raised to a power. We can simplify by evaluating this quantity raised to the exponent's coefficient.

[$2(0.5)^{3x} = 2(0.5^3)^x = 2(0.125)^x$]

PRACTICE PROBLEMS

1. Rewrite 5^{2x} as an equivalent expression with only x as the exponent.	2. Rewrite $10(1.1)^{5x}$ as an equivalent expression with only x as the exponent.
3. Rewrite 2^{3x+2} as an equivalent expression with only x as the exponent.	4. Rewrite $4(3)^{x+1}$ as an equivalent expression with only x as the exponent.

11.4 **Compare Linear and Exponential Functions**

KEY TERMS AND CONCEPTS

Using our knowledge about sequences, we can predict whether a continuous function is *linear* or *exponential* before we even graph the function. First, create a table using *equally spaced* values of the domain. Then look at the values of the function. If we can **add** a constant (a *common difference*) to each value to get the next value, the function is **linear**. If we can **multiply** each value by a constant (a *common ratio*) to get the next value, the function is **exponential**.

Example: Compare the tables of the two functions, $f(n) = 2n$ and $f(n) = 2^n$.

We will use values of n that are evenly spaced at 1 unit apart, from -2 to 3.

n	$f(n) = 2n$
-2	-4
-1	-2
0	0
1	2
2	4
3	6

Add 2

n	$f(n) = 2^n$
-2	$\frac{1}{4}$
-1	$\frac{1}{2}$
0	1
1	2
2	4
3	8

Multiply by 2

In the first table, we can add a constant, 2, to get the next function value, so this function is linear. In the second table, we can multiply each function value by 2 to get the next value, so the function is exponential. The graph of the two functions, below, confirms our findings by their shapes:

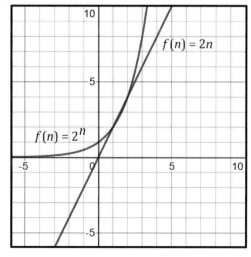

An exponential growth function $g(x)$ will *always eventually exceed* any linear function $f(x)$. That is, x will eventually reach a value k for which $g(x) > f(x)$ for all $x > k$. We can find the value of k by graphing both functions on the calculator and determining the x-value at the rightmost point of intersection.

In fact, an exponential growth function will *always eventually exceed* any polynomial function, such as quadratic functions (with an x^2 term), cubic functions (with an x^3 term), etc. We will learn more about quadratic and cubic functions later in this course.

CALCULATOR TIP

Use the calculator to find the *rightmost point of intersection* of two functions:

1. Press Y= and enter both equations.
2. Press 2nd CALC 5 for intersect .
3. Press ENTER for the "First curve?" and "Second curve?" prompts.
4. For the "Guess?" prompt, use the arrow keys to move the cursor near the rightmost point of intersection. Then press ENTER.
5. The coordinates of the point of intersection will be shown.

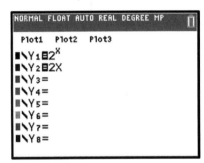
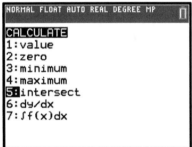
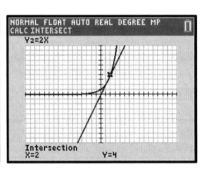

MODEL PROBLEM

Determine whether the function below is linear, exponential, or neither.

x	0	1	2	3	4
y	96	48	24	12	6

Solution:

exponential

Explanation:

For a table with equally spaced values of x:

a) if the same value is *added* to each y-value to get the next y, the function is linear *[we would need to add $-48, -24, -12,$ and -6, so it is not linear]*.

b) if each y-value is *multiplied* by the same value to get the next y, the function is exponential *[each y-value is multiplied by $\frac{1}{2}$ throughout, so it is exponential]*.

c) otherwise, the function is neither.

PRACTICE PROBLEMS

1. Identify each function as linear, exponential, or neither.

a)

x	−3	−2	−1	0	1	2	3
y	14	10	6	2	−2	−6	−10

b)

x	−3	−2	−1	0	1	2	3
y	$\frac{1}{9}$	$\frac{1}{3}$	1	3	9	27	81

c)

x	−3	−2	−1	0	1	2	3
y	$\frac{1}{2}$	1	2	4	8	16	32

d)

x	−3	−2	−1	0	1	2	3
y	−27	−9	−3	0	3	9	27

2. A tile pattern is shown below. Create an explicit formula that could be used to determine the number of squares in the nth figure.

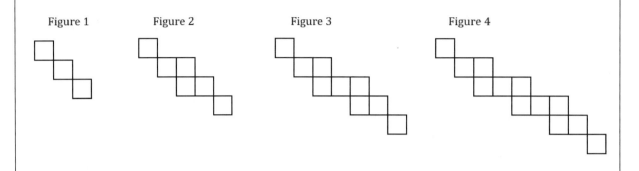

Figure 1   Figure 2   Figure 3   Figure 4

3. A tile pattern is shown below. Create an explicit formula that could be used to determine the number of black triangles in the nth figure.

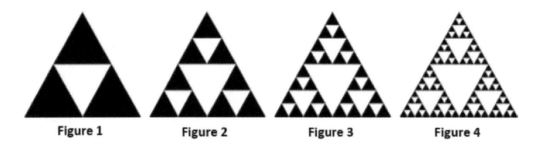

Figure 1   Figure 2   Figure 3   Figure 4

Chapter 12. Sequences

12.1 <u>Arithmetic Sequences</u>

KEY TERMS AND CONCEPTS

A **sequence** is an ordered list of numbers, called terms. If we let the integer n represent the term number in the sequence, then a_n represents the nth term in the sequence. Unless otherwise specified, you can assume that the sequence is an **infinite sequence**, meaning that the values of n are the set of all counting numbers (or sometimes, whole numbers).

Examples: 9, 11, 13, 15, ...

$$a_1, a_2, a_3, a_4, ...$$

An **explicit formula** describes how to calculate each term (a_n) based on its term number (n). The formula allows us to determine the value of a specified term. By substituting the term number for n, we can evaluate the formula just as we would for any function.

Examples: The formula for the sequence above is $a_n = 2n + 7$. We can calculate the value of any term using this formula by substituting for n; for example, to calculate what the fourth term is, $a_4 = 2(4) + 7 = 15$.

An **arithmetic sequence** is one in which each term is obtained by *adding* the same number (called the **common difference**, represented by d) to the preceding term.

Example: 9, 11, 13, 15, ...

         +2 +2 +2   so, $d = 2$

We can find the common difference of an arithmetic sequence by subtracting consecutive terms, such as $a_2 - a_1$ or $a_3 - a_2$. In general, the common difference $d = a_n - a_{n-1}$.

We can define an arithmetic sequence using the formula $a_n = a_1 + (n-1)d$ where a_1 is the first term and d is the common difference.

Example: The sequence 9, 11, 13, 15, ... can be written as $a_n = 9 + (n-1) \cdot 2$. By distributing the d and combining terms, we can simplify the formula:

$$a_n = 9 + (n-1) \cdot 2$$
$$a_n = 9 + 2n - 2$$
$$a_n = 2n + 7$$

339

An *arithmetic sequence* is always a **linear** function. The common difference, d, is its *slope*.

Example: For the arithmetic sequence 9, 11, 13, 15, ..., $a_1 = 9$ and $d = 2$, so we can define the sequence by substituting for a_1 and d in $a_n = a_1 + (n-1)d$, giving us $a_n = 9 + (n-1) \cdot 2$. By simplifying, $a_n = 2n + 7$.

The arithmetic sequence is graphed below. Since the function is discrete, the graph consists of isolated points, not a continuous line.

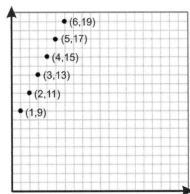

n	$a_n = 2n + 7$
1	9
2	11
3	13
4	15
5	17
6	19

As can be seen by the table, we can **add** d (the slope) to each term to obtain the next term. In this graph, the set of points that make up the discrete function lie on a straight line.

A *linear regression* of these points, using the domain of real numbers x, would have an equation of $y = 2x + 7$, representing the continuous function, $f(x) = 2x + 7$.

We can write sequence definitions in *function notation*.

Example: $a_n = 2n + 7$ can be written in function notation, such as $a(n) = 2n + 7$. Each point can also be rewritten in function notation; for example, $a_1 = 9$ can be written as $a(1) = 9$.

To find a specific term of an arithmetic sequence:
1. Determine a_1 (the first term) and d (the common difference) from the given terms.
2. In the general formula for arithmetic sequences, substitute for n, a_1, and d, and evaluate.

Example: To find the 20th term of the arithmetic sequence 32, 37, 42, 47, ...

The general formula is $a_n = a_1 + (n-1)d$ and in this case, $a_1 = 32$, $d = 5$, and $n = 20$, so $a_{20} = 32 + (20-1)(5) = 127$.

▒▒▒□ CALCULATOR TIP

If the formula for an arithmetic sequence is known, the calculator can also be used to find the value of any terms.

1. Press [2nd][LIST][5] for the seq function.
2. On the TI-84 models with Stat Wizards turned on (in the [MODE] screen), you'll be prompted to enter the formula, the variable used in the formula, the starting and ending term numbers to display, and a step of 1 (see center screenshot below).

   Then press [ENTER] twice to Paste and display the result.
   [On the TI-83, this screen is skipped, so you will need to type these directly within the parentheses of the seq function, separated by commas, and then press [ENTER].]

Example: To display the 25th term of the sequence $a_n = 2n + 7$, follow the above steps, as shown below. The variable X is used for convenience, but N could be used instead. Just be sure the variable used in the expression (Expr) is the same variable named on the next line. The display shows that 57 is the 25th term.

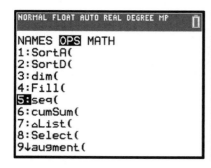  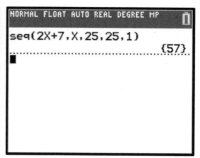

Because the common difference, d, is also the slope of the linear function, we can use the slope formula to calculate d given any two terms.

To write the formula for an arithmetic sequence given two terms:
1. Express the two terms as points. Find d, which is the slope of the line through these points, using the slope formula.
2. Substitute d, as well as n and a_n from one of the terms, into the general formula for an arithmetic sequence. Solve for a_1.
3. Write the general formula, substituting known values for a_1 and d, and simplify.

Example: To write a formula for the arithmetic sequence where $a_5 = 63$ and $a_8 = 99$, find d, which is the slope of the line through the points (5,63) and (8,99):

$$d = \frac{99 - 63}{8 - 5} = \frac{36}{3} = 12.$$ Then, substitute $d = 12$ and, using the first point,

$n = 5$ and $a_n = 63$ into the general formula $a_n = a_1 + (n - 1)d$ to find a_1:

$63 = a_1 + (5 - 1)(12)$

$63 = a_1 + 48$

$a_1 = 15$

Now that we know $a_1 = 15$ and $d = 12$, we can write the formula:

$a_n = a_1 + (n - 1)d$

$a_n = 15 + (n - 1)(12)$

$a_n = 12n + 3$

MODEL PROBLEM 1:   *FIND THE NTH TERM*

Find the 15th term of the arithmetic sequence 5, 11, 17, 23, …

Solution:	**Explanation of steps:**
(A) $a_1 = 5, d = 6$	(A) Find a_1 and d.
(B) $a_n = a_1 + (n - 1)d$	*[a₁ is the first term, d is the common difference.]*
(C) $a_{15} = 5 + (15 - 1) \cdot 6$	(B) Write the formula for arithmetic sequences.
(D) $a_{15} = 89$	(C) Substitute for a_1, d, and the term number, n.
	(D) Evaluate.

342

PRACTICE PROBLEMS

1. What is the common difference of the arithmetic sequence $5, 8, 11, 14, \ldots$?	2. What is the common difference in the sequence $8, 4, 0, -4, \ldots$?
3. Write a formula for the nth term of the arithmetic sequence, $15, 20, 25, 30, \ldots$.	4. Write a formula for the nth term of arithmetic sequence, $10, 12, 14, 16, \ldots$.
5. Find the eighth term of the arithmetic sequence for which $a_1 = 21$ and $d = 9$.	6. Find the 27th term of the arithmetic sequence, $5, 8, 11, 14, \ldots$.

MODEL PROBLEM 2:   *WRITE A FORMULA GIVEN TWO TERMS*

Two terms of an arithmetic sequence are $a_8 = 21$ and $a_{27} = 97$. Write a rule for the nth term.

Solution: **Explanation of steps:**

(A)   (8,21) and (27,97)   (A)   Express the two terms as points. Find d,
$$d = \frac{97 - 21}{27 - 8} = \frac{76}{19} = 4$$
which is the slope of the line through these
points, using the slope formula.

(B) $a_n = a_1 + (n-1)d$ (B)   Substitute d, as well as n and a_n from one of
$21 = a_1 + (8-1) \cdot 4$ the terms *[$a_8 = 21$, so use $n = 8$ and*
$21 = a_1 + 32 - 4$ *$a_n = 21$]*, into the general formula for an
$-7 = a_1$ arithmetic sequence. Solve for a_1.

(C) $a_n = a_1 + (n-1)d$ (C)   Write the general formula, substituting
$a_n = -7 + (n-1) \cdot 4$ known values for a_1 and d, and simplify.
$a_n = -7 + 4n - 4$
$a_n = 4n - 11$

PRACTICE PROBLEMS

7. Two terms of an arithmetic sequence are $a_6 = 10$ and $a_{21} = 55$. Write a formula for the nth term.	8. Two terms of an arithmetic sequence are $a_4 = -23$ and $a_{22} = 49$. Write a formula for the nth term.

12.2   **Geometric Sequences**

KEY TERMS AND CONCEPTS

A **geometric sequence** is one in which each term is obtained by *multiplying* the same number (called the **common ratio**, represented by r) to the preceding term.

Example: 5, 10, 20, 40, …

$$\underset{\times 2\ \ \times 2\ \ \times 2}{\cup\ \cup\ \cup}\qquad\qquad\text{so, } r = 2$$

We can find the common ratio by dividing consecutive terms, such as $\dfrac{a_2}{a_1}$ or $\dfrac{a_3}{a_2}$. In general, the common ratio $r = \dfrac{a_n}{a_{n-1}}$.

We can define a geometric sequence using the formula $a_n = a_1 r^{n-1}$ where a_1 is the first term and r is the common ratio $(r \neq 0)$.

Example: The formula for the above sequence can be written as $a_n = 5 \cdot 2^{n-1}$.

A *geometric sequence* is always an **exponential** function.

Example: For the geometric sequence 5, 10, 20, 40, … , $a_1 = 5$ and $r = 2$, so we can define the sequence by substituting for a_1 and r in $a_n = a_1 r^{n-1}$, giving us the formula $a_n = 5 \cdot 2^{n-1}$. This is graphed below.

n	$a_n = 5 \cdot 2^{n-1}$
1	5
2	10
3	20
4	40
5	80
6	160

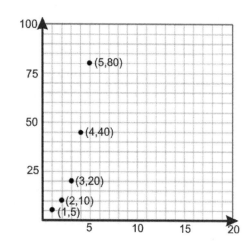

As can be seen by the table, we can **multiply** each term by r to obtain the next term. In this graph, the set of points that make up the discrete function lie on an exponential curve.

Since $r^{n-1} = \dfrac{r^n}{r}$, an alternate way of writing the geometric sequence formula is $a_n = \dfrac{a_1 r^n}{r}$.

This will allow us to simplify our formulas so that they don't include binomial exponents.

Example: $a_n = 5 \cdot 2^{n-1}$ can be rewritten as $a_n = \dfrac{5 \cdot 2^n}{2} = \dfrac{5}{2}(2)^n$ or $a_n = 2.5(2)^n$. Using

function notation, $a_n = 2.5(2)^n$ can be rewritten as $a(n) = 2.5(2)^n$.

To find a specific term of a geometric sequence:
1.   Determine a_1 (the first term) and r (the common ratio) from the given terms.
2.   In the general formula for geometric sequences, substitute for n, a_1, and r, and evaluate.

Example: To find the sixth term of the geometric sequence $8, 32, 128, \ldots$,

we know $a_1 = 8$, $r = 4$, and $n = 6$, so substitute into the general formula

$a_n = a_1 r^{n-1}$ to get $a_6 = 8(4)^{6-1} = 8(4)^5 = 8{,}192$.

 CALCULATOR TIP

If the formula for a geometric sequence is known, the calculator can also be used to find the

value of any terms, just like we saw with arithmetic sequences.

1.   Press $\boxed{\text{2nd}}\boxed{\text{LIST}}\boxed{5}$ for the seq function.
2.   On the TI-84 models, enter the formula, the variable used in the formula, the starting and ending term numbers to display, and a step of 1 next to the prompts on the next screen. Then press $\boxed{\text{ENTER}}$ twice to Paste and display the result.
     [On the TI-83, this screen is skipped, so you will need to type these directly within the parentheses of the seq function, separated by commas, and then press $\boxed{\text{ENTER}}$.]

Example: To display the 6th through 8th terms of the sequence $a_n = 5(3)^n$, follow the

above steps, as shown below. The terms are 3645, 10935, and 32805.

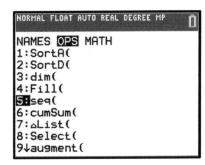  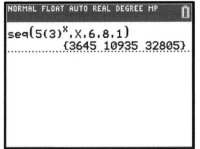

MODEL PROBLEM

Find the seventh term of the sequence: $3, -6, 12, -24, \ldots$.

Solution: **Explanation of steps:**

(A) $a_1 = 3; r = \frac{-6}{3} = -2$ (A) Determine a_1 (the first term) and r (the common ratio) from the given terms.

(B) $a_n = a_1 r^{n-1}$ (B) In the general formula for geometric sequences, substitute for n *[7]*, a_1, and r, and simplify.

$a_7 = 3(-2)^{7-1} = 192$

PRACTICE PROBLEMS

1. What is the common ratio of the geometric sequence $12, 6, 3, 1.5, \ldots$?	2. What is the common ratio of the geometric sequence $-2, 4, -8, 16, \ldots$?
3. What is the common ratio of the geometric sequence $2, -8, 32, -128, \ldots$?	4. Write a formula for the nth term of the geometric sequence, $4, 10, 25, 62.5, \ldots$.

5. Write a formula for the nth term of the geometric sequence, $-1, 2, -4, 8, \ldots$.	6. What is the fifteenth term of the geometric sequence $5, -10, 20, -40, \ldots$?
7. Find the seventh term of the geometric sequence for which $a_1 = 6$ and $r = -\frac{1}{2}$.	8. Find the thirtieth term of the geometric sequence for which the tenth term is 512 and the fifteenth term is 16,384.

12.3 **Recursively Defined Sequences [CC]**

KEY TERMS AND CONCEPTS

Sequences can often be defined using a **recursive formula**. A recursive formula first defines the starting term (called the *seed term*), and then defines the next terms based on values of previous terms.

Examples: (a) The arithmetic sequence $9, 11, 13, 15, ...$, can be defined as:

$$a_1 = 9$$
$$a_n = a_{n-1} + 2$$

common difference $d = 2$

This means the first term a_1 is 9 and the nth term a_n is defined as the value of the previous term a_{n-1} plus the common difference, 2.

(b) Similarly, the geometric sequence $5, 10, 20, 40, ...$, can be defined as:

$$a_1 = 5$$
$$a_n = 2a_{n-1}$$

common ratio $r = 2$

This means the first term a_1 is 5 and the nth term a_n is defined as 2 times the value of the previous term a_{n-1}.

Not all sequences are arithmetic or geometric. For example, this sequence has neither a common difference nor a common ratio. Each term is 2 times the previous term, plus 3.

$$10, 23, 49, 101, ...$$

However, it can still be defined using a recursive formula:

$$a_1 = 10$$
$$a_n = 2a_{n-1} + 3$$

A famous recursively defined sequence is the **Fibonacci sequence**, in which each term (after the first two seed terms) equals the sum of the two previous terms:

$$1, 1, 2, 3, 5, 8, 13, 21, 34, ...$$

We can define this as:

$$a_1 = 1$$
$$a_2 = 1$$
$$a_n = a_{n-1} + a_{n-2}$$

CALCULATOR TIP

The calculator can be used to generate the terms of a recursive sequence. The calculator names its sequences starting with u instead of a.

1. Press MODE and change from FUNCTION to SEQ mode.
2. Press Y=. Since we are in SEQ mode, this screen will look very different.
3. nMin is the number of the first term, which is usually 1.
4. Next to u(n), enter the recursive formula for u_n by pressing 2nd 7 for u and X,T,Θ,n for n. Place subscripts in parentheses (using function notation).
5. Next to u(nMin) [or u(1) on some models], enter the value of the seed term, u_1. [Some models allow a second seed term to be entered as u(2) if needed.]
6. Press 2nd [TABLE] to view the terms in a table.
7. When finished with sequences, remember to switch back to FUNCTION mode.

Example: The screens below show the calculator generating terms of the sequence,

$$u_1 = 10$$
$$u_n = 2u_{n-1} + 3$$

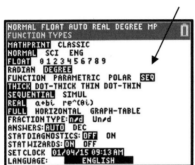

MODEL PROBLEM

The first 5 terms of an arithmetic sequence are $12, 7, 2, -3, -8$.

1. Write an explicit formula for this sequence.

2. Write a recursive formula for this sequence.

Solution:

1.

(A) $a_n = a_1 + (n-1)d$
(B) $a_n = 12 + (n-1)(-5)$
(C) $a_n = 17 - 5n$

2.

(D) $a_1 = 12$
(E) $a_n = a_{n-1} - 5$

Explanation of steps:

(A) Start with the template for explicit formulas of arithmetic sequences.
(B) Substitute for a_1 (the first term *[12]*) and d (the common difference *[-5]*).
(C) Simplify.
(D) State the value of the first term.
(E) State the value of each new term based on the previous term. *[Subtract 5 from the previous term.]*

PRACTICE PROBLEMS

1. Write a recursive formula for the arithmetic sequence, $6, 10, 14, 18, \ldots$.	2. Write a recursive formula for the geometric sequence, $8, 24, 72, 216, \ldots$.
3. Write a recursive formula for the geometric sequence, $16, -8, 4, -2, \ldots$.	4. Write the first 4 terms of the sequence, $a_1 = 3$ $a_n = 2a_{n-1} + 1$
5. Write the first 4 terms of the sequence, $a_1 = 3$ $a_n = 2a_{n-1} - 4$	6. A sequence is recursively defined as: $a_1 = 3$ and $a_n = a_{n-1} + n$ Write the first four terms of this sequence. Is this sequence arithmetic, geometric, or neither? Justify your answer.

7. Write the first 4 terms of the sequence,

$$a_1 = 2$$

$$a_n = 3a_{n-1} + n$$

8. Write the first 4 terms of the sequence,

$$a_1 = -3$$

$$a_n = 2a_{n-1} - n$$

9. Write a formula for the sequence

$$2, 3, 6, 18, 108, 1944, \ldots$$

such that $a_1 = 2, a_2 = 3$, and a_n is defined recursively for $n > 2$.

10. The first four terms in a sequence are

$$40, 8, 24, 16, \ldots$$

Each term after the first two terms is found by taking the mean (average) of the two preceding terms.

(a) Write a recursive formula for this sequence.

(b) Which term is the first odd number in this sequence?

Chapter 13.   Factoring

13.1   **Factor Out the Greatest Common Factor**

KEY TERMS AND CONCEPTS

The **distributive property** allows us to express the product of a monomial and polynomial as a single polynomial. There are times when we would like to factor a polynomial. To **factor** is to break a polynomial down into a product of its factors. Factoring is a process that reverses multiplying.

As part of this process, we may need to find the **greatest common factor (GCF)** of the terms. Remember that we found the GCF of whole numbers by listing their prime factorizations and then determining which factors they had in common.

Example: GCF of 60 and 75. $60 = 2 \cdot 2 \cdot \underline{3} \cdot \underline{5}$ and $75 = \underline{3} \cdot \underline{5} \cdot 5$.

They have $3 \cdot 5 = 15$ in common, so 15 is the GCF.

If the terms of a polynomial have any factors in common, we can use the distributive property (in reverse) to break the polynomial down into factors.

To factor out the GCF:

1. Identifying the greatest common factor (GCF) of its terms.
2. Find the other factor by either
   a. gathering up the remaining factors from each term, or
   b. dividing the original polynomial by the GCF
3. Write the result as a product of the two factors.

Example: $3x^2 + 6x$ can be rewritten as $\underline{3} \cdot \underline{x} \cdot x + 2 \cdot \underline{3} \cdot \underline{x}$, giving us a GCF of $3x$.

To find the other factor, we can either:

(a) gather up the remaining (*not underlined*) factors from the prime factorization $\underline{3} \cdot \underline{x} \cdot x + 2 \cdot \underline{3} \cdot \underline{x}$ to get $x + 2$, or

(b) we can divide the original polynomial by the GCF, as in $\dfrac{3x^2 + 6x}{3x} = x + 2$.

Write the result as the product of the two factors: $3x(x + 2)$.

Note: You can check your answer by applying the distributive property.

If all of the factors in a term's prime factorization are underlined as part of the GCF, you are left with a "hidden" factor of 1. So, you'll need to write the term 1 as part of the other factor. Remember, the other factor should have as many terms as the original polynomial.

Example: $3x^2 + 3x$ can be rewritten as $\underline{3} \cdot \underline{x} \cdot x + \underline{3} \cdot \underline{x}$, giving us a GCF of $3x$. When gathering up the remaining factors, we see that the all of the second term's factors are underlined, leaving us with just a "hidden" factor of 1. So, our other factor is $x + 1$. The result in factored form is $3x(x + 1)$.

The need to use a term of 1 is more easily seen when we divide by the GCF:

$$\frac{3x^2 + 3x}{3x} = \frac{3x^2}{3x} + \frac{3x}{3x} = x + 1$$

MODEL PROBLEM

Factor $8x^2y - 12xy + 20y^2$.

Solution:

(A) $8x^2y - 12xy + 20y^2 = 2 \cdot \underline{2} \cdot 2 \cdot x \cdot x \cdot \underline{y} - \underline{2} \cdot \underline{2} \cdot 3 \cdot x \cdot \underline{y} + \underline{2} \cdot \underline{2} \cdot 5 \cdot \underline{y} \cdot y$

(B) $= 2 \cdot 2 \cdot y \,(2 \cdot x \cdot x - 3 \cdot x + 5 \cdot y)$

(C) $= 4y(2x^2 - 3x + 5y)$

Explanation of steps:

(A) Find the GCF of the terms. One way to do this is to expand each term using the prime factorization methods. Then underline any factors that are common to <u>all terms</u>.

(B) The underlined factors represent the GCF *[2 · 2 · y = 4y]*.
The factors that remain (not underlined) should be written in parentheses as the other factor. (If all of a term's factors are underlined, write 1.)
You can also find the second factor by dividing the original polynomial by the GCF $\left[\dfrac{8x^2y - 12xy + 20y^2}{4y} = 2x^2 - 3x + 5y\right]$.

(C) Write the result in unexpanded form.

PRACTICE PROBLEMS

1. Factor: $4x^2 - 6x$	2. Factor: $5a^2 - 10a$
3. Factor: $14x^3 + 7x$	4. Factor: $x^3 + x^2 - x$
5. Factor: $12x^3y + 18xy^2$	6. Factor: $2y^3 - 4y^2 + 2y$
7. Factor: $3x^3 - 6x^2 + 6x$	8. Factor: $-2x - 2y$
9. Factor: $3m^2n + 12mn^2$	10. Factor: $6x^3y^2z - 4x^2y^2$

13.2   **Factor a Trinomial**

KEY TERMS AND CONCEPTS

When we multiply two binomials (by FOIL), the result is often a trinomial.

Example: $(x - 3)(x + 2) = x^2 + 2x - 3x - 6 = x^2 - x - 6$

Therefore, we can often **factor a trinomial** into the product of two binomial factors.

If the trinomial is a second-degree polynomial in one variable in standard form with a lead coefficient of 1 (that is, if x is the variable, then the polynomial is of the form $x^2 + bx + c$, where b and c are integers), then we can use the following method to factor the trinomial.

To factor $x^2 + bx + c$ by the product-sum method:
1. Find two integers (if any) that *multiply* to give us c and *add* to give us b.
2. Factor the trinomial into two binomials in which the variable is written as each first term and the two integers are written as the last terms.

Remember that if c is positive, the two integers must have the same signs, but if c is negative, the two integers must have different signs.

Example: To factor $x^2 - x - 6$ *[b = −1 and c = −6]*, we need two integers whose product is −6 and whose sum is −1. Those two integers are −3 and 2. So, write the result as $(x - 3)(x + 2)$.

Note: You can check your answer by multiplying the two binomials.

Note that not all trinomials can be factored. For example, $x^2 + x + 1$ cannot be factored because there are no two integers whose product is 1 and whose sum is 1. A trinomial that cannot be factored is called a **prime trinomial**.

MODEL PROBLEM

Factor $x^2 - 8x + 12$.

Solution:

$(x - 6)(x - 2)$

Explanation of steps:

Find two integers that multiply to give us c *[+12]* and add to give us b *[−8]*.

[The factors of 12 are: 12×1, 6×2, and 4×3, as well as $(-12) \times (-1)$, $(-6) \times (-2)$, and $(-4) \times (-3)$. The only pair that adds to -8 is -6 and -2. So, the answer is $(x - 6)(x - 2)$.]

PRACTICE PROBLEMS

1. Factor $x^2 + 9x + 14$	2. Factor $x^2 - 11x + 18$
3. Factor $x^2 - 6x - 27$	4. Factor $a^2 - a - 210$
5. Factor: $x^2 + 5x - 24$	6. Factor: $x^2 + 2x - 15$

7. Factor: $x^2 - 10x - 24$	8. Factor: $x^2 - 5x + 6$
9. Determine whether the following trinomial is prime: $x^2 - 3x + 15$	10. If $x + 2$ is a factor of $x^2 + bx + 10$, what is the value of b?

11. Add the trinomials. Then, factor the result: $(-3x^2 + x - 2) + (4x^2 + 3x - 10)$

13.3   Factor the Difference of Perfect Squares

KEY TERMS AND CONCEPTS

When multiplying binomials, you may have noticed an interesting result when the binomials are a sum and difference of the same two terms. The middle terms of the product cancel out, leaving us with just the difference of the squares of the terms.

Example: $(x + 3)(x - 3) = x^2 - 3x + 3x - 9 = x^2 - 9$

So, if we want to factor a **difference of two perfect squares** into its two binomial factors, we can simply take the **sum and difference of the square roots** of the two terms.

Example: $x^2 - 9$ is a difference of two perfect squares.

By taking the square root of each term (x and 3), we can factor this expression into the product of two binomials: $(x + 3)(x - 3)$.

In order to use this method, *both terms must be perfect squares* and there must be a *subtraction* sign between them.

Be sure to write the square roots in the same order that their squares appear in the problem. For example, $(x + 3)(x - 3)$ is not the same as $(3 + x)(3 - x)$; subtraction is not commutative.

MODEL PROBLEM

Factor $9x^4 - 25$.

Solution:

$(3x^2 + 5)(3x^2 - 5)$

Explanation of steps:

If the expression is the difference (subtraction) of two perfect squares, then take the square root of each term *[$\sqrt{9x^4} = 3x^2$ and $\sqrt{25} = 5$].*
Write the binomial factors as the sum *[$3x^2 + 5$]* and difference *[$3x^2 - 5$]* of the square roots, and express the answer as a product of the binomial factors *[$(3x^2 + 5)(3x^2 - 5)$].*

PRACTICE PROBLEMS

1. Factor $x^2 - 36$	2. Factor $4x^2 - 9$
3. Factor $9 - x^2$	4. Factor $a^2 - 1$
5. Factor $49x^2 - y^2$	6. Factor $4a^2 - 9b^2$
7. Factor $x^2y^2 - 16$	8. Factor $x^{10} - 100$

9. Factor $100n^2 - 1$	10. Factor $121 - x^2$
11. Factor $9a^2 - 64b^2$	12. When $9x^2 - 100$ is factored, it is equivalent to $(3x - b)(3x + b)$. What is a value for b?

13.4   <u>**Factor a Trinomial by Grouping [CC]**</u>

KEY TERMS AND CONCEPTS

In an earlier section, we saw the product-sum method for factoring a trinomial for which the lead coefficient is 1. In other words, we factored trinomials of the form $ax^2 + bx + c$, where $a = 1$ and b and c are non-zero integers, by finding two integers that multiply to give us c and add to give us b. When the lead coefficient is a non-zero integer other than 1 (that is, for $a \neq 1$), that simple method can no longer help us. However, as long as they are not prime, we can still factor these types of trinomials. First, we **expand** them into equivalent polynomials with four terms, and then **factor by grouping**.

Consider the procedure to multiply $(x - 2)(4x + 3)$ by distribution:

$(x - 2)(4x + 3)$

$x(4x + 3) - 2(4x + 3)$ Multiply each term of the first binomial by the second factor.

$4x^2 + 3x - 8x - 6$ The result is a four-term polynomial.

$4x^2 - 5x - 6$ By combining like terms, we end up with a trinomial.

This factoring method will essentially perform these steps in reverse.

To factor a trinomial $ax^2 + bx + c$ where a, b, and c are non-zero integers:
1. Find two integers that multiply to give you ac but add to give you b.
2. Break up the middle term into the sum of two terms with these coefficients.
3. Group the terms into two pairs, where each pair has a common factor.
4. Factor the GCF from each group.
5. Factor out the common binomial (reverse distribute).

MODEL PROBLEM

Factor $4x^2 - 5x - 6$.

Solution:

(A) $4x^2 - 5x - 6$

$ac = 4(-6) = -24$

and $b = -5$

$+3$ and -8

(B) $4x^2 \boxed{+3x - 8x} - 6$

(C) $\boxed{4x^2 + 3x}\ \boxed{-8x - 6}$

(D) $x(4x + 3) - 2(4x + 3)$

(E) $(x - 2)(4x + 3)$

Explanation of steps:

(A) Find two integers that multiply to give you ac but add to give you b.
$[3 \times (-8) = -24$ and $3 + (-8) = -5.]$

(B) Break up the middle term into the sum of two terms with these coefficients.
$[-5x \rightarrow +3x - 8x]$

(C) Group the terms into two pairs, where each pair has a common factor.

(D) Factor the GCF from each group. *[x and –2]*

(E) Factor out the common binomial (reverse distribute). *[The factors outside parentheses are rewritten as a binomial factor, $(x - 2).$]*

PRACTICE PROBLEMS

1. Factor: $6x^2 + x - 2$	2. Factor: $12x^2 + 5x - 2$
3. Factor: $12x^2 - 29x + 15$	4. Factor: $6x^2 - 11x + 4$

5. Factor: $15x^2 + 14x - 8$	6. Factor: $-10x^2 - 29x - 10$
7. Factor $4x^2 + 12x + 9$. What is the square root of this trinomial, written as a binomial?	8. Factor $-6 + 11x + 10x^2$

9. The product of two factors is $2x^2 + x - 6$. One of the factors is $(x + 2)$. What is the other factor?

13.5 **Factor Completely**

KEY TERMS AND CONCEPTS

Sometimes, more than one method of factoring must be performed in order to completely factor an expression. An expression is **factored completely** if all of the factors are prime.

To factor completely:

1. Factor out a greatest common factor, if there is one.
2. Factor any trinomials, if possible, or any differences of two perfect squares.
3. Repeat these steps for each factor until every factor is prime.

CALCULATOR TIP

We can use the calculator to check our factoring by a method we saw earlier.

1. Store an arbitrary, preferably non-integer, value into x. For example, we can store 12.3 into x by pressing [1][2][.][3][STO▸][X,T,Θ,n].

2. Now, test whether the two expressions are equal using [2nd][TEST][1] for the equal sign. A result of 1 means they are equal, or a result of 0 means they are not.

Example: The screenshots below show how to test whether $3x^2 - 12$ and its factored form, $3(x + 2)(x - 2)$, are equivalent.

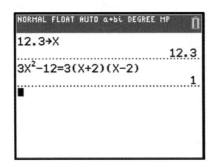

MODEL PROBLEM

Factor completely: $5x^4 - 5$

Solution:

$$5x^4 - 5 =$$

(A) $5(x^4 - 1) =$

(B) $5(x^2 + 1)(x^2 - 1) =$

(C) $5(x^2 + 1)(x + 1)(x - 1)$

Explanation of steps:

(A) Factor out the GCF, if any *[the GCF is 5]*.

(B) If any factor is a trinomial *[not here]* or a difference of two perfect squares *[$x^4 - 1$]*, then factor it.

(C) Look at each factor to see if any of them can be factored further. *[The factor $x^2 - 1$ is a difference of two perfect squares and can be factored further.]*

PRACTICE PROBLEMS

1. Factor completely: $2y^2 + 12y - 54$	2. Factor completely: $3x^2 + 15x - 42$
3. Factor completely: $3x^2 - 27$	4. Factor completely: $2x^2 - 50$

5. Factor completely: $2a^2 - 10a - 28$	6. Factor completely: $x^3 + 8x^2 + 7x$
7. Factor completely: $2x^8 + 16x^7 + 32x^6$	8. Factor completely: $3ax^2 - 27a$
9. Factor completely: $5x^2y^3 - 180y$	10. Factor completely: $2x^5 - 32x$

11. Factor completely: $2x^2 + 10x - 12$	12. Factor completely: $a^3 - 4a$
13. Factor completely: $3x^3 - 33x^2 + 90x$	14. Factor completely: $36x^2 - 100y^6$
15. Factor completely: $4x^3y^3 - 36xy$	16. Factor completely: $6x - x^3 - x^2$

Chapter 14.   Quadratic Functions

14.1   Solve Simple Quadratic Equations

KEY TERMS AND CONCEPTS

In a **linear equation**, the highest power for the variable x is 1. It is also called a first-degree equation. If an equation includes an x^2 term (and no term with x to a power higher than 2), it is called a **quadratic equation**, or a second-degree equation.

Example: $y = x^2$ is a quadratic equation; therefore, $f(x) = x^2$ is a quadratic function.

We have seen that tables of *linear* functions show a *common difference* in its values (as long as the x values change by constant amounts) and tables of *exponential* functions show a *common ratio*. To recognize quadratic functions, we will not find a common difference like we do for linear functions, but we'll find that the differences among their differences (called **second differences**) increase by a constant amount, as shown below.

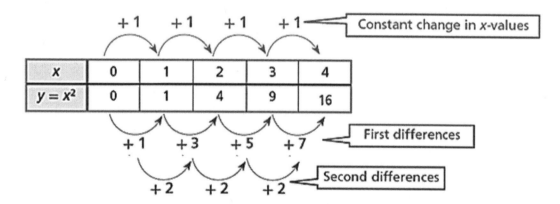

In this section, we will solve *simple* quadratic equations that have an x^2 term but no x term. The solutions to a quadratic equation are called its **roots** or **zeros**. Unlike linear equations, there are usually two solutions to a quadratic equation.

Example: For the equation $x^2 = 25$, the roots (*or zeros, or solutions*) are 5 and -5.
             After all, both $5^2 = 25$ and $(-5)^2 = 25$.

Note that when $x^2 = 0$, then zero is the only solution, and for $x^2 = -1$ (or any negative constant), there are no solutions among the real numbers. And so, it's possible for quadratic equations to have no real solutions, one solution, or two distinct solutions.

Also, based on the context, we may be able to discard one of the solutions as unreasonable.

Example: If $x^2 = 25$ represents the relationship between the length of a side of a square, x, and the area of the square, 25, a negative value for x (that is, -5) would not be a reasonable solution, so it can be discarded. The solution is 5.

One-step equations: To solve a simple quadratic equation like $x^2 = 25$, we can isolate the variable by performing the opposite of squaring – taking the **square root** – of both sides. We use the symbol, $\pm\sqrt{}$, to represent both the positive and negative square roots.

In general, for any non-negative constant c, we solve $x^2 = c$ by writing $x = \pm\sqrt{c}$. The solutions to a quadratic equation can also be written in set notation.

Example: (a) We solve $x^2 = 25$ by writing $x = \pm\sqrt{25} = \pm5$, or in set notation, $\{5, -5\}$.

(b) We solve $x^2 = 2$ by writing $x = \pm\sqrt{2}$, meaning that both $\sqrt{2}$ and $-\sqrt{2}$ are solutions to this equation. Since $\sqrt{2}$ is irrational, we cannot eliminate the radical sign, as we were able to do in the previous example. In set notation, the solutions are $\{\sqrt{2}, -\sqrt{2}\}$.

Generally, solutions are written in simplest radical form.

Example: If we find $x = \pm\sqrt{12}$, the solutions should be written as $\{2\sqrt{3}, -2\sqrt{3}\}$.

For this course, the constant c in the equation $x^2 = c$ will be non-negative.

Example: We cannot solve $x^2 = -1$ using the set of real numbers. This is because $\sqrt{-1}$, or the square root of any negative number, is not a real number.

Solving multi-step equations: It may take more than one step to solve a quadratic equation; we may need to isolate x^2 before taking the square root of both sides.

Example: $2x^2 + 1 = 33$ can be solved by subtracting 1 from both sides to get $2x^2 = 32$, then dividing both sides by 2 to get $x^2 = 16$. Finally, we can take the square root of both sides to give us $x = \pm\sqrt{16}$, or $x = \pm4$, so the roots are $\{4, -4\}$.

Finding the zeros of a function: The roots of a function are called its "zeros" because they represent the x-values at the points on its graph where $y = 0$, and therefore $f(x) = 0$. So, we can find the zeros of a quadratic function by *setting its expression equal to zero*.

Example: To find the zeros of $f(x) = x^2 - 9$, we solve the equation $x^2 - 9 = 0$. The zeros (or roots) are $\{3, -3\}$.

Literal equations: In an earlier section (see p. 32), we solved literal equations for one variable in terms of the other variables. We can solve literal equations for a squared variable by this same method: isolate the squared variable, then take the square root of both sides.

Example: Given $a = x^2 + b$, we can solve for x in terms of a and b.

First, subtract b from both sides to isolate the x^2, giving us $a - b = x^2$.

Then, take the square root of both sides, so $x = \pm\sqrt{a - b}$.

The standard form for a quadratic equation is $ax^2 + bx + c = 0$, where $a \neq 0$. The method in this section works only when $b = 0$; that is, when there is only an x^2 term in the equation. When $b \neq 0$ and the quadratic equation includes both an x^2 term and an x term, we would solve by one of the other methods in this unit (factoring, completing the square, or the quadratic formula).

MODEL PROBLEM 1:   *ONE-STEP EQUATION*

Solve $a^2 = 5$.

Solution:

$a = \pm\sqrt{5}$ Solutions are $\{\sqrt{5}, -\sqrt{5}\}$.

Explanation:

Take the square root of both sides, making sure to include both the positive and negative root.

PRACTICE PROBLEMS

1. Solve for x: $x^2 = 81$	2. Solve for y: $y^2 = 20$

MODEL PROBLEM 2:   *MULTI-STEP EQUATION*

Solve $3x^2 - 2 = 46$.

Solution: **Explanation of steps:**

$$3x^2 - 2 = 46$$

(A) $3x^2 = 48$ (A) Isolate x^2.

$$x^2 = 16$$ *[Add 2 to both sides, then divide both sides by 3]*

(B) $x = \pm\sqrt{16}$ (B) Take the square root of both sides and write the solutions.

$$\{4, -4\}$$

PRACTICE PROBLEMS

3. What is the solution set of the equation $3x^2 = 75$?	4. What is the solution set of the equation $4x^2 - 36 = 0$?
5. Solve: $2x^2 - 1 = 11$	6. Solve: $9x^2 + 5 = 9$

MODEL PROBLEM 3:   *ZEROS OF A FUNCTION*

Find the zeros of the function $f(x) = 4x^2 - 1$.

Solution:

(A) $4x^2 - 1 = 0$

(B) $4x^2 = 1$

    $x^2 = \frac{1}{4}$

(C) $x = \pm\sqrt{\frac{1}{4}}$

    $\left\{ -\frac{1}{2}, \frac{1}{2} \right\}$

Explanation of steps:

(A) Set $f(x) = 0$.

(B) Isolate x^2.

    [Add 1 to both sides and divide both sides by 4]

(C) Take the square root of both sides and write the solutions. *[The square root of ¼ is ½.]*

PRACTICE PROBLEMS

7. Find the zeros of the function, $f(x) = 5x^2 - 5$.	8. Find the zeros of the function, $g(m) = 3m^2$.

MODEL PROBLEM 4:   *LITERAL EQUATION*

The formula for the area of a circle is $A = \pi r^2$, where r is the radius. Express the radius in terms of the area.

Solution:

$$A = \pi r^2$$

(A) $\dfrac{A}{\pi} = r^2$

(B) $r = \sqrt{\dfrac{A}{\pi}}$

Explanation of steps:

(A)   Isolate the squared variable for which we are solving. *[Divide both sides by π.]*

(B)   Take the square root of both sides.
[We discard the negative square root in this case because the radius of a circle must be positive.]

PRACTICE PROBLEMS

9. Solve for h in terms of s: $s = \frac{1}{2}h^2$	10. Solve for the positive value of a in terms of b and c: $$a^2 + b^2 = c^2$$

14.2 **Solve Quadratic Equations by Factoring**

KEY TERMS AND CONCEPTS

The **standard form** for a quadratic equation is $ax^2 + bx + c = 0$, where a, b, and c are real numbers $(a \neq 0)$ and zero is on one side of the equation.

Example: $x^2 - 3x + 5 = 0$ is a quadratic equation in standard form, where $a = 1$, $b = -3$, and $c = 5$.

If both a and b are not equal to 0 (that is, if there are both an x^2 and an x term), we need a new method of solving. Here, we look at solving quadratic equations by factoring.

To solve by factoring, we can use the following fact about a product of two (or more) factors equal to 0. If $ab = 0$, then at least one of the following must be true: $a = 0$ or $b = 0$. This is known as the **zero product property**.

If we can factor a quadratic equation into **factored form**, $g(x - m)(x - n) = 0$ where $g \neq 0$, then the zero product property tells us that either $x - m = 0$ or $x - n = 0$, so $x = m$ or $x = n$. Therefore, the roots are m and n.

To solve a quadratic equation by factoring:
1. transform the equation into standard form, with zero on one side
2. factor the polynomial completely
3. set each factor that contains a variable equal to zero
4. solve each resulting equation

MODEL PROBLEM

Find the roots of the equation $x^2 + 6 = 5x$.

Solution:

(A) $x^2 + 6 = 5x$

$\underline{\quad -5x \quad - 5x \quad}$

$x^2 - 5x + 6 = 0$

(B) $(x - 3)(x - 2) = 0$

(C) $x - 3 = 0$ or $x - 2 = 0$

(D) $\quad x = 3$ or $\quad x = 2$

The roots are 2 and 3.

Explanation of steps:

(A) transform the equation into standard form, with zero on one side *[by subtracting the 5x from both sides]*.

(B) factor the polynomial completely

(C) set each factor equal to zero

(D) solve each resulting equation

It is also a good idea to check each solution on your calculator. Check the original equation using $\boxed{2}\boxed{\text{STO}\blacktriangleright}\boxed{\text{X,T,}\Theta\text{,}n}$ then check it again using $\boxed{3}\boxed{\text{STO}\blacktriangleright}\boxed{\text{X,T,}\Theta\text{,}n}$.

PRACTICE PROBLEMS

1. Solve for x: $x^2 - 5x = 0$	2. Solve for x: $x^2 + 3x - 18 = 0$
3. Solve for x (by factoring): $4x^2 - 36 = 0$	4. Solve for x: $x^2 - 4x - 32 = 0$

5. Solve for x: $x^2 - 5x = 6$	6. Solve for x: $x^2 - 3 = 2x$
7. Find the roots of the equation $x^2 - x = 6$ algebraically.	8. Find the roots of the equation $x^2 = 30 - 13x$ algebraically.
9. Solve for x: $x^2 - 4x = x + 24$	10. Solve for x: $2x^2 + 10x = 12$
11. Solve for x: $x(x + 2) = 3$	12. Solve for x: $(x + 2)(x + 3) = 12$

14.3 **Find Quadratic Equations from Given Roots**

KEY TERMS AND CONCEPTS

If given roots (zeros), then working backwards we can find an equation with those roots.

To find an equation given its roots:

1. Set x equal to each root. For a double root, the same root is used twice.
2. Get zero to one side of each equation.
3. Write as factors.
4. Multiply factors.

MODEL PROBLEM

Find a quadratic equation with roots of 5 and -1.

Solution: **Explanation of steps:**

(A) $x = 5$ *or* $x = -1$ (A)   Set x equal to each root.

(B) $x - 5 = 0$ $x + 1 = 0$ (B)   Get zero to one side of each equation.

(C) $(x - 5)(x + 1) = 0$ (C)   Write as factors.

(D) $x^2 - 4x - 5 = 0$ (D)   Multiply factors.

PRACTICE PROBLEMS

1. Write a quadratic equation in standard form with roots of 10 and -2.	2. Write a quadratic equation in standard form with roots of 0 and 3.

3. Write a quadratic equation in standard form that has roots of -12 and 2.	4. Write a quadratic equation in standard form that has roots of -3 and 5.
5. Write a quadratic equation in standard form that has the solution set $\{-5, 2\}$.	6. Write a quadratic equation in standard form that has the solution set $\{1, 3\}$.
7. Write a quadratic equation in standard form with roots of $\frac{3}{2}$ and 2.	8. Write a quadratic equation in standard form with the double root of 1.

9. Write a quadratic equation in standard form with roots of 4 and -4.

10. When a 3rd degree polynomial is set equal to zero, it is a cubic equation. A cubic equation can have 3 roots.

    Find a cubic equation with roots of 0, 1, and -1. *(We'll look at cubic equations in a later unit.)*

14.4 **Equations with the Square of a Binomial**

KEY TERMS AND CONCEPTS

In an earlier section in this unit, we saw that we can solve an equation of the form $x^2 = c$, where c is a real number, by taking the square root of both sides: $x = \pm\sqrt{c}$.

In some equations, something more than just x may be squared. We may have a variable expression in parentheses as the base of the exponent (and no other variable terms outside the parentheses). In a quadratic equation, this expression may be a monomial or binomial. We can still follow the same steps to solve these types of equations. Once we isolate the expression being squared, we eliminate the exponent and parentheses by taking the square root of both sides. Since we need to use the $\pm$ symbol, this results in two linear equations to be solved, one for the positive square root and one for the negative square root.

Examples: To solve $(2x - 6)^2 = 4$, take the square root of both sides to get

$2x - 6 = \pm\sqrt{4}$. This results in two linear equations: $2x - 6 = 2$ and $2x - 6 = -2$. Solving both equations, we find the two roots of the original quadratic equation, 4 and 2.

Irrational Roots

In some cases, the roots may be irrational. Since we cannot combine a rational number with an irrational number by addition or subtraction, the roots may be written as a sum and difference.

Example: If we solve $(x + 1)^2 = 2$ by taking the square root of both sides, we get

$x + 1 = \pm\sqrt{2}$. This represents the two equations, $x + 1 = \sqrt{2}$ and $x + 1 = -\sqrt{2}$. In each case, subtracting 1 from both sides gives us $x = -1 + \sqrt{2}$ and $x = -1 - \sqrt{2}$, so our solutions, or roots, would be written as $\{-1 + \sqrt{2}, -1 - \sqrt{2}\}$.

Note: You may not need to write out both equations. It is common practice to go directly from $x + 1 = \pm\sqrt{2}$ to writing $x = -1 \pm \sqrt{2}$ before stating the two roots.

MODEL PROBLEM 1:   *IRRATIONAL ROOTS*

Solve $3(x - 2)^2 = 15$.

Solution: **Explanation of steps:**

$$3(x - 2)^2 = 15$$

(A) $(x - 2)^2 = 5$

(B) $x - 2 = \pm\sqrt{5}$

(C) $x = 2 \pm \sqrt{5}$

(D) $\{2 - \sqrt{5}, 2 + \sqrt{5}\}$

(A) Isolate the binomial squared (ie, isolate the parentheses). *[Divide both sides by 3]*

(B) Take the square root of both sides.

(C) Isolate *x*. *[Add 2 to both sides]*

(D) Write the solution (roots) in set notation.

PRACTICE PROBLEMS

1. Solve $(x + 5)^2 = 16$.	2. Solve $(x - 4)^2 = 10$.
3. Solve $6(b - 1)^2 = 48$.	4. Solve $5 - (m + 1)^2 = -25$.

MODEL PROBLEM 2:   *ZEROS OF A FUNCTION*

Find the zeros of the function $f(x) = (x + 1)^2 - 1$.

Solution:

(A) $(x + 1)^2 - 1 = 0$

(B) $(x + 1)^2 = 1$

   $x + 1 = \pm\sqrt{1}$

   $x + 1 = \pm 1$

   $x = -1 \pm 1$

(C) $\{-2, 0\}$

Explanation of steps:

(A)   Set $f(x) = 0$.

(B)   Solve the equation.

   [Isolate the parentheses by adding 1 to both sides; take the square root of both sides; and isolate x by subtracting 1 from both sides]

(C)   Write the zeros. *[-1 + 1 = 0 and -1 - 1 = -2]*

PRACTICE PROBLEMS

5. Find the zeros of the function $f(x) = (x - 2)^2$.	6. Find the zeros of the function $g(x) = 2(x + 5)^2 - 50$.

14.5 **Complete the Square**

KEY TERMS AND CONCEPTS

Another method for solving quadratic equations is called **completing the square**. This method converts a quadratic equation into one of the form, $(x + p)^2 = q$, where p and q are constants, allowing the resulting equation to be easily solved by taking the square root of both sides. We do this by manipulating the equation so that one side is a **perfect square trinomial** that can be factored into the *square of a binomial*, $(x + p)^2$, for some p. For a perfect square trinomial of the form $x^2 + bx + c$, the value of p will be $\frac{b}{2}$.

A trinomial $x^2 + bx + c$ is a perfect square if $\left(\frac{b}{2}\right)^2 = c$.

Example: $x^2 - 10x + 25$ is a perfect square trinomial because $\left(-\frac{10}{2}\right)^2 = (-5)^2 = 25$.

Therefore, it can be written as the square of a binomial, $(x - 5)^2$.

To solve a quadratic equation $x^2 + bx + c = 0$ by completing the square:

1. Add the opposite of c to both sides.

2. Add $\left(\frac{b}{2}\right)^2$ to both sides.

3. Factor the trinomial into a binomial squared.

4. Take the square root of both sides. Use the ± symbol on the right side and simplify radicals.

5. Solve for x, remembering that ± gives two possible solutions.

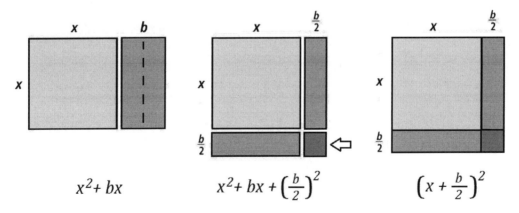

$$x^2 + bx \qquad\qquad x^2 + bx + \left(\frac{b}{2}\right)^2 \qquad\qquad \left(x + \frac{b}{2}\right)^2$$

The advantage of this method is that it can be used when trinomials cannot be factored. When we use this method on quadratic equations in which *prime trinomials* are set equal to zero, the roots (if there are any real roots) will be *irrational* (they will include *radicals*).

MODEL PROBLEM 1:   *RATIONAL ROOTS*

Solve $x^2 + 6x - 7 = 0$ by completing the square.

Solution:

(A) $x^2 + 6x - 7 = 0$

  $x^2 + 6x = 7$

(B) $\left(\frac{b}{2}\right)^2 = \left(\frac{6}{2}\right)^2 = 3^2 = 9$

  $x^2 + 6x + 9 = 7 + 9$

(C) $(x + 3)^2 = 16$

(D) $x + 3 = \pm\sqrt{16}$

  $x + 3 = \pm 4$

(E) $x = -3 \pm 4$

  $\{1, -7\}$

Explanation of steps:

(A) Add the opposite of c to both sides.
  [add 7 to both sides]

(B) Find $\left(\frac{b}{2}\right)^2$ and add it *[9]* to both sides of the equation.

(C) Factor the trinomial into a binomial squared.
  [$x^2 + 6x + 9 = (x + 3)^2$].

(D) Take the square root of both sides. Use the $\pm$ symbol on the right side and simplify radicals.
  [$\pm\sqrt{16} = \pm 4$]

(E) Solve for x, remembering that $\pm$ gives two solutions *[$-3 + 4 = 1$ and $-3 - 4 = -7$].*

PRACTICE PROBLEMS

1. Solve $x^2 - 8x + 16 = 0$.	2. Solve $x^2 + 10x - 11 = 0$ by completing the square.

MODEL PROBLEM 2:   *IRRATIONAL ROOTS*

Solve $x^2 - 2x - 1 = 0$ by completing the square.

Solution:

(A) $x^2 - 2x - 1 = 0$

      $x^2 - 2x = 1$

(B) $\left(\frac{b}{2}\right)^2 = \left(\frac{-2}{2}\right)^2 = (-1)^2 = 1$

      $x^2 - 2x + 1 = 1 + 1$

(C) $(x - 1)^2 = 2$

(D) $x - 1 = \pm\sqrt{2}$

(E) $x = 1 \pm \sqrt{2}$

      $\{1 + \sqrt{2}, 1 - \sqrt{2}\}$

Explanation of steps:

(A)   Add the opposite of c to both sides.

(B)   Add $\left(\frac{b}{2}\right)^2$ to both sides of the equation *[add 1 to both sides].*

(C)   Factor the left side into a binomial squared. *[$x^2 - 2x + 1 = (x - 1)^2$].*

(D)   Take the square root of both sides. Use the $\pm$ symbol on the right side and simplify radicals. *[$\pm\sqrt{2}$ cannot be simplified.]*

(E)   Solve for x, remembering that $\pm$ gives two solutions *[we are left with two irrational roots].*

PRACTICE PROBLEMS

3. Solve $x^2 + 4x + 2 = 0$ by completing the square.	4. Solve $x^2 - 4x - 8 = 0$ by completing the square.

5. Solve $2x^2 - 12x + 4 = 0$ by completing the square.

6. Use completing the square to show that $x^2 - 2x + 3 = 0$ has no real solutions.

7. A rectangular pool has an area of 880 square feet. The length is 10 feet longer than the width. Find the dimensions of the pool, to the *nearest tenth of a foot*.

14.6 **Quadratic Formula and the Discriminant**

KEY TERMS AND CONCEPTS

Another method for solving quadratic equations of the form $ax^2 + bx + c = 0$ is by the use

of the **quadratic formula**, $x = \dfrac{-b \pm \sqrt{b^2 - 4ac}}{2a}$.

Example: To solve $x^2 - 2x - 1 = 0$ by the quadratic formula, write the formula but
substitute 1 for a, –2 for b, and –1 for c, then evaluate:

$$x = \frac{-(-2) \pm \sqrt{(-2)^2 - 4(1)(-1)}}{2(1)} = \frac{2 \pm \sqrt{8}}{2} = \frac{2 \pm 2\sqrt{2}}{2} = 1 \pm \sqrt{2}$$

For quadratic equations that cannot be solved by factoring, you may prefer this method
over completing the square, especially when b is odd (to avoid fractions) or when $a \neq 1$.

The formula is derived by completing the square on the equation, $ax^2 + bx + c = 0$. The $\pm$
symbol in the formula allows for the possibility of two solutions (*roots*).

CALCULATOR TIP

You can check your solutions using the calculator; however, be aware that the calculator will display irrational numbers as decimal approximations.

First, store the values of a, b, and c in variables, then type and evaluate each part of the formula. Since $\pm$ can't be entered as an operation, the formula needs to be entered twice, first with $\boxed{+}$ and then with $\boxed{-}$.

Example: To check that the roots of $x^2 - 2x - 1 = 0$ are $1 \pm \sqrt{2}$,

1) Store 1 into A, –2 into B, and –1 into C by pressing $\boxed{1}\boxed{\text{STO}\blacktriangleright}\boxed{\text{ALPHA}}[A]$
   $\boxed{\text{ALPHA}}[:]\boxed{(\text{-})}\boxed{2}\boxed{\text{STO}\blacktriangleright}\boxed{\text{ALPHA}}[B]\ \boxed{\text{ALPHA}}[:]\boxed{(\text{-})}\boxed{1}\boxed{\text{STO}\blacktriangleright}\boxed{\text{ALPHA}}[C]\ \boxed{\text{ENTER}}$.
   Multiple instructions, separated by colons, may be entered on one line.

2) Find $\dfrac{-b + \sqrt{b^2 - 4ac}}{2a}$ by typing $\boxed{(}\boxed{(\text{-})}\boxed{\text{ALPHA}}[B]\boxed{+}\boxed{\text{2nd}}\boxed{\sqrt{\ }}$
   $\boxed{\text{ALPHA}}[B]\boxed{x^2}\boxed{-}\boxed{4}\boxed{\text{ALPHA}}[A]\boxed{\text{ALPHA}}[C]\boxed{\blacktriangleright}\boxed{)}\ \boxed{\div}\ \boxed{(}\boxed{2}\boxed{\text{ALPHA}}[A]\boxed{)}\ \boxed{\text{ENTER}}$.

3) To find $\dfrac{-b - \sqrt{b^2 - 4ac}}{2a}$, recall the formula by pressing $\boxed{\text{2nd}}[\text{ENTRY}]$, then use the arrows to move to the $\boxed{+}$ and change it to a $\boxed{-}$. Press $\boxed{\text{ENTER}}$ again.

4) Check if the decimal approximations match the exact answers, $1 \pm \sqrt{2}$, by calculating $\boxed{1}\boxed{+}\boxed{\text{2nd}}\boxed{\sqrt{\ }}\boxed{2}\boxed{\blacktriangleright}\boxed{\text{ENTER}}$ and $\boxed{1}\boxed{-}\boxed{\text{2nd}}\boxed{\sqrt{\ }}\boxed{2}\boxed{\blacktriangleright}\boxed{\text{ENTER}}$.

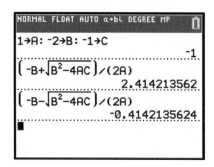

The part of the quadratic formula that is under the square root symbol, $b^2 - 4ac$, is called the *discriminant.*

The **discriminant** $b^2 - 4ac$ tells us about the **number and nature of the roots**.

- If the **discriminant is negative**, then the formula includes the square root of a negative number, so there are **no real roots**.
  (You will learn about imaginary roots in Algebra II.)
- If the **discriminant is zero**, the square root term "disappears" from the formula ($\sqrt{0} = 0$), leaving just $x = \dfrac{-b}{2a}$. Therefore, the equation has only **one distinct real root**. As long as a and b are both rational, the root will be rational.
  *(Note: Since a quadratic generally has two roots, some people prefer to say that when the discriminant is zero, there are **two equal roots**.)*
- If the **discriminant is positive**, the $\pm$ symbol before the radical causes **two different real roots** to be produced by the formula.
  - If the discriminant is a *perfect square*, the radical sign will be eliminated, meaning the *two roots are rational* (assuming a and b are rational), which means the equation could have been factored over the integers.
  - If the discriminant is *not a perfect square*, the radical sign cannot be eliminated, so the *two roots are irrational*.

We can relate these situations to the graphs of the corresponding parabolas. The discriminant determines how many *x*-intercepts (*roots*) there are.

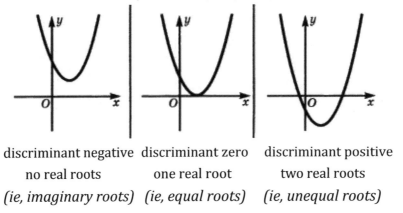

discriminant negative   discriminant zero   discriminant positive
no real roots   one real root   two real roots
(ie, imaginary roots)   *(ie, equal roots)*   *(ie, unequal roots)*

▓▓▓ CALCULATOR TIP

If you plan on using the quadratic formula more than once, it may be convenient to store the formula in your calculator as a reusable program. *Be aware, however, that if your calculator is placed into Test Mode prior to an exam, you will no longer have access to the program.*

To create a program to calculate the quadratic formula:

1. Press PRGM NEW 1 for Create New.

2. Type a name, such as QUAD, using the letter keys, and press ENTER. Alpha lock is on, so you don't have to press the ALPHA key.

3. Press PRGM I/O 2 for Prompt. Type ALPHA [A] , ALPHA [B] , ALPHA [C] ENTER.

4. To create the formula, $m = \dfrac{-b + \sqrt{b^2 - 4ac}}{2a}$, type ((-) ALPHA [B] + 2nd [√]

   ALPHA [B] x^2 − 4 ALPHA [A] ALPHA [C])) ÷ (2 ALPHA [A]) STO▸ ALPHA [M] ENTER.

5. To create the formula, $n = \dfrac{-b - \sqrt{b^2 - 4ac}}{2a}$, type ((-) ALPHA [B] − 2nd [√]

   ALPHA [B] x^2 − 4 ALPHA [A] ALPHA [C])) ÷ (2 ALPHA [A]) STO▸ ALPHA [N] ENTER.

6. Press PRGM I/O 3 for Disp. Type the line "X=",M,N using the keys,

   ALPHA ["] X,T,Θ,*n* 2nd MATH 1 ALPHA ["] , ALPHA [M] , ALPHA [N] ENTER.

7. Press 2nd [QUIT]. This will save your program.

8. Press PRGM, select the QUAD program, and press ENTER ENTER.

9. Enter a value for each prompt and press ENTER. For example, to find the roots of $x^2 - 2x - 1 = 0$, enter 1, –2, and –1.

10. The roots are shown.

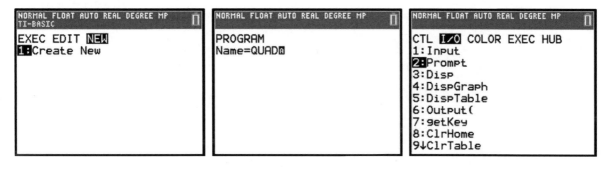

continued on the next page ...

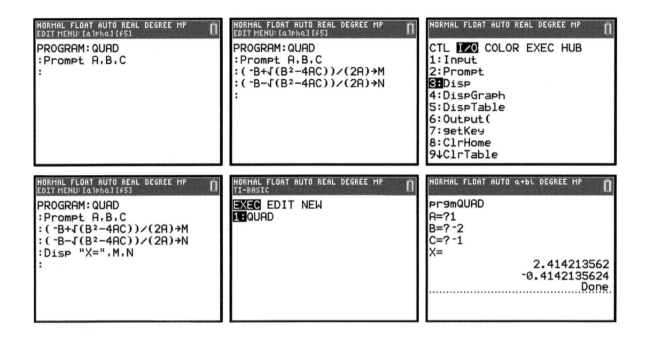

MODEL PROBLEM

In the diagram to the right, a smaller rectangle with a length of x and width of 2 is enclosed inside a larger rectangle with a length of $2x + 3$ and a width of x. The shaded area is 21 square units. Find the length of the smaller rectangle.

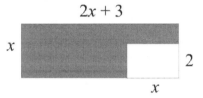

Solution:

(A)   area of large rectangle – area of small rectangle = shaded area

(B)

$$x(2x + 3) - 2x = 21$$
$$2x^2 + 3x - 2x = 21$$
$$2x^2 + x = 21$$
$$2x^2 + x - 21 = 0$$

(C)

$$x = \frac{-b \pm \sqrt{b^2 - 4ac}}{2a} = \frac{-1 \pm \sqrt{1^2 - 4(2)(-21)}}{2(2)}$$

$$= \frac{-1 \pm \sqrt{1 + 168}}{4} = \frac{-1 \pm \sqrt{169}}{4} = \frac{-1 \pm 13}{4}$$

$x = \frac{12}{4} = 3$ or $x = \frac{-14}{4} = -3.5$ (*rejected*)

The length of the smaller rectangle is 3 units.

Explanation of steps:

(A) Write an equation for the shaded area.

(B) Substitute expressions for the areas (products of the lengths and widths) of the rectangles. Simplify and express in standard form.

(C) Substitute a, b and c *[2, 1, and −21]* into the quadratic formula, and evaluate. Reject any negative roots, since the length cannot be negative.

PRACTICE PROBLEMS

1. A quadratic function has two real roots. How many times does the graph of the function cross the x-axis? (1) 1 (3) 0 (2) 2 (4) Cannot be determined	2. The roots of $x^2 + 4x + 7$ are (1) not real (2) equal (3) rational (4) irrational
3. The roots of the equation $9x^2 + 3x - 4 = 0$ are (1) not real (2) real, rational, and equal (3) real, rational, and unequal (4) real, irrational, and unequal	4. The roots of the equation $2x^2 + 4 = 9x$ are (1) real, rational, and equal (2) real, rational, and unequal (3) real, irrational, and unequal (4) not real
5. Solve the equation $6x^2 - 2x - 3 = 0$ and express the answer in simplest radical form.	6. Solve the equation $2x^2 + 7x - 3 = 0$ and express the answer in simplest radical form.
7. Solve $x^2 + 7x + 8 = 0$ by the quadratic formula.	8. Solve $2x^2 - 8x + 3 = 0$ by the quadratic formula.

14.7   <u>**Solve Quadratics with a≠1 [CC]**</u>

KEY TERMS AND CONCEPTS

In this chapter, we will look at three methods for solving a quadratic equation of the form $ax^2 + bx + c = 0$, where $a \neq 1$.

The Transforming Method allows you to write a new equation where $a = 1$, solve this simpler equation, and then divide the results by a when you're done.

<u>**Method 1: The Transforming Method**</u>

1. Write a new equation of the form $n^2 + bn + ac = 0$, where n is a new variable and a, b, and c are taken from the original equation.
2. Solve the new equation for n.
3. For each solution for n, a solution of the original equation is $x = \dfrac{n}{a}$.

The Transforming Method is a relatively new method and not as commonly known as the next three. To see why the transforming method works, we can look at the quadratic

formula, $x = \dfrac{-b \pm \sqrt{b^2 - 4ac}}{2a}$. For the new equation, $n^2 + bn + ac = 0$, we've replaced x

with n, a with 1, and c with ac. Substituting these into the quadratic formula results in

$n = \dfrac{-b \pm \sqrt{b^2 - 4(1)(ac)}}{2(1)} = \dfrac{-b \pm \sqrt{b^2 - 4ac}}{2}$. The resulting formula for n is the same as the

formula for x except that it is missing the division by a. Therefore, $x = \dfrac{n}{a} = \dfrac{-b \pm \sqrt{b^2 - 4ac}}{2a}$.

<u>**Method 2: Factor by Grouping**</u>

1. Find two integers that multiply to give you ac but add to give you b.
2. Break up the middle term into the sum of two terms with these coefficients.
3. Group the terms into two pairs, where each pair has a common factor.
4. Factor the GCF from each group.
5. Factor out the common binomial (reverse distribute).
6. Set each factor equal to zero and solve for x.

The first two methods require a trinomial that is factorable, and not all trinomials are. The advantage of the next two methods is that they will also work when factoring isn't possible.

Method 3: Complete the Square

1. Divide both sides (*each term*) by the leading coefficient, resulting in a new equation of the form $x^2 + bx + c = 0$.
2. Add the opposite of c to both sides.
3. Add $\left(\frac{b}{2}\right)^2$ to both sides.
4. Factor the trinomial into a binomial squared.
5. Take the square root of both sides. Use the ± symbol on the right side and simplify radicals.
6. Solve for x, remembering that ± gives two possible solutions.

Method 4: Quadratic Formula

1. Write the quadratic formula: $x = \dfrac{-b \pm \sqrt{b^2 - 4ac}}{2a}$.
2. Substitute for a, b, and c, and simplify.

MODEL PROBLEM 1:   *TRANSFORMING METHOD*

Solve $3x^2 + 5x - 2 = 0$ by the transforming method.

Solution:

$$3x^2 + 5x - 2 = 0$$

(A) $n^2 + 5n - 6 = 0$

(B) $(n + 6)(n - 1) = 0$

$n + 6 = 0 \quad n - 1 = 0$

$n = -6 \;$ or $\; n = 1$

(C) $x = -\dfrac{6}{3} \;$ or $\; x = \dfrac{1}{3}$

$\left\{-2, \dfrac{1}{3}\right\}$

Explanation of steps:

(A) Write a new equation of the form $n^2 + bn + ac = 0$, where n is a new variable and a, b, and c are taken from the original equation. *[ac = 3(−2) = −6]*

(B) Solve the new equation for n.

(C) For each solution for n, a solution of the original equation is $x = \dfrac{n}{a}$. *[a = 3]*

PRACTICE PROBLEMS

1. Solve by the transforming method: $10x^2 + 9x + 2 = 0$	2. Solve by the transforming method: $2x^2 - 3x - 2 = 0$
3. Solve by the transforming method: $12x^2 + 29x + 15 = 0$	4. Solve by the transforming method: $4x^2 + 109x + 225 = 0$

MODEL PROBLEM 2:   FACTOR BY GROUPING

Factor by grouping to solve $3x^2 + 5x - 2 = 0$.

Solution: **Explanation of steps:**

(A) $3x^2 + 5x - 2 = 0$ (A)   Find two integers that multiply to give you ac

        $ac = 3(-2) = -6$ *[−6]* but add to give you b *[5]*.

        and $b = 5$ (B)   Break up the middle term into the sum of two

        −1 and +6   terms with these coefficients.

(B) $3x^2 \boxed{-x + 6x} - 2 = 0$ *[+5x ⇒ −x + 6x]*

(C) $\boxed{3x^2 - x}\ \boxed{+6x - 2} = 0$ (C)   Group the terms into two pairs, where each pair

(D) $x(3x - 1) + 2(3x - 1) = 0$ has a common factor.

(E) $(x + 2)(3x - 1) = 0$ (D)   Factor the GCF from each group. *[x and 2]*

(F) $x + 2 = 0$ $3x - 1 = 0$ (E)   Factor out the common binomial (reverse

        $x = -2$ $x = \frac{1}{3}$ distribute). *[The factors outside parentheses are*

                                        rewritten as a binomial factor, (x + 2).]

(G) $\left\{-2, \frac{1}{3}\right\}$ (F)   Set each factor equal to zero and solve.

                                   (G)   State the solution.

PRACTICE PROBLEMS

5.   Factor by grouping to solve for x:
 	
     $10x^2 + 9x + 2 = 0$
	6. Factor by grouping to solve for x:
	
	     $3x^2 - 14x + 8 = 0$

7. Factor by grouping to solve for x: $2x^2 - 3x - 2 = 0$	8. Factor by grouping to solve for x: $4x(x-1) = 15$

MODEL PROBLEM 3: *COMPLETE THE SQUARE*

Solve $3x^2 + 5x - 2 = 0$ by completing the square.

Solution:

$$3x^2 + 5x - 2 = 0$$

(A) $x^2 + \frac{5}{3}x - \frac{2}{3} = 0$

(B) $x^2 + \frac{5}{3}x = \frac{2}{3}$

(C) $\left(\frac{b}{2}\right)^2 = \left(\frac{5}{3 \cdot 2}\right)^2 = \left(\frac{5}{6}\right)^2 = \frac{25}{36}$

     $x^2 + \frac{5}{3}x + \frac{25}{36} = \frac{49}{36}$

(D) $\left(x + \frac{5}{6}\right)^2 = \frac{49}{36}$

(E) $x + \frac{5}{6} = \pm\sqrt{\frac{49}{36}} = \pm\frac{7}{6}$

(F) $x = -\frac{5}{6} \pm \frac{7}{6} = -\frac{12}{6} \text{ or } \frac{2}{6}$

     $\left\{-2, \frac{1}{3}\right\}$

Explanation of steps:

(A)   Divide both sides (*each term*) by the leading coefficient. *[Divide both sides – each term – by 3.]*

(B)   Add the opposite of c to both sides.

(C)   Add $\left(\frac{b}{2}\right)^2$ to both sides.

     [Add $\frac{25}{36}$. The right side evaluates to $\frac{2}{3} + \frac{25}{36} = \frac{49}{36}$.]

(D)   Factor the trinomial into a binomial squared.

(E)   Take the square root of both sides. Use the $\pm$ symbol on the right side and simplify radicals.

(F)   Solve for x, remembering that $\pm$ gives two solutions

PRACTICE PROBLEMS

9. Solve $4x^2 + 8x = 45$ by completing the square.	10. Solve $3x^2 - 2x - 1 = 0$ by completing the square.

MODEL PROBLEM 4: *QUADRATIC FORMULA*

Solve $3x^2 + 5x - 2 = 0$ by the quadratic formula.

Solution:

(A) $x = \dfrac{-b \pm \sqrt{b^2 - 4ac}}{2a}$

(B) $x = \dfrac{-5 \pm \sqrt{5^2 - 4(3)(-2)}}{2(3)}$

$x = \dfrac{-5 \pm \sqrt{49}}{6} = \dfrac{-5 \pm 7}{6}$

$x = \left\{ -2, \dfrac{1}{3} \right\}$

Explanation of steps:

(A) Write the quadratic formula.

(B) Substitute for a, b, and c, and simplify.

399

PRACTICE PROBLEMS

11. Solve $10x^2 + 9x + 2 = 0$ by the quadratic formula.	12. Solve $-3x^2 + 4x - 1 = 0$ by the quadratic formula.

14.8 **Word Problems – Quadratic Equations**

KEY TERMS AND CONCEPTS

Some verbal problems will require writing and solving quadratic equations. As with any type of verbal problem, try to represent the situation by writing an equation (or system of equations). If the equation is quadratic (in at least one term the variable is squared), then use the methods for solving a quadratic equation.

Geometric area problems often result in quadratic equations.

Example: If the length and width of a rectangle are expressions in terms of the same variable, say x, then the area, as the product of these expressions, would include that variable squared (x^2).

Important: If either root of the equation is not possible in the given situation, reject it.

Example: When finding the length of a side of a rectangle, reject any negative solutions.

MODEL PROBLEM

Find two consecutive whole numbers such that their product is 42.

Solution:

(A) Let x represent the smaller number. The larger number is $x + 1$.

(B) $x(x + 1) = 42$

(C) $x^2 + x = 42$

(D) $x^2 + x - 42 = 0$

(E) $(x + 7)(x - 6) = 0$

(F) $x + 7 = 0 \ or \ x - 6 = 0$

(G) $x = -7 \ or \ x = 6$

(H) Numbers are 6 and 7.

Explanation of steps:

(A) Represent an unknown quantity as a variable and express other quantities in terms of this variable.

(B) Write an equation for the given situation.

(C) Simplify both sides of the equation.

(D) Since the equation is quadratic *[there's a x² term]*, transform it into standard form by getting zero to one side *[by subtracting 42 from both sides]*.

(E) Factor completely.

(F) Set each factor containing a variable equal to 0.

(G) Solve each resulting equation. Reject any impossible solutions. *[The problem asked for whole numbers, so –7 is not a possible solution].*

(H) Be sure to answer the problem. *[If x, the smaller number, is 6, then the larger, next consecutive whole number is 7.]*

PRACTICE PROBLEMS

1. The square of a positive number decreased by twice the number is 48. Find the number.	2. The larger of two positive numbers is 8 more than the smaller. The sum of their squares is 104. Find the two numbers.
3. When 36 is subtracted from the square of a number, the result is five times the number. What is the positive solution?	4. The square of a positive number is 24 more than 5 times the number. What is the value of the number?
5. The area of the rectangular playground enclosure at South School is 500 square meters. The length of the playground is 5 meters longer than the width. Find the dimensions of the playground, in meters.	6. Tamara has two sisters. One of the sisters is 7 years older than Tamara. The other sister is 3 years younger than Tamara. The product of Tamara's two sisters' ages is 24. How old is Tamara?

7. Find two negative consecutive odd integers such that their product is 63.

8. Find three consecutive odd integers such that the product of the first and the second exceeds the third by 8.

9. Find two consecutive whole numbers where the product of the larger and 10 more than the smaller is 90.

10. Three brothers have ages that are consecutive even integers. The product of the first and third boys' ages is 20 more than twice the second boy's age. Find the age of *each* of the three boys.

11. The hypotenuse of a right triangle is 6 meters long. One leg is 1 meter longer than the other. Find the lengths of *both* legs of the triangle, to the *nearest hundredth of a meter.*

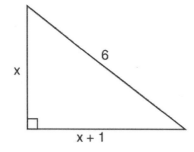

12. From ground level, a projectile is shot into the air. Its height, in feet, is modeled by $p(x) = -16x^2 + 32x$, where x is the number of elapsed seconds. Determine the total number of seconds that the projectile will be in the air.

13. A pump is used to drain water from a pool. The amount of water in the pool is modeled by the function $w(t) = -5t^2 - 8t + 120$, where $w(t)$ represents the number of gallons of water in the pool after the pump has operated for t minutes.

a) How many gallons of water were in the pool when the pump was first turned on?

b) Determine, to the _nearest tenth of a minute_, the amount of time it takes for all the water in the pool to drain.

14. In the accompanying diagram, the large rectangle $ABCD$ is made up of four smaller rectangles with dimensions as indicated.

a) Represent, in terms of x, the area of $ABCD$.

b) Find the area of _each_ of rectangles I, II, III, and IV.

c) Show that the area obtained in part (a) above is equal to the sum of the areas obtained in part (b) above.

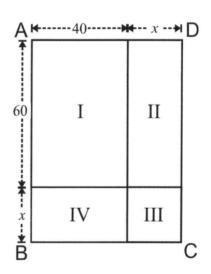

Chapter 15. Parabolas

15.1 <u>Find Roots Given a Parabolic Graph</u>

KEY TERMS AND CONCEPTS

The **standard form** of a quadratic function is $y = ax^2 + bx + c$ where $a \neq 0$.

Example: $y = x^2 - 4x + 3$ or $f(x) = -2x^2 - x + 1$

The graph of a quadratic function is a U-shaped curve called a **parabola**.

The points on the parabola represent the (x, y) values for which the quadratic equation is true. As we saw with linear equations (page 69), we can **determine whether a point is on a graph** by substituting the x-value and y-value for the variables x and y in the equation of the graph and then checking if these values make the equation true. If a point is on a graph, it is a solution to the equation represented by the graph.

Example: (3,4) is on the graph represented by $y = x^2 - 2x + 1$ because by substituting
3 for x and 4 for y, we get $4 = 3^2 - 2(3) + 1$, which is true.

In a quadratic function, if $a > 0$, then the parabola "**opens up**" like the letter U, but if $a < 0$, then the parabola "**opens down**" like an upside-down U.

Example: The graph of $y = x^2 - 4x + 3$ opens up, but $y = -2x^2 - x + 1$ opens down.

Just as we have for other functions, the **y-intercept** of $y = ax^2 + bx + c$ is the constant, c. We know this because the graph of the function crosses the y-axis when $x = 0$, which gives us $y = c$.

When $y = 0$, we can find the **roots** or **zeros** algebraically by solving for x.

Example: The roots of $y = x^2 - 4x + 3$ are the solutions to the equation
$x^2 - 4x + 3 = 0$. Factoring the trinomial, we get $(x - 1)(x - 3) = 0$, so the
roots are 1 and 3.

Graphically, $y = 0$ for all points along the x-axis. Therefore, the **roots** or **zeros** are the x-coordinates of the points **where the parabola crosses the x-axis**, also called the **x-intercepts**.

Example: Since the roots of the quadratic function $y = x^2 - 4x + 3$ are 1 and 3, the
parabola will cross the x-axis at points (1,0) and (3,0).

MODEL PROBLEM 1:   *DETERMINING WHETHER A POINT IS ON THE GRAPH*

Does the graph whose equation is $y = -x^2 - x + 3$ contain the point $(2, -3)$?

Solution:

(A) $-3 = -2^2 - 2 + 3$?

(B) $-3 = -4 - 2 + 3 = -3$, so yes, $(2, -3)$ is in the solution set.

Explanation of steps:

(A) Substitute for x and y.

(B) Evaluate both sides of the equation to determine if the equation is true.

PRACTICE PROBLEMS

1. Which of the following points is *not* on the graph of the parabola whose equation is $y = 2x^2 + x - 1$?	2. If $(h,11)$ is a point on the graph of $y = x^2 - 3x + 1$, which of the following can be the value of h?
(a) $(-1,0)$ (c) $(-2,-9)$ (b) $(0,-1)$ (d) $(2,9)$	(a) -2 (c) 1 (b) 0 (d) 2

MODEL PROBLEM 2:   *DETERMINING THE ROOTS*

What are the root(s) of the quadratic equation associated with this graph?

Solution:

The roots are 0 and 4.

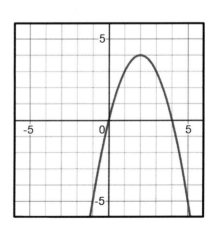

Explanation of steps:

The x-intercepts, or the x-coordinates of the points where the parabola crosses the x-axis, are the roots of the equation. *[Since the parabola crosses the x-axis at $(0,0)$ and $(4,0)$, the roots are 0 and 4.]*

PRACTICE PROBLEMS

3. What are the root(s) of the quadratic equation associated with this graph? 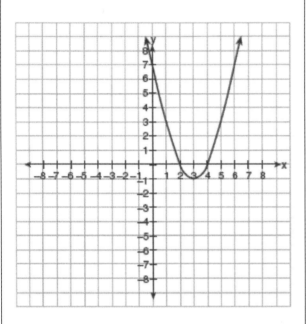	4. What are the root(s) of the quadratic equation associated with this graph? 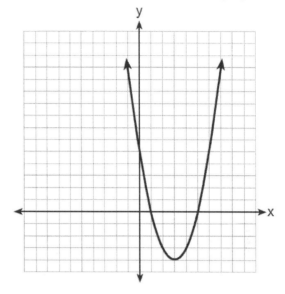
5. What are the root(s) of the quadratic equation associated with this graph? 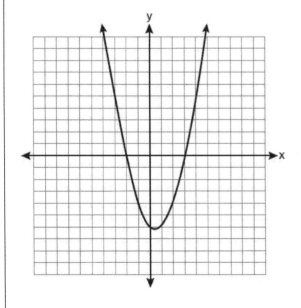	6. What are the root(s) of the quadratic equation associated with this graph? 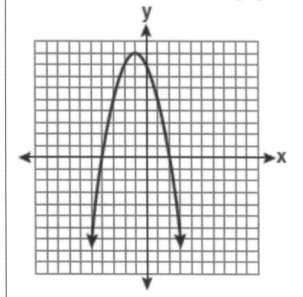

7. What are the root(s) of the quadratic equation associated with this graph?

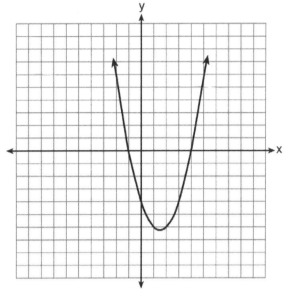

8. What are the root(s) of the quadratic equation associated with this graph?

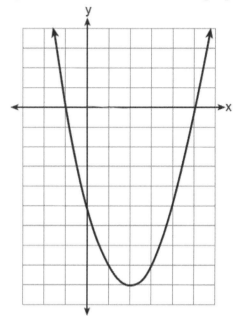

9. What are the root(s) of the quadratic equation associated with this graph?

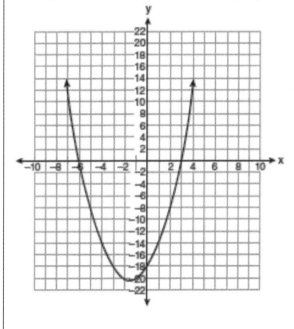

10. What are the root(s) of the quadratic equation associated with this graph?

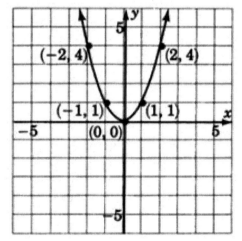

15.2 **Find Vertex and Axis Graphically**

KEY TERMS AND CONCEPTS

A **parabola** is a graph of a quadratic function of the form $y = ax^2 + bx + c$ where $a \neq 0$.

The **vertex** of a parabola is the minimum or maximum point, or turning point, on the graph. It is the lowest point on the curve if the parabola opens up ($a > 0$), or the highest point if the parabola opens down ($a < 0$).

The **axis of symmetry** is the vertical line that crosses through the vertex. Its equation is in the form $x =$ *[the x-coordinate of the vertex]*. The axis of symmetry divides the parabola into two parts that are mirror images of each other.

Example: If the vertex of a parabola is $(-2, 3)$, its x-coordinate is -2, so the axis of symmetry is a line whose equation is $x = -2$. In other words, a vertical line drawn from the vertex to the x-axis would cross the axis at -2.

MODEL PROBLEM

What are the vertex and axis of symmetry of the following parabola?

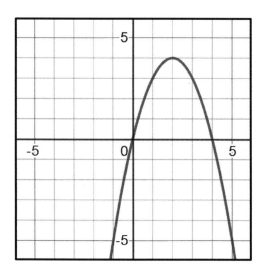

Solution:

(A)   The vertex is (2,4).

(B)   The axis of symmetry is $x = 2$.

Explanation of steps:

(A)   The vertex is the turning point of the parabola. *[Since this parabola opens down, the vertex is the highest point, (2,4).]*

(B)   The axis of symmetry is a vertical line through the vertex.

[Given that the vertex is (2,4), a vertical line through this point would include all points where x equals 2, and would cross the x-axis at 2, so the equation of the axis of symmetry is x = 2.]

409

PRACTICE PROBLEMS

1. What are the vertex and the axis of symmetry of the parabola shown below? 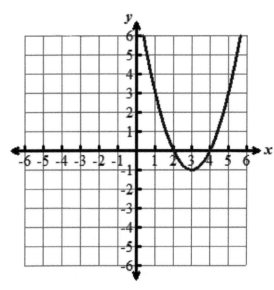	2. What are the vertex and the axis of symmetry of the parabola shown below? 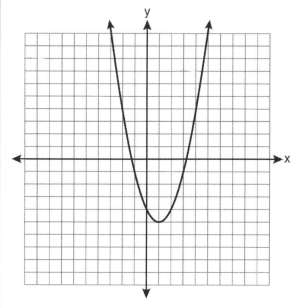
3. What are the vertex and the axis of symmetry of the parabola shown below? 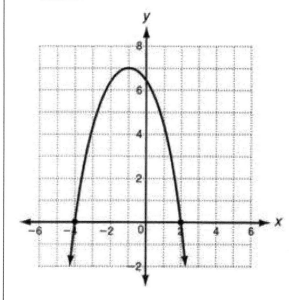	4. What are the vertex and the axis of symmetry of the parabola shown below? 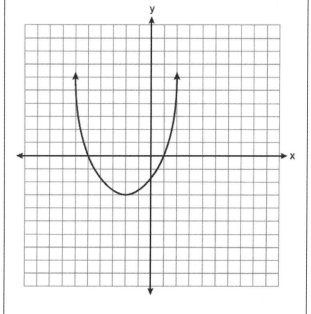

5. What are the vertex and the axis of symmetry of the parabola shown below?

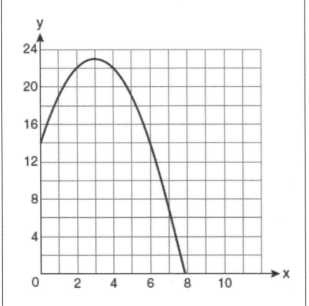

6. What are the vertex and the axis of symmetry of the parabola shown below?

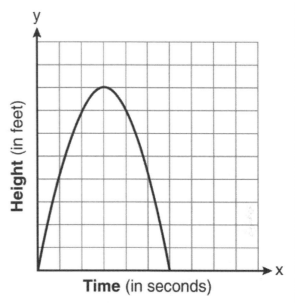

7. What are the vertex and the axis of symmetry of the parabola shown below?

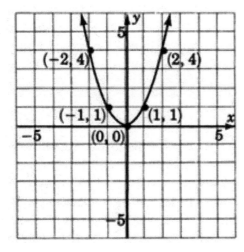

8. If the equation of the axis of symmetry of a parabola is $x = 2$, at which pair of points could the parabola intersect the x-axis?

(1) (3,0) and (5,0)

(2) (3,0) and (2,0)

(3) (3,0) and (1,0)

(4) (−3,0) and (−1,0)

15.3 **Find Vertex and Axis Algebraically**

KEY TERMS AND CONCEPTS

A **parabola** is a graph of a quadratic function of the form $y = ax^2 + bx + c$ where $a \neq 0$.

Example: For $y = x^2 - 4x + 3$, $a = 1$, $b = -4$, and $c = 3$.

The **axis of symmetry** is a vertical line that divides the parabola into two parts that are mirror images of each other. The **equation for the axis of symmetry** is: $x = \dfrac{-b}{2a}$.

Example: The axis of symmetry for the parabola whose equation is $y = x^2 - 4x + 3$

is the line $x = \dfrac{-b}{2a} = \dfrac{-(-4)}{2(1)} = 2$, or simply $x = 2$.

An alternate method for finding the *equation for the axis of symmetry* is to find the *average of the roots*. This may be easier if the quadratic function is already factored. The **factored form** of a quadratic equation is $y = g(x - m)(x - n)$, where m and n are the roots.

Example: If we factor $y = x^2 - 4x + 3$, we get $y = (x - 3)(x - 1)$, so the roots are

$\{3, 1\}$. Therefore, the axis of symmetry is at $x = \dfrac{m + n}{2} = \dfrac{3 + 1}{2} = 2$.

The **vertex** (or turning point) of the parabola is the lowest point (*minimum*) on the curve if the parabola *opens up* ($a > 0$), or the highest point (*maximum*) if the parabola *opens down* ($a < 0$). Since the minimum or maximum point for a parabola is at its vertex, we will often need to find the vertex to determine the largest or smallest value of a real world quadratic function.

The vertex lies on the axis of symmetry. The *x*-**coordinate of the vertex** is determined by the equation for the axis of symmetry. The *y*-**coordinate of the vertex** can be found by substituting for x in the quadratic equation.

Example: For $y = x^2 - 4x + 3$, the axis of symmetry is $x = 2$, so substitute 2 for x.
$y = (2)^2 - 4(2) + 3 = -1$, so the vertex is the point $(2, -1)$.

MODEL PROBLEM 1:   *GIVEN AN EQUATION*

Find the axis of symmetry and vertex for the parabola with equation $y = x^2 + 12x + 32$.

Solution:

(A) $a = 1$ and $b = 12$

(B) $x = \dfrac{-b}{2a} = \dfrac{-(12)}{2(1)} = -6$

(C) $y = x^2 + 12x + 32$
     $y = (-6)^2 + 12(-6) + 32$
     $y = -4$

(D) Axis of symmetry: $x = -6$.
     Vertex: $(-6, -4)$.

Explanation of steps:

(A) The values for a and b come from the coefficients of the x^2 and x terms of the equation.

(B) Substitute for a and b in the axis of symmetry equation $x = \dfrac{-b}{2a}$ and evaluate.

(C) Substitute the value of x found in the previous step into the original equation to find the value of y. You now have the coordinates of the vertex.

(D) State your answers.

PRACTICE PROBLEMS

1. Find the axis of symmetry and vertex of the parabola whose equation is $y = -x^2 + 4x - 8$.	2. Find the axis of symmetry and vertex of the parabola whose equation is $y = x^2 - 6x + 10$.

3. What is the vertex of the parabola whose equation is $y = 3x^2 + 6x - 1$?	4. What is the minimum point of the parabola whose equation is $y = 2x^2 + 8x + 9$?
5. Find the axis of symmetry and vertex of the parabola whose equation is $y = x^2 + 2x$.	6. Find the axis of symmetry and vertex of the parabola whose equation is $y = 3x^2 + 1$.
7. Find the axis of symmetry and vertex of the parabola whose equation is $y = -2x^2 - 8x + 3$	8. Find the axis of symmetry and vertex of the parabola whose equation is $y = -x^2 - 2x + 1$

MODEL PROBLEM 2:   *VERBAL PROBLEM*

You have a 500-ft. roll of chain link fencing and a large field. You want to fence in a rectangular playground area. What is the largest such playground area you can enclose?

Solution:

(A)   The perimeter $P = 2l + 2w$, so $500 = 2l + 2w$, or $250 = l + w$.

(B)   Therefore, $l = -w + 250$.

(C)   The area $A = lw$, so $A = (-w + 250)(w)$, or $A = -w^2 + 250w$.

(D)   The axis of symmetry is at $w = \dfrac{-b}{2a} = \dfrac{-250}{2(-1)} = 125$.

(E)   When $w = 125$, $l = -w + 250 = -125 + 250 = 125$.

(F)   So the maximum area is $A = lw = (125)(125) = 15{,}625$ sq. ft.

Explanation of steps:

(A)   The amount of fencing tells us the perimeter *[500 ft.]*. Write the formula and substitute.

(B)   From the perimeter equation, we can solve for *l* in terms of *w*.

(C)   Now, we can substitute for *l* and *w* into the area formula, resulting in a quadratic function.

(D)   Since this quadratic function graphs as a parabola that opens down *[a = −1]*, the maximum area is at its vertex. Finding the axis of symmetry will find us the value of *w* when the area is at its maximum. *[w = 125 ft.]*

(E)   Once we have *w*, we can find *l*. *[Substitute into the formula from step B.]*

(F)   With both dimensions known, calculate the area.

PRACTICE PROBLEMS

9. A manufacturer has daily production costs of $C(x) = 0.25x^2 - 8x + 800$ where C is the total cost, in dollars, and x is the number of units produced. What is the minimum daily cost, and how many units should be produced to yield the minimum cost?

10. A business owner estimates her weekly profits, p, in dollars, by the function $p(w) = -4w^2 + 160w$, where w represents the number of workers she hires. What is the number of workers she should hire in order to earn the greatest profit?

15.4   <u>Graph Parabolas</u>

KEY TERMS AND CONCEPTS

The **standard form** of a quadratic function is $y = ax^2 + bx + c$ where $a \neq 0$.

Example: For $y = x^2 - 4x + 3$, $a = 1$, $b = -4$, and $c = 3$.

The graph of a quadratic function is called a **parabola**. If $a > 0$, then the parabola "**opens up**" like the letter U, but if $a < 0$, then the parabola "**opens down**" like an upside-down U.

Example: For $y = x^2 - 4x + 3$, $a = 1$, so the parabola opens up.

We can **graph the parabola** by:

1. drawing the axis of symmetry as a dashed line for reference only
2. plotting the vertex
3. plotting the y-intercept and its reflection
4. plotting any additional points
5. connecting the points with a solid curve

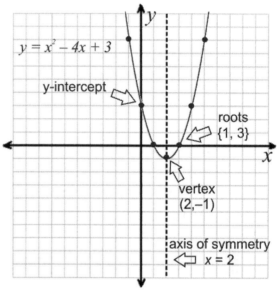

The **equation for the parabola's axis of symmetry**, a vertical line that divides the parabola into two parts that are mirror images of each other, is $x = \dfrac{-b}{2a}$.

Example: The axis of symmetry for the parabola whose equation is $y = x^2 - 4x + 3$ is the line

$$x = \frac{-b}{2a} = \frac{-(-4)}{2(1)} = 2, \text{ or simply } x = 2.$$

The axis of symmetry gives us the **x-coordinate of the vertex**. You can find **y-coordinate of the vertex** by substituting for x in the quadratic equation.

Example: For $y = x^2 - 4x + 3$, the axis of symmetry is $x = 2$, so substitute 2 for x.

$y = (2)^2 - 4(2) + 3 = -1$, so the vertex is the point $(2, -1)$.

The **y-intercept of the parabola** (the y coordinate of the point where the parabola crosses the y-axis), is c. The **reflection of the y-intercept** over the axis of symmetry (as long as the axis of symmetry is not $x = 0$) is another point on the parabola.

Example: For $y = x^2 - 4x + 3$, $c = 3$, so the y-intercept is 3.

The reflection of $(0,3)$ over the axis of symmetry is $(4,3)$.

We can **plot additional points** on the curve by substituting any integer value of x into the equation to find the corresponding value for y. We can also plot its reflection.

Example: For $y = x^2 - 4x + 3$, we substitute 5 for x to get $y = (5)^2 - 4(5) + 3 = 8$.

So, the point $(5,8)$ is on the parabola. Its reflection is the point $(-1,8)$.

For graphs of any non-linear functions, you are required to plot and label at least 3 points.

▥▤ CALCULATOR TIP

You can use the graphing calculator to **graph a parabola**.

Example: To graph $y = x^2 - 4x + 3$, press [Y=]. Then, next to "Y1 =", type in the

quadratic expression $x^2 - 4x + 3$ using [X,T,Θ,n] for the variable, x, and the [x^2]

button for the exponent, 2. Then. press [GRAPH] to view the parabola.

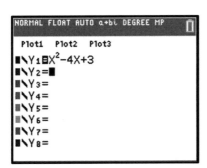
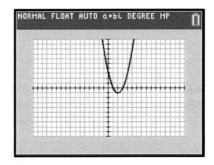

CALCULATOR TIP

The calculator can help you find the **roots** of a graphed parabola:

- Using the [TABLE] feature:

  Press [2nd][TABLE] to see a table of (x, y) coordinates of points on the parabola. Press the [▼] key to scroll down for more points. You can find the roots by looking for the values of x when **y equals 0** *[for the equation $y = x^2 - 4x + 3$, the roots are 1 and 3]*.

- Using the [CALC] feature:

  Press [2nd][CALC][2] for zero. Look for the first point where the parabola crosses the x-axis. For the "Left Bound?" prompt, use the [◄][►] keys to move the cursor to left of this point and press [ENTER]. For the "Right Bound?" prompt, use the [►] key to move the cursor to right of this point (near the vertex) and press [ENTER] twice. The coordinates are shown; the value of x is the root. If there is a second point where the parabola crosses the x-axis, repeat these steps, moving the cursor to the left and right of the point to find its coordinates; the value of x is another root.

The calculator can also help you find the **vertex** of a graphed parabola:

  Press [2nd][CALC] and then press either [3] for minimum if the parabola opens up $(a > 0)$ or [4] for maximum if the parabola opens down $(a < 0)$. For the "Left Bound?" prompt, use the [◄][►] keys to move the cursor to any point along the left side of the parabola and press [ENTER]. For the "Right Bound?" prompt, use the [►] key to move the cursor to any point along the right side of the parabola and press [ENTER] twice. The coordinates of the vertex (or a close approximation) will be shown. You may need to round to find the actual coordinates of the vertex.

MODEL PROBLEM

Graph the equation $y = -x^2 + 2x + 3$.

Solution:

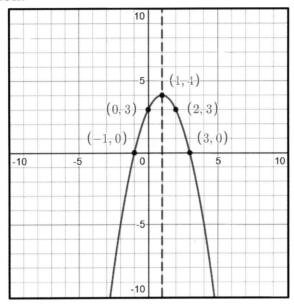

Explanation of steps:

(A)   The axis of symmetry is $x = \dfrac{-b}{2a} = \dfrac{-(2)}{2(-1)} = 1$. A dashed vertical line, $x = 1$, is drawn.

(B)   Substituting $x = 1$, $y = -(1)^2 + 2(1) + 3 = 4$, so the vertex is $(1, 4)$.

(C)   The y-intercept, c, is 3, so $(0,3)$ and its reflection $(2,3)$ are plotted.

(D)   When $x = 3$, $y = -(3)^2 + 2(3) + 3 = 0$, so the point $(3,0)$ and its reflection $(-1,0)$ can be plotted as additional points. Connect the points to draw the parabola.

PRACTICE PROBLEMS

1. Graph the parabola whose equation is $y = 2x^2 - 8x + 4$. 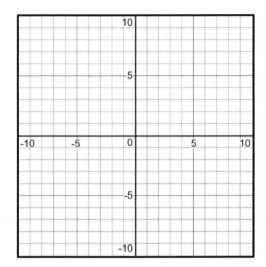	2. Graph the parabola whose equation is $y = -x^2 + 6x - 5$. 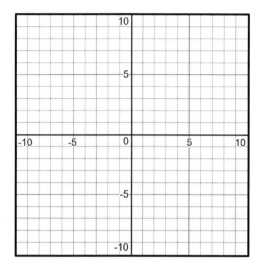
3. Graph the parabola whose equation is $y = -x^2 + 4x - 8$. 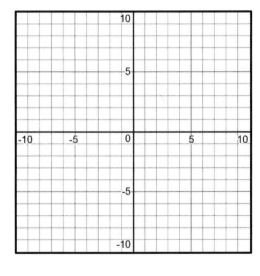	4. Graph the parabola whose equation is $y = x^2 - 6x + 10$. 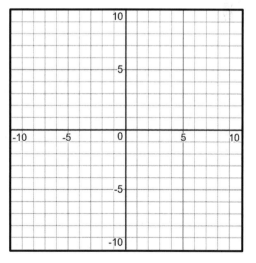

5. Graph the parabola whose equation is $y = 3x^2 + 6x - 1$.

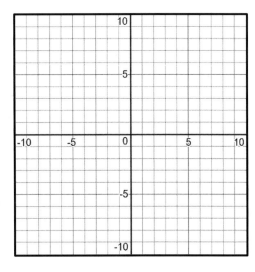

6. Graph the parabola whose equation is $y = 2x^2 + 8x + 9$.

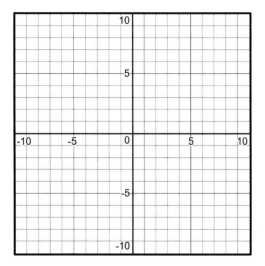

7. Graph the parabola whose equation is $y = x^2 + 2x$.

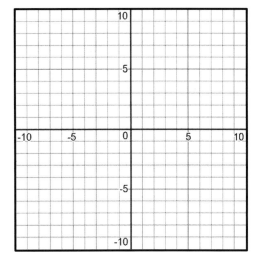

8. Graph the parabola whose equation is $y = 3x^2 + 1$.

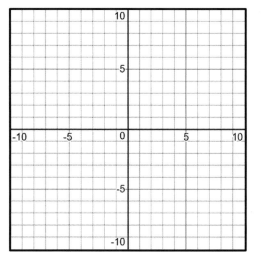

9. Graph the equation $y = x^2 - 2x - 3$. Using the graph, determine the roots of the equation $x^2 - 2x - 3 = 0$.

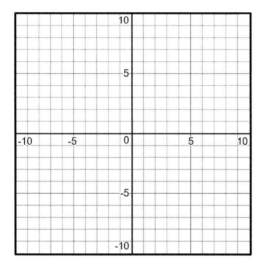

10. Graph the equation $y = x^2 + 2x - 8$. Using the graph, determine the roots of the equation $x^2 + 2x - 8 = 0$.

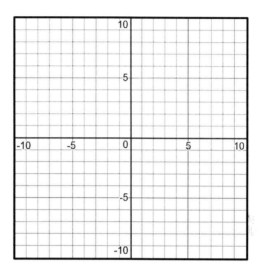

11. A ball is tossed in the air so that the path of the ball is modeled by the equation $y = -x^2 + 6x$, where y represents the height of the ball in feet and x is the time in seconds.

a) Graph $y = -x^2 + 6x$ for $0 \le x \le 6$ on the grid below.

b) At what time, x, is the ball at its highest point?

12. A ball is tossed in the air so that the path of the ball is modeled by the equation $h = -8t^2 + 40t$, where h represents the height of the ball in feet and t is the time in seconds.

a) Graph $h = -8t^2 + 40t$ for $0 \le t \le 5$ on the grid below.

b) At what time, t, is the ball at its highest point?

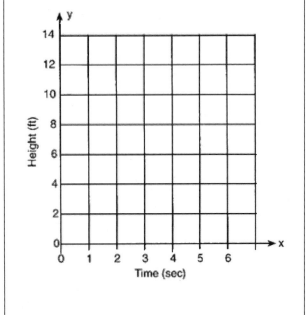

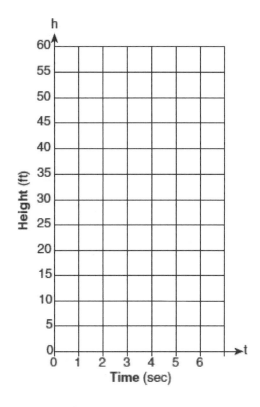

13. The shape of a parabolic arch is represented by the equation $y = -2x^2 + 12x$, where y is the height of the arch in feet. The arch is 6 feet wide at its base.

   a) Graph the parabola below.

   b) What is the maximum height of the arch?

14. The shape of a parabolic arch is represented by the equation $y = -x^2 + 20x$, where y is the height of the arch in feet. The arch is 20 feet wide at its base.

   a) Graph the parabola below.

   b) What is the maximum height of the arch?

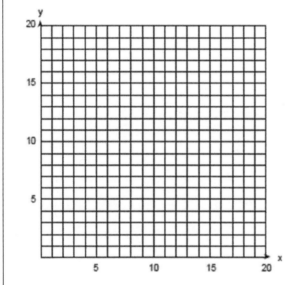

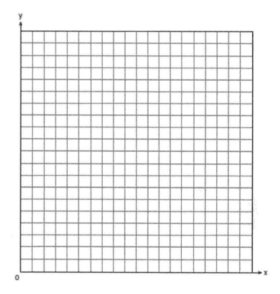

15.5   **Vertex Form**

KEY TERMS AND CONCEPTS

It is sometimes helpful to transform an equation, $y = x^2 + bx + c$, into **vertex form**: $y = (x - h)^2 + k$. In vertex form, the values of h and k represent the coordinates of the vertex (h, k) of the parabola. This allows us to more easily determine the vertex from the equation.

To transform a quadratic equation into vertex form, we use the steps for **completing the square**, which we have learned previously.

To convert a quadratic function $y = x^2 + bx + c$ into vertex form:

1. Add the opposite of c to both sides.
2. Add $\left(\frac{b}{2}\right)^2$ to both sides.
3. Factor the trinomial into a binomial squared.
4. Isolate y. Write the equation in vertex form, as $y = (x - h)^2 + k$.
5. The vertex is the point (h, k).

Once we have an equation in vertex form, we can **state the vertex**. However, be careful about the signs of the coordinates. Since there's subtraction inside the parentheses of $y = (x - h)^2 + k$, we need to negate the sign of the second term in parentheses to find h. Outside parentheses, the sign of k can be taken as is.

Examples: For $y = (x - 3)^2 + 2$, the vertex is $(3, 2)$.

                    For $y = (x + 1)^2 - 1$, the vertex is $(-1, -1)$.

To graph a function in vertex form as a parabola, start by plotting the vertex, then use a table to plot points for values of x that are just above or below h (we usually choose consecutive integers).

Example: To graph $y = (x - 2)^2 - 1$, plot the vertex $(2, -1)$, then plot additional points using a table. As a parabola, the points should reflect over the axis of symmetry.

x	$(x - 2)^2 - 1$	y
−1	$(-1 - 2)^2 - 1$	8
0	$(0 - 2)^2 - 1$	3
1	$(1 - 2)^2 - 1$	0
2	$(2 - 2)^2 - 1$	−1
3	$(3 - 2)^2 - 1$	0
4	$(4 - 2)^2 - 1$	3
5	$(5 - 2)^2 - 1$	8

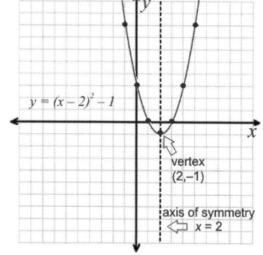

MODEL PROBLEM

Transform the equation $y = x^2 + 4x + 1$ into vertex form. State the coordinates of the vertex.

Solution:

$$y = x^2 + 4x + 1$$
(A) $y - 1 = x^2 + 4x$

(B) $\left(\dfrac{b}{2}\right)^2 = \left(\dfrac{4}{2}\right)^2 = 2^2 = 4$

$$y - 1 + 4 = x^2 + 4x + 4$$
(C) $y + 3 = (x + 2)^2$

(D) $y = (x + 2)^2 - 3$

(E) Vertex is $(-2, -3)$.

Explanation of steps:

(A) Add the opposite of c to both sides.

(B) Add $\left(\dfrac{b}{2}\right)^2$ to both sides.

(C) Factor the trinomial into a binomial squared.

(D) Isolate y. Write the equation in vertex form, as $y = (x - h)^2 + k$.

(E) The vertex is the point (h, k).

427

PRACTICE PROBLEMS

1. Transform the equation $y = x^2 + 6x + 10$ into vertex form and state the coordinates of the vertex.	2. Transform the equation of the function $f(x) = x^2 + 10x + 21$ into vertex form and state the coordinates of the vertex.
3. Graph the parabola $y = (x - 3)^2 + 1$. 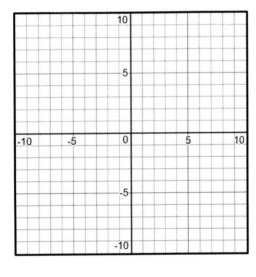	4. Graph the parabola $y = (x - 1)^2 - 3$. 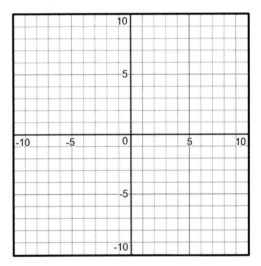

15.6 **Vertex Form with a≠1 [CC]**

KEY TERMS AND CONCEPTS

The standard form for a quadratic equation is $y = ax^2 + bx + c$. Even when $a \neq 1$, equations in this form can be transformed into *vertex form*, $y = a(x - h)^2 + k$, where h and k represent the coordinates of the vertex (h, k) of the parabola. As with the standard form, the value of a tells us whether the parabola opens up (a is positive) or down (a is negative). Changing the absolute value of a will stretch the parabola.

To convert $y = ax^2 + bx + c$ into vertex form, complete the square:
1. Divide both sides (*each term*) by the leading coefficient, a.
2. Add the opposite of c to both sides.
3. Add $\left(\dfrac{b}{2}\right)^2$ to both sides.
4. Factor the trinomial into a binomial squared.
5. Isolate y. Write the equation in vertex form, as $y = a(x - h)^2 + k$.
6. The vertex is the point (h, k).

MODEL PROBLEM

Transform the equation $y = -2x^2 + 4x + 1$ into vertex form. State the coordinates of the vertex.

Solution:

$$y = -2x^2 + 4x + 1$$
(A) $-\dfrac{y}{2} = x^2 - 2x - \dfrac{1}{2}$
(B) $-\dfrac{y}{2} + \dfrac{1}{2} = x^2 - 2x$
(C) $\left(\dfrac{b}{2}\right)^2 = \left(\dfrac{-2}{2}\right)^2 = 1$
$$-\dfrac{y}{2} + \dfrac{1}{2} + 1 = x^2 - 2x + 1$$
(D) $-\dfrac{y}{2} + \dfrac{3}{2} = (x - 1)^2$
(E) $-\dfrac{y}{2} = (x - 1)^2 - \dfrac{3}{2}$
$$y = -2(x - 1)^2 + 3$$
(F)   Vertex is (1,3).

Explanation of steps:

(A)   Divide both sides by a. *[Divide by –2.]*

(B)   Move the constant term c to the opposite side.

(C)   Add $\left(\dfrac{b}{2}\right)^2$ to both sides.

(D)   Factor the trinomial into a binomial squared.

(E)   Isolate y. Write the equation in vertex form, as $y = a(x - h)^2 + k$.

(F)   The vertex is the point (h, k).

PRACTICE PROBLEMS

1. Transform the equation
   $y = 2x^2 + 4x + 6$ into vertex form and state the coordinates of the vertex.

2. Transform the equation of the function $f(x) = 3x^2 + 18x + 26$ into vertex form and state the coordinates of the vertex.

3. The French Bakery sells more croissants when it reduces its price. The profit, in dollars, is modeled by the function
   $y = -0.2(x - 60)^2 + 150$
   where x is the number of croissants sold per day. What is the maximum profit the bakery can make?

4. The daily profit of a custom T-shirt shop can be modeled by
   $P(n) = -n^2 + 60n - 400$
   where n is the number of T-shirts produced each day and $P(n)$ is the profit, in dollars, made on that number. Rewrite this function in vertex form and determine the maximum daily profit.

5. Graph the parabola
    $y = 2(x + 1)^2 + 3$.

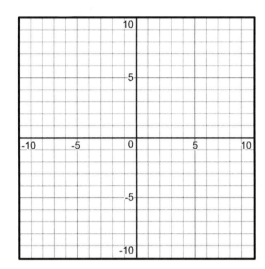

6. Graph the parabola
    $y = -0.5(x - 1)^2 - 3$.

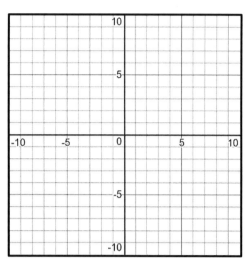

Chapter 16.   Quadratic-Linear Systems

16.1   Solve Quadratic-Linear Systems Algebraically

KEY TERMS AND CONCEPTS

A system of equations that includes one quadratic equation and one linear equation can be solved algebraically using the **substitution method**.

1. First solve each equation for y so that y is set equal to both a quadratic expression and a linear expression in terms of x.
2. Then, since both expressions are equal to y, set them equal to each other, and solve the resulting quadratic equation for x.
3. Once you have the value(s) of x, find the corresponding value(s) of y by substituting into one of the original equations.

MODEL PROBLEM

Solve the following system of equations algebraically:

$$y = x^2 - x - 6$$
$$y = 2x - 2$$

Solution:

(A)   By substitution, $x^2 - x - 6 = 2x - 2$.

(B) $x^2 - x - 6 = 2x - 2$

$\underline{-2x + 2 \quad -2x + 2}$

$x^2 - 3x - 4 = 0$

$(x - 4)(x + 1) = 0$

$x = \{-1, 4\}$

(C)   When $x = -1$, $y = 2(-1) - 2 = -4$.

When $x = 4$, $y = 2(4) - 2 = 6$.

(D)   Solutions: $(-1, -4)$ and $(4, 6)$

Explanation of steps:

(A)   Since both expressions are equal to y, set them equal to each other. That is, substitute the linear expression for y in the quadratic equation.

(B)   Solve the quadratic equation by getting zero to one side, then factoring.

(C)   For each root, substitute for x in the linear equation to find the corresponding value of y.

(D)   Express the solutions as ordered pairs.

▦▢ CALCULATOR TIP

We can check each solution using the calculator. For example, to check whether $(-1, -4)$ is a solution to the system above, enter:

[(-)][1][STO▸][X,T,Θ,*n*] [ALPHA][:][(-)][4][STO▸][ALPHA][Y] [ENTER]

[ALPHA][Y] [2nd][TEST][1] [X,T,Θ,*n*][*x²*][−][X,T,Θ,*n*][−][6] [ENTER]   (1 means true)

[ALPHA][Y] [2nd][TEST][1] [2][X,T,Θ,*n*][−][2] [ENTER]   (1 means true)

Repeat these steps for $(4,6)$ by storing 4 in x and 6 in y and testing both equations again.

PRACTICE PROBLEMS

1. Solve the following system of equations algebraically: $$y = x^2 - 5$$ $$y = -4x$$	2. Solve the following system of equations algebraically: $$y = x^2 + 4x + 1$$ $$y = 5x + 3$$
3. Solve the following system of equations algebraically: $$y = x^2 + 2x - 1$$ $$y = 3x + 5$$	4. Solve the following system of equations algebraically: $$y = x^2 + 4x - 2$$ $$y = 2x + 1$$

5. Solve the following system of equations algebraically:

$$y = x^2 + 7x + 22$$
$$y + 3x = 1$$

6. Solve the following system of equations algebraically:

$$y + 3x = 6$$
$$x^2 = y + 2x + 6$$

7. Solve the following system of equations algebraically:

$$y = x^2 + 2x - 8$$
$$y = 2x + 1$$

8. Solve the following system of equations algebraically:

$$y = x^2 - 6x + 9$$
$$y = -9x + 19$$

9. Solve the following system of equations algebraically:

$$y = x^2 + 5x - 17$$
$$y = x - 5$$

10. Solve the following system of equations algebraically:

$$y = 3x - 6$$
$$y = x^2 - x - 6$$

16.2 **Solve Quadratic-Linear Systems Graphically**

KEY TERMS AND CONCEPTS

To solve a system of equations graphically, **graph both equations** on the same set of axes and determine the **point(s) of intersection**. These points are the solutions to the system.

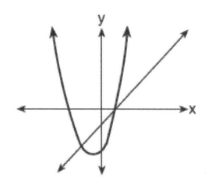

The graph of a quadratic-linear system consists of a **parabola** (from a quadratic equation) and a **line** (from a linear equation). The parabola and line may intersect at two points, so there may be two solutions to the system.

Example: The graph below shows that the solutions to the system, $y = x^2 - 4x + 3$ and $y = -2x + 6$, are the points of intersection, $(-1, 8)$ and $(3, 0)$.

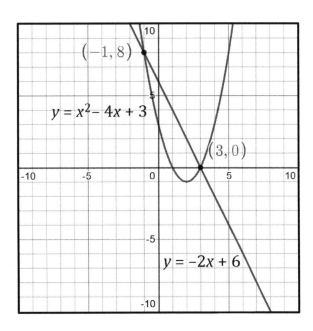

Although you are not required to label the two graphs when they have different degrees (such as one linear and one quadratic), it is still helpful to do so.

CALCULATOR TIP

You can also use the calculator to find the point(s) of intersection:

1. Press [Y=] and enter both equations.

2. Press [2nd][CALC][5] for intersect.

3. Press [ENTER] for the "First curve?" and "Second curve?" prompts.

4. For the "Guess?" prompt, use the arrow keys to move the cursor near one of the points of intersection and press [ENTER]. The coordinates of the closest point of intersection will be shown.

5. If there appears to be a second point of intersection, repeat steps 2 to 4 but move the cursor near the second point in response to the "Guess?" prompt.

Example: The screenshots below show that the soltuions to the system of equations, $y = x^2 - 4x + 3$ and $y = -2x + 6$, are $(-1,8)$ and $(3,0)$.

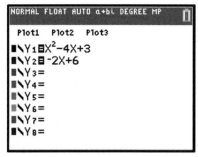
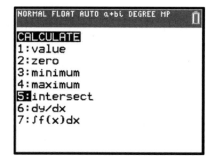
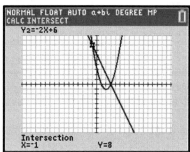
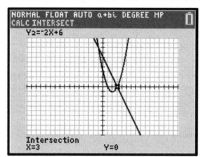

MODEL PROBLEM

Solve the following system of equations graphically:

$$y = x^2 - 4x + 3$$
$$y + 1 = x$$

Solution:

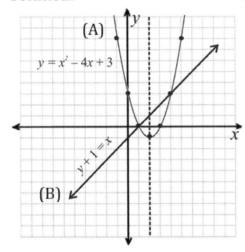

(C) Solutions: (1,0) and (4,3)

Explanation of steps:

(A) Graph the quadratic equation as a parabola. Include at least 3 points with integer values of x on each side of the axis of symmetry. *[The axis of symmetry is $x = 2$ and vertex is $(2, -1)$. Plot additional points with x-coordinates of 3, 4, and 5, plus their reflections.]*

(B) Graph the linear equation as a line. *[First transform the equation into slope-intercept form, $y = x - 1$.]*

(C) State the point(s) of intersection as the solutions

PRACTICE PROBLEMS

1. Which point is a solution of the system of equations shown on the graph?

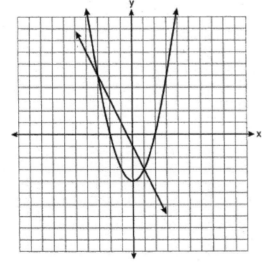

(1) $(-3, 1)$ (3) $(0, -1)$

(2) $(-3, 5)$ (4) $(0, -4)$

2. Which point is a solution of the system of equations shown on the graph?

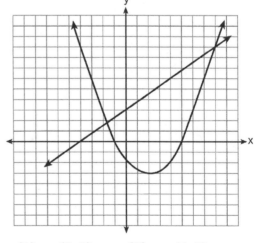

(1) $(8, 9)$ (3) $(0, 3)$

(2) $(5, 0)$ (4) $(2, -3)$

437

3. Solve the following system graphically:

$$y = x^2 + 4x - 2$$
$$y = 2x + 1$$

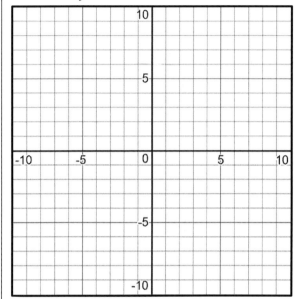

4. Solve the following system graphically:

$$y = x^2 + 2x - 1$$
$$y = 3x + 5$$

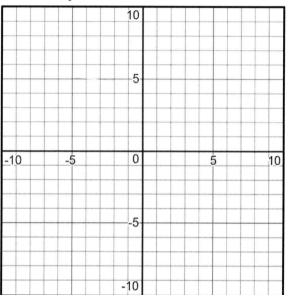

5. Solve the following system graphically:

$$y = x^2 + 4x + 1$$
$$y = 5x + 3$$

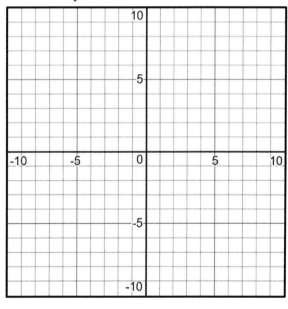

6. Solve the following system graphically:

$$y = x^2 + 4x - 1$$
$$y + 3 = x$$

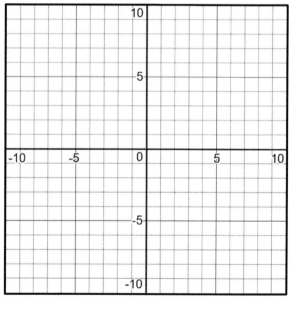

7. Solve the following system graphically:

$$y = x^2 - 6x + 5$$

$$2x + y = 5$$

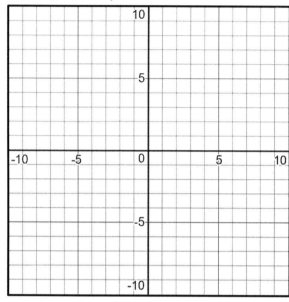

8. Solve the following system graphically:

$$y = x^2 + 4x - 5$$

$$y = x - 1$$

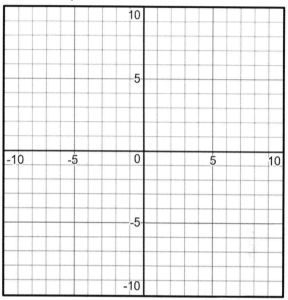

9. Solve the following system graphically:

$$y = x^2 - 6x + 1$$

$$y + 2x = 6$$

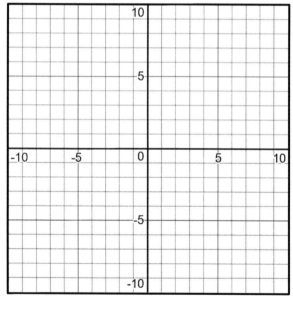

10. Solve the following system graphically:

$$y = -x^2 + 6x - 3$$

$$x + y = 7$$

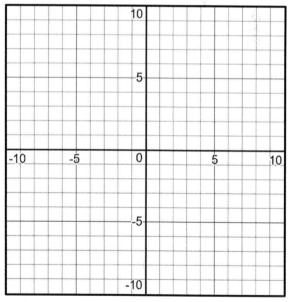

11. Solve the following system graphically:

$$y = -x^2 - 4x + 12$$
$$y = -2x + 4$$

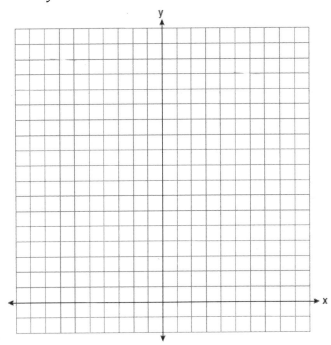

Chapter 17.　Cubic and Radical Functions

17.1　Cubic Functions

KEY TERMS AND CONCEPTS

A **cubic function** is one that is defined by a polynomial with a degree of three; that is, it includes an x^3 term. The graph of the simplest (*parent*) cubic function, $y = x^3$, is shown below.

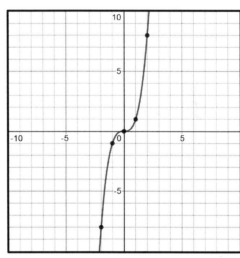

x	y
-2	-8
-1	-1
0	0
1	1
2	8

The general form of a cubic function is
$$f(x) = ax^3 + bx^2 + cx + d.$$

It is sometimes possible to find the **roots** (zeros) of a cubic function by factoring.

Example:　For $f(x) = x^3 - x^2 - 2x$, the roots can be found by factoring.
$$x^3 - x^2 - 2x = 0$$
$$x(x^2 - x - 2) = 0$$
$$x(x + 1)(x - 2) = 0$$
So, the roots are $\{-1, 0, 2\}$.

Some cubic functions can be factored by grouping.

Example:　For $g(x) = x^3 + 2x^2 - x - 2$, we can begin to factor by grouping.
$$\boxed{x^3 - x} + \boxed{2x^2 - 2} = 0$$
$$x(x^2 - 1) + 2(x^2 - 1) = 0$$
$$(x + 2)(x^2 - 1) = 0$$
$$(x + 2)(x + 1)(x - 1) = 0$$
So, the roots are $\{-2, -1, 1\}$.

441

As with quadratic functions, you can see the real roots of the function as the **x-intercepts** on the graph. For example, the function to the right has roots of -4, -1, and 2. This means it has **factors** of $x + 4$, $x + 1$, and $x - 2$:

$$x = -4 \qquad x = -1 \qquad x = 2$$
$$x + 4 = 0 \qquad x + 1 = 0 \qquad x - 2 = 0$$
$$(x + 4)(x + 1)(x - 2) = 0$$

Multiplying the factors, we get the equation of this cubic function: $f(x) = x^3 + 3x^2 - 6x - 8$.

However, this is not the only cubic function with these factors. The function below has the same roots but an additional constant factor of $\frac{1}{4}$, which "flattens" the graph.

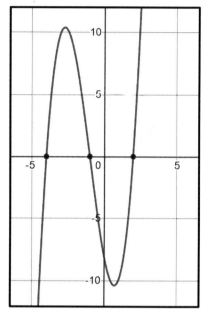

$$f(x) = x^3 + 3x^2 - 6x - 8$$

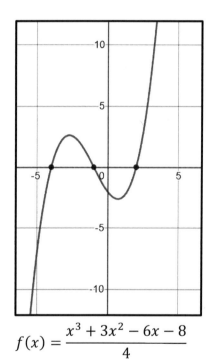

$$f(x) = \frac{x^3 + 3x^2 - 6x - 8}{4}$$

MODEL PROBLEM

Which of the following could represent the graph of $f(x)$ shown below?

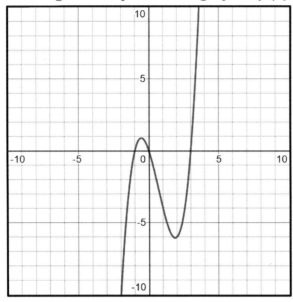

(1) $f(x) = (x - 1)(x + 3)$ (3) $f(x) = (x + 1)(x - 3)$

(2) $f(x) = x(x - 1)(x + 3)$ (4) $f(x) = x(x + 1)(x - 3)$

Solution: (4)

Explanation of steps:

   (A)   The x-intercepts *[−1, 0, and 3]* represent the real roots.

   (B)   If a is a root, then $(x - a)$ is a factor. *[If 3 is a root, then $(x - 3)$ is a factor; if 0 is a root, x is a factor; and if −1 is a root, $(x + 1)$ is a factor.]*

443

PRACTICE PROBLEMS

1. Graph $y = x^3 + 3$ by completing the table for integers $-2 \leq x \leq 2$.

    Based on the graph, how many real roots does the function appear to have?

x	y
-2	
-1	
0	
1	
2	

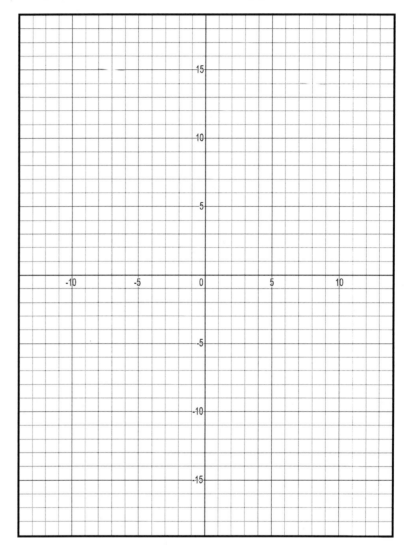

2. Graph $y = x^3 - 9x + 5$ by completing the table for integers $-3 \le x \le 3$.

   Based on the graph, how many real roots does the function appear to have?

x	y
−3	
−2	
−1	
0	
1	
2	
3	

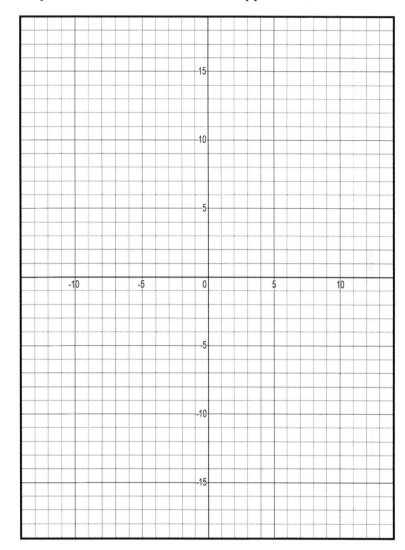

17.2 **Square Root Functions**

KEY TERMS AND CONCEPTS

A **square root function** is a function that has the independent variable, x, in the radicand.

Examples:　　$y = \sqrt{x} + 2$ or $y = \sqrt{x - 3}$

The simplest (*parent*) square root function, $y = \sqrt{x}$, can be graphed as follows:

x	y
0	0
1	1
4	2
9	3
16	4

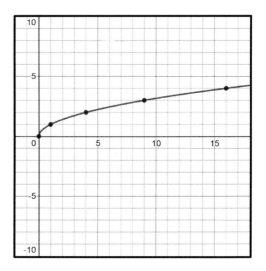

Note that for real numbers, the radicand cannot be negative. This is because there are no real numbers that have negative squares: the square of a positive number is positive and the square of a negative number is positive. So, the domain of a square root function is restricted to only values of x for which the radicand is at least zero.

🖩 CALCULATOR TIP

To enter a square root on the calculator, press 2nd[√], followed by the radicand.

On the TI-84 in MathPrint mode, exit the radicand by pressing the ▶ key.

On the TI-83, end the radicand by pressing) to close the parentheses.

MODEL PROBLEM

Which function is represented by the graph below?

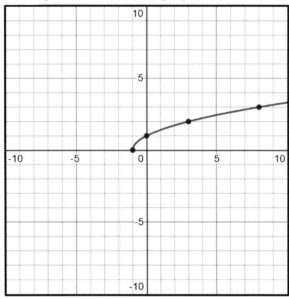

   (1) $f(x) = \sqrt{x} + 1$ (3) $f(x) = \sqrt{x+1}$

   (2) $f(x) = \sqrt{x} - 1$ (4) $f(x) = \sqrt{x-1}$

Solution: (3)

Explanation of steps:
Test the given points to determine which function they satisfy.
[The points $(-1,0)$, $(0,1)$, $(3,2)$, and $(8,3)$ satisfy $y = \sqrt{x+1}$ by substituting each pair of x and y values into the equation. For example, $(8,3)$ satisfies the equation because $3 = \sqrt{8+1}$.]

[Note: In Chapter 18, we will also see that the graph could be recognized as a translation of the parent function $y = \sqrt{x}$ by one unit to the left.]

PRACTICE PROBLEMS

1. Which of the following graphs represent the function $y = \sqrt{x} - 1$?

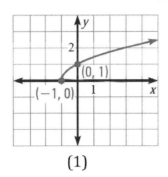
(1)

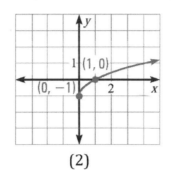
(2)

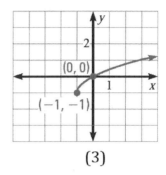
(3)

2. Williams High School relocated into a larger building and immediately began recruiting students to increase enrollment. The number of students enrolled, y, is modeled by the function $y = 90\sqrt{3x} + 400$, where x is the number of months the new school building has been open.

a) Construct a table of values.

b) Sketch the function on the grid.

c) Find the number of students enrolled exactly 3 months after the building opened.

d) After how many months will 940 students be enrolled?

17.3 **Cube Root Functions [CC]**

KEY TERMS AND CONCEPTS

A **cube root function** is similar to a square root function in definition except that a cube root symbol is used.

Examples: $y = \sqrt[3]{x} + 2$ or $y = \sqrt[3]{x - 3}$

The **cube root** of a number is a factor whose cube equals that number.

Example: $\sqrt[3]{8} = 2$ because $2 \cdot 2 \cdot 2 = 8$

▦▯ CALCULATOR TIP

To enter a cube root on the calculator, press $\boxed{\text{MATH}}\boxed{4}$ for $^3\sqrt($, followed by the radicand.

Be sure to end the radicand by pressing $\boxed{\blacktriangleright}$ or $\boxed{)}$.

The simplest (*parent*) cube root function, $y = \sqrt[3]{x}$, can be graphed as follows:

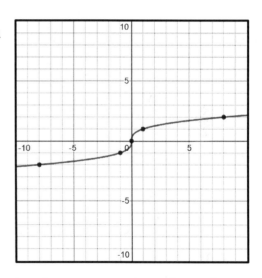

x	y
−8	−2
−1	−1
0	0
1	1
8	2
27	3

Note that the domain of a cube root function is *not* restricted to non-negative values of *x*. This is because the cube root of a negative number is a real, negative number.

Example: $\sqrt[3]{-8} = -2$ because $(-2)(-2)(-2) = -8$.

MODEL PROBLEM

What are the real solutions to the system of equations $y = \sqrt{x}$ and $y = \sqrt[3]{x}$?

Solution: (0,0) and (1,1)

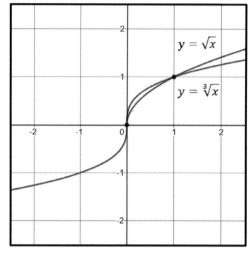

Explanation:

Graph both functions on the same plane and look for intersections.

[These functions intersect at only two points, (0,0) and (1,1). These points of intersection show that $\sqrt{0} = \sqrt[3]{0} = 0$ and $\sqrt{1} = \sqrt[3]{1} = 1$.]

PRACTICE PROBLEMS

1. Which of the following graphs represent the function $y = \sqrt[3]{x} + 3$?

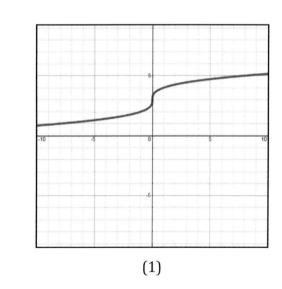

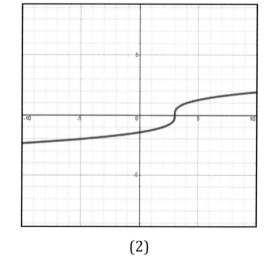

(1)   (2)

Chapter 18.   Transformations of Functions

18.1   Translations

KEY TERMS AND CONCEPTS

The absolute value function $y = |x|$ and the quadratic function $y = x^2$ are graphed below.

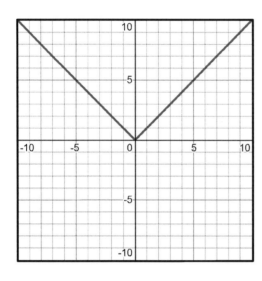 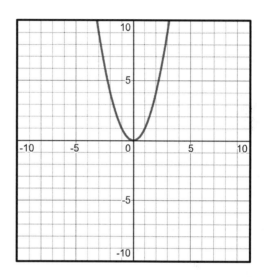

The functions above are called parent functions. A **parent function** is the simplest function of a family of functions that preserves the definition or shape of the entire family.

Example: $y = x^2$ is the parent function for the entire family of quadratic functions that have the general form $y = ax^2 + bx + c$ where $a \neq 0$, since these are all quadratic by definition and are all shaped as parabolas.

A function $f(x)$ may be:

- **translated** by adding/subtracting a constant, as in $f(x) + k$ or $f(x + k)$
- **reflected** by negation, as in $-f(x)$ or $f(-x)$
- **stretched** by multiplying/dividing by a constant, as in $k \cdot f(x)$ or $f(kx)$

A summary of the types of transformations we will cover in this chapter is given below.

$f(x) + k$	$(x, y) \rightarrow (x, y + k)$	vertically shifts the graph up $(k > 0)$ or down $(k < 0)$
$f(x + k)$	$(x, y) \rightarrow (x - k, y)$	horizontally shifts the graph left $(k > 0)$ or right $(k < 0)$
$-f(x)$	$(x, y) \rightarrow (x, -y)$	reflects the graph over the x-axis
$f(-x)$	$(x, y) \rightarrow (-x, y)$	reflects the graph over the y-axis
$k \cdot f(x)$	$(x, y) \rightarrow (x, ky)$	vertically stretches by a factor of k
$f(kx)$	$(x, y) \rightarrow (kx, y)$	horizontally stretches by a factor of $\frac{1}{k}$

In this section, we will look at translations. Reflections and stretches will be covered later in this chapter.

In a **translation**, the graph of a function is shifted up, down, left, or right.

Vertical shifts

If we add a constant k to a function's output expression, as in $f(x) + k$, its graph will shift **up** (if $k > o$) or **down** (if $k < 0$). In a vertical shift, each point (x, y) maps to $(x, y + k)$.

Example:　　The parent functions $y = |x|$ and $y = x^2$ may be translated as follows:

$y = |x| + k$ or $y = x^2 + k$. Adding k to the function's output vertically shifts the function *up* (for a <u>positive k</u>) or *down* (for a <u>negative k</u>).

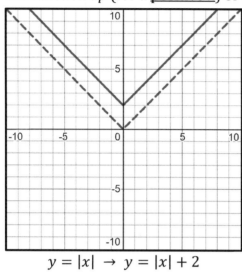
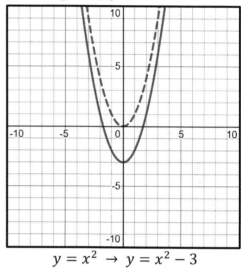

$$y = |x| \; \rightarrow \; y = |x| + 2 \qquad\qquad y = x^2 \; \rightarrow \; y = x^2 - 3$$

Horizontal shifts

If we add a constant k to a function's input expression, as in $f(x + k)$, its graph will shift **left** (if $k > o$) or **right** (if $k < 0$). In a horizontal shift, each point (x, y) maps to $(x - k, y)$.

Example:　　The parent functions $y = |x|$ and $y = x^2$ may be translated as follows:

$y = |x + k|$ or $y = (x + k)^2$. Adding k to the function's input horizontally shifts the function **left** (for a <u>positive k</u>) or **right** (for a <u>negative k</u>).

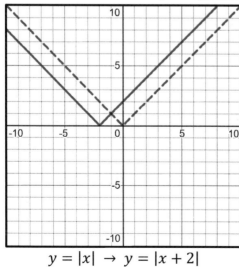
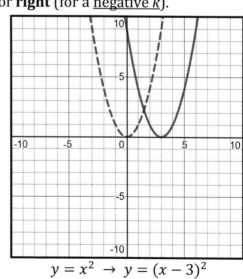

$$y = |x| \; \rightarrow \; y = |x + 2| \qquad\qquad y = x^2 \; \rightarrow \; y = (x - 3)^2$$

453

MODEL PROBLEM

Below is a graph of the parent function $y = \sqrt{x}$. Draw a graph of $y = \sqrt{x - 1} + 2$.

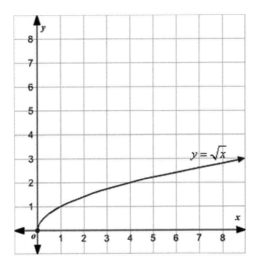

Solution:

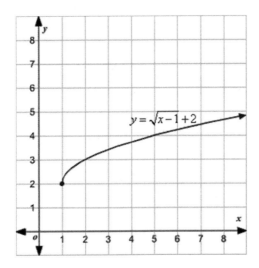

Explanation of steps:

The graph of $f(x) = \sqrt{x - a} + b$ can be obtained by translating the graph of the parent function $f(x) = \sqrt{x}$ by a units to the right and b units up.

[For $y = \sqrt{x - 1} + 2$, this means 1 unit to the right and 2 units up.]

Note that this also changes the *domain* and *range*, from $x \geq 0$ and $y \geq 0$, to $x \geq a$ and $y \geq b$, respectively.

PRACTICE PROBLEMS

1. What is the equation of a graph translated up 3 units, if the original graph is $y = x^2$? (1) $y = (x - 3)^2$ (2) $y = (x + 3)^2$ (3) $y = x^2 - 3$ (4) $y = x^2 + 3$	2. Describe how the graph $g(x) = (x + 2)^2$ is related to the graph of $f(x) = x^2$. (1) a translation 2 units down of $f(x)$ (2) a translation 2 units left of $f(x)$ (3) a translation 2 units up of $f(x)$ (4) a translation 2 units right of $f(x)$
3. If the original graph is $y = |x|$, then the graph of $y = |x - 2|$ has been (1) shifted up 2 units (2) shifted down 2 units (3) shifted right 2 units (4) shifted left 2 units	4. If the graph of $y = |x| + 2$ is shifted 3 units down, what is the equation of the new graph?
5. Write the equation of the graph $y = |x|$ after it is shifted 4 units to the left.	6. Write the equation of the graph $y = x^2$ after it is shifted 5 units up and 2 units to the right.

18.2　**Reflections**

KEY TERMS AND CONCEPTS

In a **reflection**, the graph of a function is reflected over the x-axis or the y-axis.

Vertical reflections

If we negate a function's output expression, as in $-f(x)$, its graph will reflect vertically over the x-axis. In a reflection over the x-axis, each point (x, y) maps to $(x, -y)$.

Example:　　The parent functions $y = |x|$ and $y = x^2$ may be reflected as follows:

　　　　　　$y = -|x|$ or $y = -x^2$ would flip the graph upside down over the x-axis.

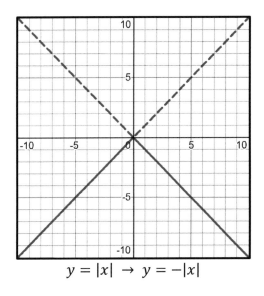

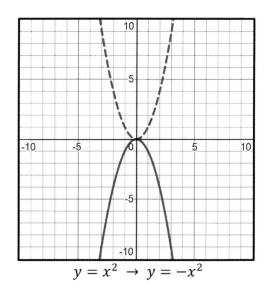

$$y = |x| \;\rightarrow\; y = -|x|$$ 　　　　　 $$y = x^2 \;\rightarrow\; y = -x^2$$

Horizontal reflections

If we negate a function's input expression, as in $f(-x)$, its graph will reflect horizontally over the y-axis. In a reflection over the y-axis, each point (x, y) maps to $(-x, y)$.

Example:　　Since the parent functions $y = |x|$ and $y = x^2$ are symmetric over the y-axis, reflecting them by $y = |-x|$ or $y = (-x)^2$ merely maps the graphs over themselves.

For a **sequence of transformations**, perform the transformations in this order:

1. vertical reflections
2. translations
3. horizontal reflections

Example: Here is a graph of $y = (x + 2)^2 - 3$. It is the graph of $y = x^2$ after it is translated vertically left by 2 and horizontally down by 3.

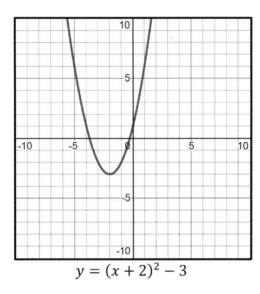

$$y = (x + 2)^2 - 3$$

Here are the graphs of $y = -(x + 2)^2 - 3$, which reflects $y = x^2$ over the x-axis (vertically) *before* the translations, and of $y = (-x + 2)^2 - 3$, which reflects $y = x^2$ over the y-axis (horizontally) *after* the translations.

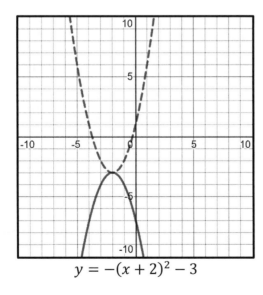

$$y = -(x + 2)^2 - 3$$

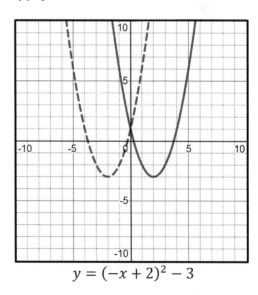

$$y = (-x + 2)^2 - 3$$

MODEL PROBLEM

Write the equation of the graph $y = \sqrt{x}$ after it is reflected over the *x*-axis and shifted 5 units to the left.

Solution:

$$y = -\sqrt{x + 5}$$

Explanation of steps:

To reflect vertically, negate the <u>output</u> *[place the negation sign <u>outside</u> the radical]*. To shift horizontally, add to (or subtract from) the <u>input</u> *[add 5 <u>inside</u> the radical]*.

PRACTICE PROBLEMS

1. If the original graph is $y = \sqrt{x}$ and the transformed graph is $y = -\sqrt{x} - 1$, then the graph has been

    (1)   reflected over the *x*-axis and shifted down 1

    (2)   reflected over the *x*-axis and shifted right 1

    (3)   reflected over the *y*-axis and shifted down 1

    (4)   reflected over the *y*-axis and shifted right 1

2. The graph of $y = |x + 2|$ is shown below.

    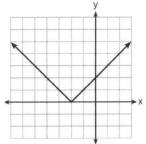

    Which graph represents $y = -|x + 2|$?

    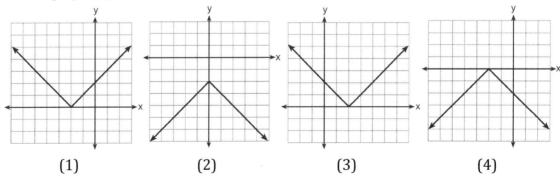

    (1)   (2)   (3)   (4)

3. The diagram below shows the graph of $y = -x^2 - c$.

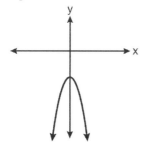

Which graph represents $y = x^2 - c$?

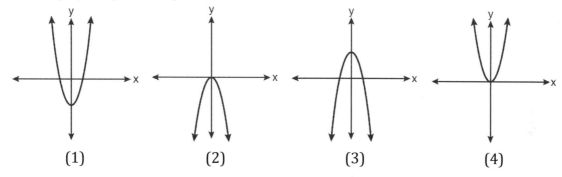

(1)   (2)   (3)   (4)

4. Write the equation of the graph $y = x^2$ after it is reflected over the x-axis and shifted 1 unit to the right.

5. Write the equation of the graph $y = \sqrt{x}$ after it is shifted 3 units left and then reflected over the y-axis.

6. Write the equation of the graph $y = x^3$ after it is shifted 2 units down and 1 unit to the right and then reflected over the y-axis.

18.3 **Stretches**

KEY TERMS AND CONCEPTS

In a **stretch**, the graph of a function is stretched vertically or horizontally. When a graph is vertically expanded or horizontally contracted, it becomes **more narrow**. However, when a graph is vertically contracted or horizontally expanded, it becomes **wider**.

Vertical stretches

If we multiply or divide a function's output expression by a constant k, as in $k \cdot f(x)$, its graph will **vertically stretch** by expanding (if $k > 1$) or contracting (if $0 < k < 1$) by a factor of k. In a vertical stretch, each point (x, y) maps to (x, ky).

Example: The parent functions $y = |x|$ and $y = x^2$ may be stretched as follows:

$y = k|x|$ or $y = kx^2$ would vertically stretch the graph by k and make it more narrow (for $k > 1$) or vertically shrink the graph and make it flatter and wider (for $0 < k < 1$).

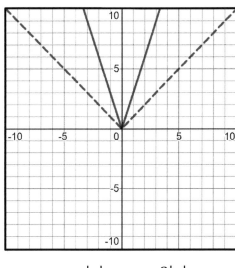

$$y = |x| \ \rightarrow \ y = 3|x|$$

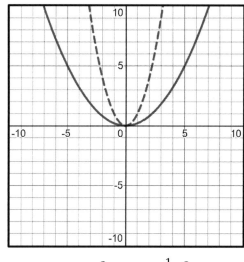

$$y = x^2 \ \rightarrow \ y = \frac{1}{5}x^2$$

Horizontal stretches

If we multiply or divide a function's input expression by a constant k, as in $f(kx)$, its graph will **horizontally stretch** by contracting (if $k > 1$) or expanding (if $0 < k < 1$) by a factor of $\frac{1}{k}$. In a horizontal stretch, each point (x, y) maps to (kx, y).

Example: The parent functions $y = |x|$ and $y = x^2$ may be stretched as follows:

$y = |kx|$ or $y = (kx)^2$ would horizontally contract the graph by $\frac{1}{k}$ and make it more narrow (for $k > 1$) or horizontally expand the graph by $\frac{1}{k}$ and make it flatter and wider (for $0 < k < 1$).

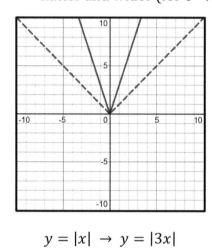   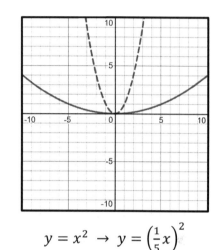

$$y = |x| \;\rightarrow\; y = |3x| \qquad\qquad y = x^2 \;\rightarrow\; y = \left(\tfrac{1}{5}x\right)^2$$

For a **sequence of transformations**, perform the transformations in this order:
1. vertical stretches and/or reflections
2. translations
3. horizontal stretches and/or reflections

Order of transformations:

If $g(x) = a \cdot f(dx + c) + b$, then $g(x)$ is a transformation of $f(x)$ *in this order*:
1. vertically stretched by a (and also reflected over the x-axis if a is negative)
2. vertically translated by b and/or horizontally translated by c
3. horizontally stretched by $\frac{1}{d}$ (and also reflected over the y-axis if d is negative)

Example: If $f(x) = \sqrt{x}$ and $g(x) = 2\sqrt{3x + 1} + 4$, then g is a transformation of f which is first vertically stretched by a factor of 2, then translated up by 4 and left by 1, and finally horizontally stretched by a factor of ⅓.

These rules apply only if $f(x)$ is written using a single x-variable term.

461

Example: We could *not* apply these transformation rules to get $g(x) = 3x^2 + 2x - 1$.

MODEL PROBLEM

The graph of the function $y = \sqrt{x}$ is vertically stretched by a factor of 4 and flipped (reflected) over the *x*-axis. What is the equation of the resulting graph?

Solution:

    (A)   (B)   (C)

$$y = \sqrt{x} \ \rightarrow \ y = 4\sqrt{x} \ \rightarrow \ y = -4\sqrt{x}$$

Explanation of steps:

  (A)   Start with the original equation.

  (B)   Perform the first transformation *[stretch by multiplying by the given factor]*.

  (C)   Perform the next transformation on the result *[negating will flip it over the x-axis]*.

PRACTICE PROBLEMS

1.   What is the relationship between the graphs of $f(x) = x^2$ and $g(x) = -3x^2$?

    (1) The graph of $g(x)$ is wider and opens in the opposite direction from the graph of $f(x)$.

    (2) The graph of $g(x)$ is narrower and opens in the opposite direction from the graph of $f(x)$.

    (3) The graph of $g(x)$ is wider and is three units below the graph of $f(x)$.

    (4) The graph of $g(x)$ is narrower and is three units to the left of the graph of $f(x)$.

2. How is the graph of $y = x^2 + 4x + 3$ affected when the coefficient of x^2 is changed to a smaller positive number?

    (1)   The graph becomes wider, and the y-intercept changes.

    (2)   The graph becomes wider, and the y-intercept stays the same.

    (3)   The graph becomes narrower, and the y-intercept changes.

    (4)   The graph becomes narrower, and the y-intercept stays the same.

3. The graph of $y = x^2$ is shown below.

    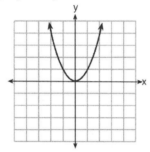

    Which graph represents $y = 2x^2$?

    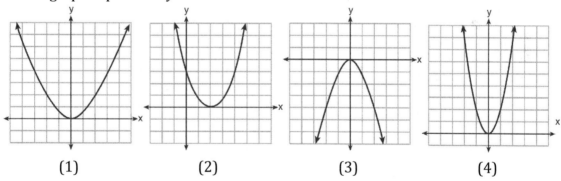

    (1)   (2)   (3)   (4)

4. The graph of the equation $y = |x|$ is shown in the diagram below.

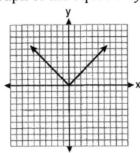

Which diagram could represent a graph of the equation $y = a|x|$ when $-1 < a < 0$?

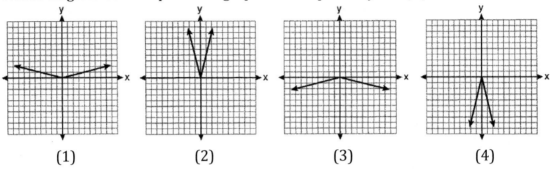

      (1)   (2)   (3)   (4)

5. To vertically compress the graph of $y = x^2$ by a factor of $\frac{1}{2}$ would result in what new equation? Will the new graph be wider or narrower than the original?

6. Graph and label the functions $y = |x|$ and $y = |2x|$ on the set of axes below.

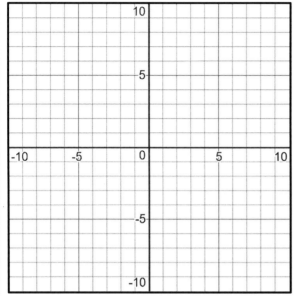

Explain how increasing the coefficient of x affects the graph of $y = |x|$.

7. Graph and label the functions $y = |x|$ and $y = \left|\frac{1}{2}x\right|$ on the set of axes below.

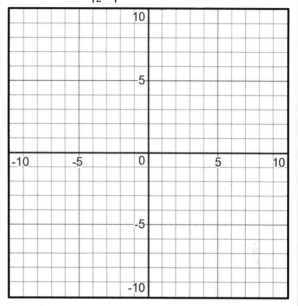

Explain how decreasing the coefficient of x affects the graph of $y = |x|$.

8. On the set of axes below, graph and label the equations $y = |x|$ and $y = 3|x|$ for the interval $-3 \leq x \leq 3$.

   Explain how changing the coefficient of the absolute value from 1 to 3 affects the graph.

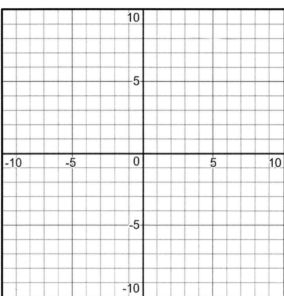

Chapter 19.   Discontinuous Functions

19.1   Piecewise Functions

KEY TERMS AND CONCEPTS

We often need to define functions in parts. These are called **piecewise functions**. We define these functions using two or more pieces, each for a different part of the function's domain, using a large brace symbol, {.

Example: The graph below is made up of two pieces. For values of $x < 0$, we see part of the parabola whose equation is $f(x) = x^2$. But for values of $x \geq 0$ the graph shows the square root function $f(x) = \sqrt{x}$. The function is defined as:

$$f(x) = \begin{cases} x^2 & x < 0 \\ \sqrt{x} & x \geq 0 \end{cases}$$

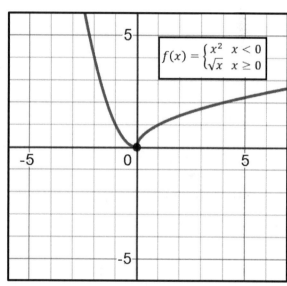

CALCULATOR TIP

To graph a piecewise function on most calculator models, you'll need to use a workaround.

1. Press MODE and change the graphing mode from Connected to Dot (or from Thick to Dot-Thick on some models). Just remember to change it back when you're done.

2. Press Y= and enter the first piece next to Y1 using the format (*piece* 1)(*condition* 1) and the second piece next to Y2 as (*piece* 2)(*condition* 2), and so on.

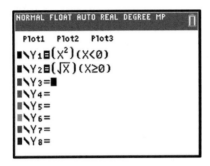 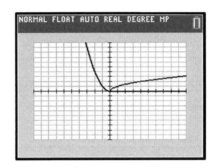

This is not exactly graphed as a piecewise function. It is graphed as two (or more) separate functions but with $f(x) = 0$ for values of x within the function's domain for which the condition is false. For these values of x outside of the condition, the points are drawn along the x-axis; be aware that these points are *not* part of the piecewise function.

To type a relational operator in a condition, press 2nd[TEST] followed by the appropriate number. To type a compound condition such as $0 < x < 1$, type it as two conditions with the logical operator "and" between them, as in 0 < X and X < 1. The logical operators, including "and," are listed under 2nd[TEST] LOGIC .

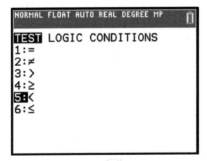 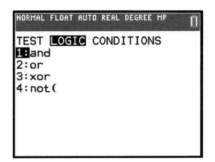

▦▯ CALCULATOR TIP

On some TI-84 models, a piecewise function is available, so the workaround isn't needed.

1. Press [Y=] and, while the cursor is next to Y1, press [MATH][ALPHA][B].

2. Select the number of pieces using the [◄] and [►] keys and select OK.

3. Enter the expressions and condtions into the template, and press [GRAPH].

 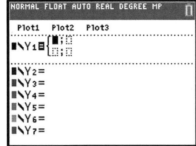 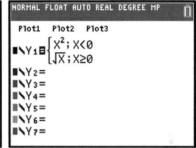

A **discontinuous** function is a function that is not continuous which, by a loose definition, means that you would not be able to draw or trace the function on a plane without lifting your pencil off the paper. The funcion above is *continuous*, since the two parts meet at and include (0,0), allowing us to draw the graph without lifting our pencil. However, piecewise functions are often discontinuous.

Example: The graph to the right shows the function defined as pieces of two lines:

$$f(x) = \begin{cases} x+1 & x < 1 \\ x-1 & x \geq 1 \end{cases}$$

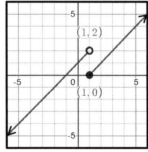

Note that for $f(-1)$ we apply the $x+1$ piece of the definition, $f(-1) = (-1) + 1 = 0$, giving the point $(-1,0)$. But for $f(1)$, we apply the $x-1$ piece of the definition, giving $f(1) = 1 - 1 = 0$ and the point $(1,0)$. Also note that the point $(1,2)$ is an open circle. That is because the top piece of the definition, $f(x) = x + 1$, is only for $x < 1$ and not for $x = 1$. When $x \geq 1$, the bottom piece of the definition, $f(x) = x - 1$, applies.

The **absolute value functions** can also be piecewise defined.

Example: $f(x) = |x|$ can be defined as $f(x) = \begin{cases} -x & x < 0 \\ x & x \geq 0 \end{cases}$

469

MODEL PROBLEM

Graph the piecewise function:

$$f(x) = \begin{cases} x^2 & x < 2 \\ 6 & x = 2 \\ 10 - x & 2 < x \le 6 \end{cases}$$

Solution:

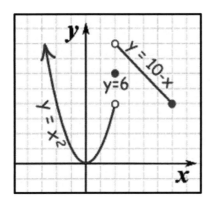

Explanation:

Graph each piece separately, using closed circles at the closed ends of the intervals (where x is =, ≤, or ≥ some value) and open circles at the open ends (where x is < or > some value). _[Graph the top piece as part of the parabola $y = x^2$, but ending at an open circle at (2,4) to show that $x = 2$ ($y = x^2 = 2^2 = 4$) is not part of that piece. The middle piece defines (2,6) as a point on the graph. The bottom piece defines a line segment graphed as $y = 10 - x$ starting at but not including (2,8) – hence the open circle – and ending at and including (6,4).]_

PRACTICE PROBLEMS

1. Given $f(x) = \begin{cases} -x & x < 0 \\ x + 1 & x \geq 0 \end{cases}$

   find $f(-3)$, $f(0)$, and $f(2)$.

2. Graph $f(x) = \begin{cases} -x & x < 0 \\ x + 1 & x \geq 0 \end{cases}$

   Is this a continuous function?

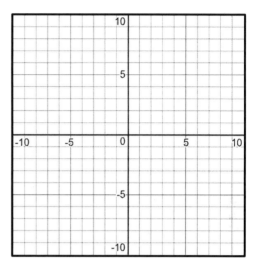

3. Graph $f(x) = \begin{cases} -1 & x < 1 \\ 1 & x = 1 \\ 2x - 2 & x > 1 \end{cases}$

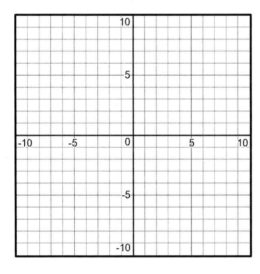

4. Graph $f(x) = \begin{cases} -x + 1 & x < 0 \\ 2^x & x \geq 0 \end{cases}$

   Is this a continuous function?

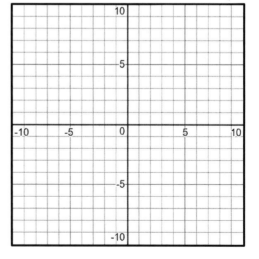

5. Graph $f(x) = |x + 1| + 1$. Is this a continuous function? Write an equivalent function using a piecewise definition instead of an absolute value symbol.

6. A garage charges the following rates for parking (with an 8 hour limit):

   $4 per hour for the first 2 hours
   $2 per hour for the next 4 hours
   No charge for the next 2 hours

   Write a piecewise function that gives the parking cost c (in dollars) in terms of the time t (in hours) that a car is parked.

19.2 <u>**Step Functions**</u>

KEY TERMS AND CONCEPTS

A **step function** is a discontinuous function that, when graphed, appears as a series of disconnected line segments resembling steps on a staircase.

Two common step functions are called the floor and ceiling functions. The **floor function** uses special bracket symbols ⌊ ⌋ with serifs only at the bottom, which represents the greatest integer less than or equal to the value inside the brackets. The **ceiling function** uses similar bracket symbols ⌈ ⌉ but with serifs only at the top, which represents the least integer that is greater than or equal to the value inside the brackets.

Examples: (a) For the floor function $f(x) = \lfloor x \rfloor$, $f(2.9) = 2$ but $f(3) = 3$.
          (b) For the ceiling function $g(x) = \lceil x \rceil$, $g(5.3) = 6$ and $g(6) = 6$.

The graphs of floor and ceiling functions are shown below. The graph is made up of disconnected line segments with open or closed circles at their ends. Just as we saw when graphing inequalities, an **open circle** means the point is *excluded*, but a **closed circle** means the point is *included*.

Example: On the graph of $y = \lfloor x \rfloor$ to the left below, $y = \lfloor x \rfloor = 1$ for all real values of x between 1 and 2, including 1 but excluding 2. In other words, $y = 1$ for all values of x such that $1 \le x < 2$, even for values very close to 2 such as 1.99999, but not including 2. For $x = 2$, $y = \lfloor 2 \rfloor = 2$, so the point $(2,2)$ is closed while the point $(2,1)$ is open.

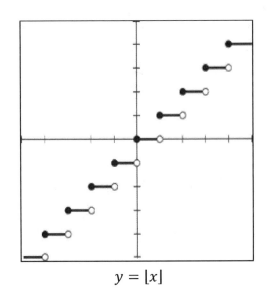
$$y = \lfloor x \rfloor$$

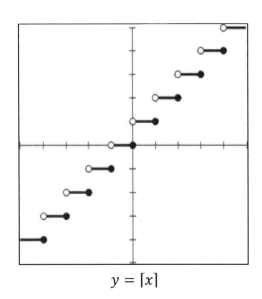
$$y = \lceil x \rceil$$

Step functions are used in various real world situations. For example, the graph below shows the cost of mailing a letter way back in 2006. For letters of up to 1 ounce in weight, the postage cost 39 cents. The cost was 41 cents for letters that were more than 1 ounce but up to 2 ounces in weight. For weights of x ounces in the interval $2 < x \leq 3$, the cost was 43 cents. This pattern continued so that each additional ounce, or fraction of an ounce, cost an additional 2 cents.

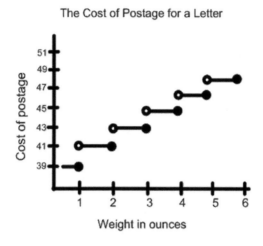

This function is a type of ceiling function, defined as $y = 2\lceil x \rceil + 37$ for all $x > 0$.

Although it is not continuous, it is still a function, as we can see by applying the vertical line test, shown to the right.

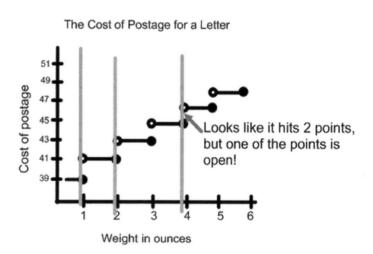

MODEL PROBLEM

A famous step function, called the Heaviside step function, is defined as:

$$H(x) = \begin{cases} 0 & x < 0 \\ 0.5 & x = 0 \\ 1 & x > 0 \end{cases}$$

Graph the function, $H(x)$.

Solution:

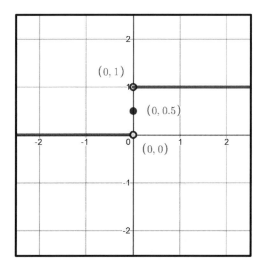

Explanation of steps:

Graph each piece separately. _[Graph $y = 0$ for $x < 0$ and $y = 1$ for $x > 0$. For both of these pieces, use an open dot at $x = 0$ because $H(0)$ does not equal 0 or 1. Instead, $H(0) = 0.5$, so graph the point (0,0.5).]_

PRACTICE PROBLEMS

1.   Given $f(x) = 3\lfloor x \rfloor + 5$, find $f(6.25)$.

2.   Graph $f(x) = \lfloor x \rfloor + 1$.

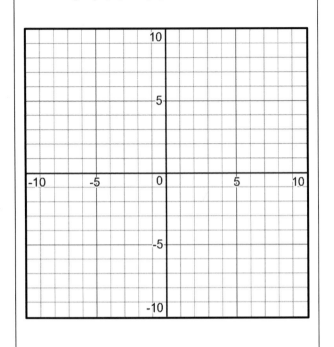

Appendix I.   Index

34401505R00267